Kaplan Publishing are constantly finding new ways to support students looking for exam success and our online resources really do add an extra dimension to your studies.

This book comes with free MyKaplan online resources so that you can study anytime, anywhere. **This free online resource is not sold separately and is included in the price of the book.**

Having purchased this book, you have access to the following online study materials:

CONTENT	AAT	
	Text	Kit
Electronic version of the book	✓	✓
Knowledge Check tests with instant answers	✓	
Mock assessments online	✓	✓
Material updates	✓	✓

How to access your online resources

Kaplan Financial students will already have a MyKaplan account and these extra resources will be available to you online. You do not need to register again, as this process was completed when you enrolled. If you are having problems accessing online materials, please ask your course administrator.

If you are not studying with Kaplan and did not purchase your book via a Kaplan website, to unlock your extra online resources please go to www.mykaplan.co.uk/add-online-resources (even if you have set up an account and registered books previously). You will then need to enter the ISBN number (on the title page and back cover) and the unique pass key number contained in the scratch panel below to gain access. You will also be required to enter additional information during this process to set up or confirm your account details.

If you purchased through the Kaplan Publishing website you will automatically receive an e-mail invitation to MyKaplan. Please register your details using this email to gain access to your content. If you do not receive the e-mail or book content, please contact Kaplan Publishing.

Your Code and Information

This code can only be used once for the registration of one book online. This registration and your online content will expire when the final sittings for the examinations covered by this book have taken place. Please allow one hour from the time you submit your book details for us to process your request.

Please scratch the film to access your unique code.

Please be aware that this code is case-sensitive and you will need to include the dashes within the passcode, but not when entering the ISBN.

KAPLAN

PUBLISHING

PERSONAL TAX

STUDY TEXT

Qualifications and Credit Framework

Q2022

Finance Act 2021

For assessments from February 2022 to end January 2023

This Study Text supports study for the following AAT qualifications:

AAT Level 4 Diploma in Professional Accounting

AAT Diploma in Professional Accounting at SCQF Level 8

KAPLAN PUBLISHING'S STATEMENT OF PRINCIPLES

LINGUISTIC DIVERSITY, EQUALITY AND INCLUSION

We are committed to diversity, equality and inclusion and strive to deliver content that all users can relate to.

We are here to make a difference to the success of every learner.

Clarity, accessibility and ease of use for our learners are key to our approach.

We will use contemporary examples that are rich, engaging and representative of a diverse workplace.

We will include a representative mix of race and gender at the various levels of seniority within the businesses in our examples to support all our learners in aspiring to achieve their potential within their chosen careers.

Roles played by characters in our examples will demonstrate richness and diversity by the use of different names, backgrounds, ethnicity and gender, with a mix of sexuality, relationships and beliefs where these are relevant to the syllabus.

It must always be obvious who is being referred to in each stage of any example so that we do not detract from clarity and ease of use for each of our learners.

We will actively seek feedback from our learners on our approach and keep our policy under continuous review. If you would like to provide any feedback on our linguistic approach, please use this form (you will need to enter the link below into your browser).

https://forms.gle/U8oR3abiPpGRDY158

We will seek to devise simple measures that can be used by independent assessors to randomly check our success in the implementation of our Linguistic Equality, Diversity and Inclusion Policy.

British Library Cataloguing-in-Publication Data

A catalogue record for this book is available from the British Library.

Published by
Kaplan Publishing UK
Unit 2, The Business Centre
Molly Millars Lane
Wokingham
Berkshire
RG41 2QZ

ISBN 978-1-83996-050-5

CONTENTS

STUDY TEXT AND WORKBOOK

KAPLAN PUBLISHING

INTRODUCTION

HOW TO USE THESE MATERIALS

These Kaplan Publishing learning materials have been carefully designed to make your learning experience as easy as possible and to give you the best chance of success in your AAT assessments.

They contain a number of features to help you in the study process.

The sections on the Unit Guide, the Assessment and Study Skills should be read before you commence your studies.

They are designed to familiarise you with the nature and content of the assessment and to give you tips on how best to approach your studies.

STUDY TEXT

This Study Text has been specially prepared for the revised AAT qualification introduced in February 2022.

It is written in a practical and interactive style:

- Key terms and concepts are clearly defined.

- All topics are illustrated with practical examples with clearly worked solutions based on sample tasks provided by the AAT in the new examining style.

- Frequent practice activities throughout the chapters ensure that what you have learnt is regularly reinforced.

- 'Pitfalls' and 'examination tips' help you avoid commonly made mistakes and help you focus on what is required to perform well in your examination.

- 'Test your understanding' activities are included within each chapter to apply your learning and develop your understanding.

ICONS

The chapters include the following icons throughout.

They are designed to assist you in your studies by identifying key definitions and the points at which you can test yourself on the knowledge gained.

 Definition

These sections explain important areas of knowledge which must be understood and reproduced in an assessment.

 Example

The illustrative examples can be used to help develop an understanding of topics before attempting the activity exercises.

 Test your understanding

These are exercises which give the opportunity to assess your understanding of all the assessment areas.

 Reference material/tax tables

These boxes will direct you to the AAT reference material that you can access during the real assessment. A copy of the professional conduct in relation to taxation is included as an appendix at the end of Chapter 1 and the rest of the reference material is included at the end of this section.

 Foundation activities

These are questions to help ground your knowledge and consolidate your understanding on areas you're finding tricky.

 Extension activities

These questions are for if you're feeling confident or wish to develop your higher level skills.

Quality and accuracy are of the utmost importance to us so if you spot an error in any of our products, please send an email to mykaplanreporting@kaplan.com with full details.

Our Quality Coordinator will work with our technical team to verify the error and take action to ensure it is corrected in future editions.

Progression

There are two elements of progression that we can measure: first how quickly learners move through individual topics within a subject; and second how quickly they move from one course to the next. We know that there is an optimum for both, but it can vary from subject to subject and from learner to learner. However, using data and our experience of learner performance over many years, we can make some generalisations.

A fixed period of study set out at the start of a course with key milestones is important. This can be within a subject, for example 'I will finish this topic by 30 June', or for overall achievement, such as 'I want to be qualified by the end of next year'.

Your qualification is cumulative, as earlier papers provide a foundation for your subsequent studies, so do not allow there to be too big a gap between one subject and another.

We know that exams encourage techniques that lead to some degree of short term retention, the result being that you will simply forget much of what you have already learned unless it is refreshed (look up Ebbinghaus Forgetting Curve for more details on this). This makes it more difficult as you move from one subject to another: not only will you have to learn the new subject, you will also have to relearn all the underpinning knowledge as well. This is very inefficient and slows down your overall progression which makes it more likely you may not succeed at all.

In addition, delaying your studies slows your path to qualification which can have negative impacts on your career, postponing the opportunity to apply for higher level positions and therefore higher pay.

You can use the following diagram showing the whole structure of your qualification to help you keep track of your progress.

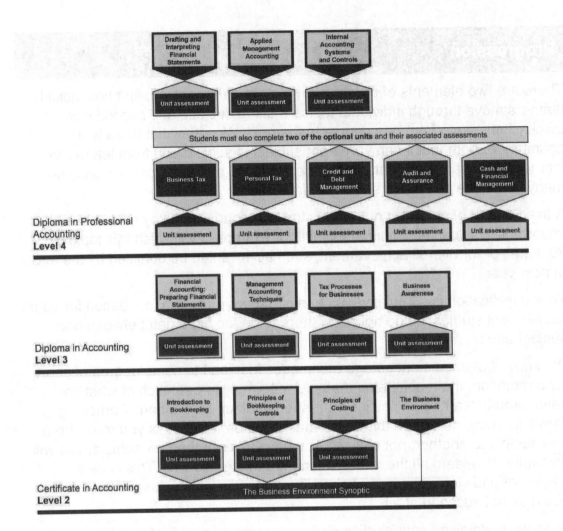

UNIT GUIDE

Introduction

This unit provides students with the fundamental knowledge of the three most common taxes that affect taxpayers in the United Kingdom (UK): income tax, capital gains tax and inheritance tax. With this knowledge, students will be equipped to prepare not only the computational aspects where appropriate of these taxes, but also appreciate how taxpayers can legally minimise their overall taxation liability.

Students will study the underpinning theory of taxation and will gain knowledge of taxes that affect every taxpayer in the UK. Within income tax, students will cover employment income, income from investments and income from property. Deductions and reliefs that apply to income tax are covered so that students can compute net income tax liability for a UK taxpayer. National Insurance completes this topic area.

Students will also study capital gains tax and inheritance tax. The fundamental principles of these taxes will be covered so that students can appreciate how they may affect UK taxpayers.

With their knowledge of these three taxes, students will then understand the taxation implications of decisions made by clients, and understand that advice and guidance may be offered to ensure that the taxpayer is complying with tax legislation.

The overall learning aim of the unit is to equip students with a knowledge of taxation as it applies to UK taxpayers so that accurate and fair taxation liabilities can be computed. It also enables students to appreciate the theory behind taxation, including the ethical aspects as it specifically applies to a taxation practitioner.

Learning outcomes

On completion of this unit the learner will be able to:

- Understand principles and rules that underpin taxation systems

- Calculate UK taxpayers' total income

- Calculate income tax and National Insurance contributions (NICs) payable by UK taxpayers

- Calculate capital gains tax payable by UK taxpayers

- Understand the principles of inheritance tax

Scope of content

The unit consists of five learning outcomes, which are further broken down into assessment criteria. These are set out in the following table with reference to the relevant chapter within the text.

Learners may not be assessed on all content, or on the full depth or breadth of a piece of content. Content assessed may change over time to ensure the validity of assessment.

		Chapter
1	**Understand principles and rules that underpin taxation systems**	
1.1	**Objectives and functions of taxation**	
	Learners need to understand:	
	• principles underpinning tax systems	1
	• definitions of progressive, regressive and proportional tax.	1
1.2	**Tax planning, tax avoidance and tax evasion**	
	Learners need to understand:	
	• the definitions of tax planning, tax avoidance and tax evasion	1
	• ethical implications of tax avoidance and tax evasion	1
	• requirements to report suspected tax evasion.	1

KAPLAN PUBLISHING

Links with other units

This unit has close links with:

- Level 3 Tax Process for Businesses
- Level 4 Business Tax

THE ASSESSMENT

Test specification for this unit assessment

Assessment type	**Marking type**	**Duration of exam**
Computer based unit assessment	Partially computer/ partially human marked	2 hours

The assessment for this unit consists of 10 compulsory, independent, tasks.

The competency level for AAT assessment is 70%.

Learning outcomes		**Weighting**
1	Understand principles and rules that underpin taxation systems	10%
2	Calculate UK taxpayers' total income	20%
3	Calculate income tax and National Insurance contributions payable by UK taxpayers	30%
4	Calculate capital gains tax payable by UK taxpayers	30%
5	Understand the principles of inheritance tax	10%
Total		100%

Sample assessment

The sample assessment has 10 tasks.

An analysis of the AAT sample assessment is set out below.

Task	Learning outcome	Topic
1	1.1, 1.2, 1.3, 1.4	Principles and rules underpinning tax
2	2.1	Income from employment
3	2.2, 2.3	Income from investments and property
4	3.1	Income tax payable
5	3.2	National insurance contributions
6	3.3	Tax planning
7	4.1	Capital gains tax principles
8	4.2	Capital gains tax: disposal of shares
9	4.3, 4.4	Capital gains tax: reliefs and exemptions
10	5.1	Inheritance tax

STUDY SKILLS

Preparing to study

Devise a study plan

Determine which times of the week you will study.

Split these times into sessions of at least one hour for study of new material. Any shorter periods could be used for revision or practice.

Put the times you plan to study onto a study plan for the weeks from now until the assessment and set yourself targets for each period of study – in your sessions make sure you cover the whole course, activities and the associated test your understanding activities.

If you are studying more than one unit at a time, try to vary your subjects as this can help to keep you interested and see subjects as part of wider knowledge.

When working through your course, compare your progress with your plan and, if necessary, re-plan your work (perhaps including extra sessions) or, if you are ahead, do some extra revision/practice questions.

Effective studying

Active reading

You are not expected to learn the text by rote, rather, you must understand what you are reading and be able to use it to pass the assessment and develop good practice.

A good technique is to use SQ3Rs – Survey, Question, Read, Recall, Review:

1 **Survey the chapter**

   Look at the headings and read the introduction, knowledge, skills and content, so as to get an overview of what the chapter deals with.

2 **Question**

   Whilst undertaking the survey ask yourself the questions you hope the chapter will answer for you.

3 **Read**

   Read through the chapter thoroughly working through the activities and, at the end, making sure that you can meet the learning objectives highlighted on the first page.

4   Recall

At the end of each section and at the end of the chapter, try to recall the main ideas of the section/chapter without referring to the text. This is best done after a short break of a couple of minutes after the reading stage.

5   Review

Check that your recall notes are correct.

You may also find it helpful to re-read the chapter to try and see the topic(s) it deals with as a whole.

Note taking

Taking notes is a useful way of learning, but do not simply copy out the text.

The notes must:

*   be in your own words

*   be concise

*   cover the key points

*   be well organised

*   be modified as you study further chapters in this text or in related ones.

Trying to summarise a chapter without referring to the text can be a useful way of determining which areas you know and which you don't.

Three ways of taking notes

1   Summarise the key points of a chapter

2   Make linear notes

A list of headings, subdivided with sub-headings listing the key points.

If you use linear notes, you can use different colours to highlight key points and keep topic areas together.

Use plenty of space to make your notes easy to use.

3   Try a diagrammatic form

The most common of which is a mind map.

To make a mind map, put the main heading in the centre of the paper and put a circle around it.

Draw lines radiating from this to the main sub-headings which again have circles around them.

Continue the process from the sub-headings to sub-sub-headings.

Annotating the text

You may find it useful to underline or highlight key points in your study text – but do be selective.

You may also wish to make notes in the margins.

Revision phase

Kaplan has produced material specifically designed for your final assessment preparation for this unit.

These include pocket revision notes and practice questions that include a bank of questions specifically in the style of the new syllabus.

Further guidance on how to approach the final stage of your studies is given in these materials.

Further reading

In addition to this text, you should also read the 'Accounting Technician' magazine every month to keep abreast of any guidance from the assessors.

Reference material

Reference material is provided in this assessment. During your assessment you will be able to access reference material through a series of clickable links on the right of every task. These will produce pop-up windows which can be moved or closed.

The reference material has been included in this study text (below). This is based on the version of the reference material that was available at the time of going to print.

The full version of the reference material is available for download from the AAT website.

Level 4 Personal Tax (PNTA)
Reference material

Finance Act 2021 – for Q2022 assessments in 2022 and 2023

Reference material for AAT assessment of Personal Tax

Introduction

This document comprises data that you may need to consult during your Personal Tax computer-based assessment.

The material can be consulted during the practice and live assessments by using the reference materials section at each task position. It's made available here so you can familiarise yourself with the content before the assessment.

Do not take a print of this document into the exam room with you*.

This document may be changed to reflect periodical updates in the computer-based assessment, so please check you have the most recent version while studying. This version is based on **Finance Act 2021** and is for use in AAT Q2022 assessments in 2022 and 2023.

*Unless you need a printed version as part of reasonable adjustments for particular needs, in which case you must discuss this with your tutor at least six weeks before the assessment date.

Contents

1. Tax rates and bands

Tax rates	Tax bands	Normal rates %	Dividend rates %
Basic rate	£ 1–£37,700	20	7.5
Higher rate	£37,701–£150,000	40	32.5
Additional rate	£150,001 and over	45	38.1

2. Allowances

		£
Personal allowance		12,570
Savings allowance:	Basic rate taxpayer	1,000
	Higher rate taxpayer	500
Dividend allowance		2,000
Income limit for personal allowances*		100,000

* Personal allowances are reduced by £1 for every £2 over the income limit.

3. Property income allowance

	£
Annual limit	1,000

4. Individual savings accounts

	£
Annual limit	20,000

AAT is a registered charity. No. 1050724

5. Deemed domicile

Deemed domicile	Criteria
Condition A	Was born in the UK
	Domicile of origin was in the UK
	Was resident in the UK for 2017 to 2018 or later years
Condition B	Has been UK resident for at least 15 of the 20 tax years immediately before the relevant tax year

6. Residence

Residence	Criteria
Automatically resident	Spend 183 or more days in the UK in the tax year; or
	Only home is in the UK; and
	You owned, rented or lived in the home for at least 91 days and spent at least 30 days there in the tax year.
Automatically not resident	Spend fewer than 16 days in the UK (or 46 days if you have not been classed as UK resident for the three previous tax years; or
	Work abroad full time (averaging at least 35 hours a week) and spend less than 91 days in the UK, of which no more than 30 are spent working
Resident by number of ties	If UK resident for one or more of the previous three tax years: • 4 ties needed if spend 16-45 days in the UK • 3 ties needed if spend 46-90 days in the UK • 2 ties needed if spend 91-120 days in the UK • 1 tie needed if spend over 120 days in the UK.
	If UK resident in none of the previous three tax years: • 4 ties needed if spend 46-90 days in the UK • 3 ties needed if spend 91-120 days in the UK • 2 ties needed if spend over 120 days in the UK.

7. Car benefit percentage

CO₂ Emissions for petrol engines g/km	Electric range miles	Cars first registered from 6 April 2020 %
Nil		1
1 to 50	130 or more	1
1 to 50	70-129	4
1 to 50	40-69	7
1 to 50	30-39	11
1 to 50	Less than 30	13
51 to 54		14
55 or more		15 + 1% for every extra 5g/km above 55g/km
Registration pre 6 April 2020*		Additional 1%
Diesel engines**		Additional 4%

* The additional 1% is not applied where the CO₂ emissions are Nil.

**The additional 4% will not apply to diesel cars which are registered after 1 September 2017 and meet the RDE2 standards.

8. Car fuel benefit

	£
Base figure	24,600

9. Approved mileage allowance payments (employees and residential landlords)

First 10,000 miles	45p per mile
Over 10,000 miles	25p per mile
Additional passengers	5p per mile per passenger
Motorcycles	24p per mile
Bicycles	20p per mile

10. Van benefit charge

	£
Basic charge	3,500
Private fuel charge	669
Benefit charge for zero emission vans	NIL

11. Other benefits in kind

Benefit	Notes
Expensive accommodation limit	£75,000
Health screening	One per year
Incidental overnight expenses: within UK	£5 per night
Incidental overnight expenses: overseas	£10 per night
Job-related accommodation	£Nil
Living expenses where job-related exemption applies	Restricted to 10% of employees net earnings
Loan of assets annual charge	20%
Low-rate or interest free loans	Up to £10,000
Mobile telephones	One per employee
Non-cash gifts from someone other than the employer	£250 per tax year
Non-cash long service award	£50 per year of service
Pay whilst attending a full-time course	£15,480 per academic year
Provision of eye tests and spectacles for VDU use	£Nil
Provision of parking spaces	£Nil
Provision of workplace childcare	£Nil
Provision of workplace sports facilities	£Nil
Removal and relocation expenses	£8,000
Staff party or event	£150 per head
Staff suggestion scheme	Up to £5,000
Subsidised meals	£Nil
Working from home	£6 per week/£26 per month

12. HMRC official rate

	%
HMRC official rate	2

13. National insurance contributions

		%
Class 1 Employee:	Below £9,568	0
	Above £9,568 and Below £50,270	12
	£50,270 and above	2
Class 1 Employer:	Below £8,840	0
	£8,840 and above	13.8
Class 1A		13.8

	£
Employment allowance	4,000

14. Capital gains tax

	£
Annual exempt amount	12,300

15. Capital gains tax – tax rates

	%
Basic rate	10
Higher rate	20

16. Inheritance tax – tax rates

	£
Nil rate band	325,000
Additional residence nil-rate band*	175,000

		%
Excess taxable at:	Death rate	40
	Lifetime rate	20

* Applies when a home is passed on death to direct descendants of the deceased after 6 April 2017. Any unused band is transferrable to a spouse or civil partner.

17. Inheritance tax – tapering relief

	% reduction
3 years or less	0
Over 3 years but less than 4 years	20
Over 4 years but less than 5 years	40
Over 5 years but less than 6 years	60
Over 6 years but less than 7 years	80

18. Inheritance tax – exemptions

		£
Small gifts		250 per transferee per tax year
Marriage or civil partnership:	From parent	5,000
	Grandparent	2,500
	One party to the other	2,500
	Others	1,000
Annual exemption		3,000

The Association of Accounting Technicians
140 Aldersgate Street
London
EC1A 4HY
t: +44 (0)20 7397 3000
f: +44 (0)20 7397 3009
e: aat@aat.org.uk
aat.org.uk

Level 4 Personal Tax (PNTA)
reference material

Professional conduct in relation to taxation

Finance Act 2021 – for Q2022 assessments in 2022 and 2023

Reference material for AAT assessment of Personal Tax

Introduction

This document comprises data that you may need to consult during your Personal Tax computer-based assessment. The material can be consulted during the practice and live assessments by using the reference material section at each task position. It is made available here so you can familiarise yourself with the content before the assessment.

Do not take a print of this document into the exam room with you*.

This document may be changed to reflect periodical updates in the computer-based assessment, so please check you have the most recent version while studying. This version is based on **Finance Act 2021** and is for use in AAT assessments in 2022 and 2023.

* Unless you need a printed version as part of reasonable adjustments for particular needs, in which case you must discuss this with your tutor at least six weeks before the assessment date.

Contents

1. Interpretation and abbreviations

Context

Tax advisors operate in a complex business and financial environment. The increasing public focus on the role of taxation in wider society means a greater interest in the actions of tax advisors and their clients.

This guidance, written by the professional bodies for their members working in tax, sets out the hallmarks of a good advisor, and in particular the fundamental principles of behaviour that members are expected to follow.

Interpretation

1.1   In this guidance:
- 'Client' includes, where the context requires, 'former client'
- 'Member' (and 'members') includes 'firm' or 'practice' and the staff thereof
- Words in the singular include the plural and words in the plural include the singular.

Abbreviations

1.2   The following abbreviations have been used:

AML	Anti-Money Laundering
CCAB	Consultative Committee of Accountancy Bodies
DOTAS	Disclosure of Tax Avoidance Schemes
GAAP	Generally Accepted Accounting Principles
GAAR	General Anti-Abuse Rule in Finance Act 2013
GDPR	General Data Protection Regulation
HMRC	Her Majesty's Revenue and Customs
MTD	Making Tax Digital
MLRO	Money Laundering Reporting Officer
NCA	National Crime Agency (previously the Serious Organised Crime Agency, SOCA)
POTAS	Promoters of Tax Avoidance Schemes
PCRT	Professional Conduct in Relation to Taxation
SRN	Scheme Reference Number

2. Fundamental principles

Overview of the fundamental principles

1. Ethical behaviour in the tax profession is critical. The work carried out by a member needs to be trusted by society at large as well as by clients and other stakeholders. What a member does reflects not just on themselves but on the profession as a whole.

2. A member must comply with the following fundamental principles:

Integrity
To be straightforward and honest in all professional and business relationships.

Objectivity
To not allow bias, conflict of interest or undue influence of others to override professional or business judgements.

Professional competence and due care
To maintain professional knowledge and skill at the level required to ensure that a client or employer receives competent professional service based on current developments in practice, legislation and techniques and act diligently and in accordance with applicable technical and professional standards.

Confidentiality
To respect the confidentiality of information acquired as a result of professional and business relationships and, therefore, not disclose any such information to third parties without proper and specific authority, unless there is a legal or professional right or duty to disclose, nor use the information for the personal advantage of the member or third parties.

Professional behaviour
To comply with relevant laws and regulations and avoid any action that discredits the profession.

3. PCRT Help sheet A: Submission of tax information and 'Tax filings'

Definition of filing of tax information and tax filings (filing)

1. For the purposes of this guidance, the term 'filing' includes any online submission of data, online filing or other filing that is prepared on behalf of the client for the purposes of disclosing to any taxing authority details that are to be used in the calculation of tax due by a client or a refund of tax due to the client or for other official purposes. It includes all taxes, NIC and duties.

2. A letter, or online notification, giving details in respect of a filing or as an amendment to a filing including, for example, any voluntary disclosure of an error should be dealt with as if it was a filing.

Making Tax Digital and filing

3. Tax administration systems, including the UK's, are increasingly moving to mandatory digital filing of tax information and returns.

4. Except in exceptional circumstances, a member will explicitly file in their capacity as agent. A member is advised to use the facilities provided for agents and to avoid knowing or using the client's personal access credentials.

5. A member should keep their access credentials safe from unauthorised use and consider periodic change of passwords.

6. A member is recommended to forward suspicious emails to phishing@hmrc.gsi.gov.uk and then delete them. It is also important to avoid clicking on websites or links in suspicious emails, or opening attachments.

7. Firms should have policies on cyber security, AML and GDPR.

Taxpayer's responsibility

8. The taxpayer has primary responsibility to submit correct and complete filings to the best of their knowledge and belief. The final decision as to whether to disclose any issue is that of the client but in relation to your responsibilities see paragraph 12 below.

9. In annual self-assessment returns or returns with short filing periods the filing may include reasonable estimates where necessary.

Member's responsibility

10. A member who prepares a filing on behalf of a client is responsible to the client for the accuracy of the filing based on the information provided.

11. In dealing with HMRC in relation to a client's tax affairs a member should bear in mind their duty of confidentiality to the client and that they are acting as the agent of their client. They have a duty to act in the best interests of their client.

12. A member should act in good faith in dealings with HMRC in accordance with the fundamental principle of integrity. In particular the member should take reasonable care and exercise appropriate professional scepticism when making statements or asserting facts on behalf of a client.

13. Where acting as a tax agent, a member is not required to audit the figures in the books and records provided or verify information provided by a client or by a third party. However, a member should take care not to be associated with the presentation of facts they know or believe to be incorrect or misleading, not to assert tax positions in a tax filing which they consider to have no sustainable basis.

14. When a member is communicating with HMRC, they should consider whether they need to make it clear to what extent they are relying on information which has been supplied by the client or a third party.

Materiality

15. Whether an amount is to be regarded as material depends upon the facts and circumstances of each case.

16. The profits of a trade, profession, vocation or property business should be computed in accordance with GAAP subject to any adjustment required or authorised by law in computing profits for those purposes. This permits a trade, profession, vocation or property business to disregard non-material adjustments in computing its accounting profits.

17. The application of GAAP, and therefore materiality does not extend beyond the accounting profits. Thus, the accounting concept of materiality cannot be applied when completing tax filings.

18. It should be noted that for certain small businesses an election may be made to use the cash basis instead; for small property businesses the default position is the cash basis. Where the cash basis is used, materiality is not relevant.

Disclosure

19. If a client is unwilling to include in a tax filing the minimum information required by law, the member should follow the guidance in Help sheet C: Dealing with Errors. The paragraphs below (paras 20 – 24) give guidance on some of the more common areas of uncertainty over disclosure.

20. In general, it is likely to be in a client's own interests to ensure that factors relevant to their tax liability are adequately disclosed to HMRC because:

    - their relationship with HMRC is more likely to be on a satisfactory footing if they can demonstrate good faith in their dealings with them. HMRC notes in 'Your Charter' that 'We want to give you a service that is fair, accurate and based on mutual trust and respect'
    - they will reduce the risk of a discovery or further assessment and may reduce exposure to interest and penalties.

21. It may be advisable to consider fuller disclosure than is strictly necessary. Reference to 'The Standards for Tax Planning' in PCRT may be relevant. The factors involved in making this decision include:
    - a filing relies on a valuation
    - the terms of the applicable law
    - the view taken by the member
    - the extent of any doubt that exists
    - the manner in which disclosure is to be made
    - the size and gravity of the item in question.

22. When advocating fuller disclosure than is necessary a member should ensure that their client is adequately aware of the issues involved and their potential implications. Fuller disclosure should only be made with the client's consent.

7

23. Cases will arise where there is doubt as to the correct treatment of an item of income or expenditure, or the computation of a gain or allowance. In such cases a member ought to consider what additional disclosure, if any, might be necessary. For example, additional disclosure should be considered where:

- there is inherent doubt as to the correct treatment of an item, for example, expenditure on repairs which might be regarded as capital in whole or part, or the VAT liability of a particular transaction, or
- HMRC has published its interpretation or has indicated its practice on a point, but the client proposes to adopt a different view, whether or not supported by Counsel's opinion. The member should refer to the guidance on the Veltema case and the paragraph below. See also HMRC guidance.

24. A member who is uncertain whether their client should disclose a particular item or of its treatment should consider taking further advice before reaching a decision. They should use their best endeavours to ensure that the client understands the issues, implications and the proposed course of action. Such a decision may have to be justified at a later date, so the member's files should contain sufficient evidence to support the position taken, including timely notes of discussions with the client and/or with other advisors, copies of any second opinion obtained and the client's final decision. A failure to take reasonable care may result in HMRC imposing a penalty if an error is identified after an enquiry.

Supporting documents

25. For the most part, HMRC does not consider that it is necessary for a taxpayer to provide supporting documentation in order to satisfy the taxpayer's overriding need to make a correct filing. HMRC's view is that, where it is necessary for that purpose, explanatory information should be entered in the 'white space' provided on the filing. However, HMRC does recognise that the taxpayer may wish to supply further details of a particular computation or transaction in order to minimise the risk of a discovery assessment being raised at a later time. Following the uncertainty created by the decision in Veltema, HMRC's guidance can be found in SP1/06 – Self Assessment: Finality and Discovery.

26. Further HMRC guidance says that sending attachments with a tax filing is intended for those cases where the taxpayer 'feels it is crucial to provide additional information to support the filing but for some reason cannot utilise the white space'.

Reliance on HMRC published guidance

27. Whilst it is reasonable in most circumstances to rely on HMRC published guidance, a member should be aware that the Tribunal and the courts will apply the law even if this conflicts with HMRC guidance.

28. Notwithstanding this, if a client has relied on HMRC guidance which is clear and unequivocal and HMRC resiles from any of the terms of the guidance, a Judicial Review claim is a possible route to pursue.

Approval of tax filings

29. The member should advise the client to review their tax filing before it is submitted.

30. The member should draw the client's attention to the responsibility which the client is taking in approving the filing as correct and complete. Attention should be drawn to any judgmental areas or positions reflected in the filing to ensure that the client is aware of these and their implications before they approve the filing.

31. A member should obtain evidence of the client's approval of the filing in electronic or non-electronic form.

4. PCRT Help sheet B: Tax advice

The Standards for Tax Planning

1. The Standards for Tax Planning are critical to any planning undertaken by members. They are:

   - Client Specific

     Tax planning must be specific to the particular client's facts and circumstances. Clients must be alerted to the wider risks and implications of any courses of action.

   - Lawful

     At all times members must act lawfully and with integrity and expect the same from their clients. Tax planning should be based on a realistic assessment of the facts and on a credible view of the law.

     Members should draw their client's attention to where the law is materially uncertain, for example because HMRC is known to take a different view of the law. Members should consider taking further advice appropriate to the risks and circumstances of the particular case, for example where litigation is likely.

   - Disclosure and transparency

     Tax advice must not rely for its effectiveness on HMRC having less than the relevant facts. Any disclosure must fairly represent all relevant facts.

   - Tax planning arrangements

     Members must not create, encourage or promote tax planning arrangements or structures that i) set out to achieve results that are contrary to the clear intention of Parliament in enacting relevant legislation and/or ii) are highly artificial or highly contrived and seek to exploit shortcomings within the relevant legislation.

   - Professional judgement and appropriate documentation

   - Applying these requirements to particular client advisory situations requires members to exercise professional judgement on a number of matters. Members should keep notes on a timely basis of the rationale for the judgements exercised in seeking to adhere to these requirements

Guidance

2. The paragraphs below provide guidance for members when considering whether advice complies with the Fundamental Principles and Standards for Tax Planning.

Tax evasion

3. A member should never be knowingly involved in tax evasion, although, of course, it is appropriate to act for a client who is rectifying their affairs.

Tax planning and advice

4. In contrast to tax evasion, tax planning is legal. However, under the Standard members 'must not create, encourage or promote tax planning arrangements that (i) set out to achieve results that are contrary to the clear intention of Parliament in enacting relevant legislation and/or (ii) are highly artificial or highly contrived and seek to exploit shortcomings within the relevant legislation'.

5. Things to consider:
   - have you checked that your engagement letter fully covers the scope of the planning advice?
   - have you taken the Standards for Tax Planning and the Fundamental Principles into account? Is it client specific? Is it lawful? Will all relevant facts be disclosed to HMRC? Is it creating, encouraging or promoting tax planning contrary to the 4th Standard for Tax Planning?
   - how tax sophisticated is the client?
   - has the client made clear what they wish to achieve by the planning?
   - what are the issues involved with the implementation of the planning?
   - what are the risks associated with the planning and have you warned the client of them? For example:
     - the strength of the legal interpretation relied upon
     - the potential application of the GAAR
     - the implications for the client, including the obligations of the client in relation to their tax return, if the planning requires disclosure under DOTAS or DASVOIT and the potential for an accelerated payment notice or partner payment notice?
     - the reputational risk to the client and the member of the planning in the public arena
     - the stress, cost and wider personal or business implications to the client in the event of a prolonged dispute with HMRC. This may involve unwelcomed publicity, costs, expenses and loss of management time over a significant period
     - if the client tenders for government contracts, the potential impact of the proposed tax planning on tendering for and retaining public sector contracts
     - the risk of counteraction. This may occur before the planning is completed or potentially there may be retrospective counteraction at a later date
     - the risk of challenge by HMRC. Such challenge may relate to the legal interpretation relied upon, but may alternatively relate to the construction of the facts, including the implementation of the planning
     - the risk and inherent uncertainty of litigation. The probability of the planning being overturned by the courts if litigated and the potential ultimate downside should the client be unsuccessful
     - is a second opinion necessary/advisable?
   - are the arrangements in line with any applicable code of conduct or ethical guidelines or stances for example the Banking Code, and fit and proper tests for charity trustees and pension administrators?
   - are you satisfied that the client understands the planning proposed?
   - have you documented the advice given and the reasoning behind it?

5. PCRT Help sheet C: Dealing with errors

Introduction

1. For the purposes of this guidance, the term 'error' is intended to include all errors and mistakes whether they were made by the client, the member, HMRC or any other party involved in a client's tax affairs, and whether made innocently or deliberately.

2. During a member's relationship with the client, the member may become aware of possible errors in the client's tax affairs. Unless the client is already aware of the possible error, they should be informed as soon as the member identifies them.

3. Where the error has resulted in the client paying too much tax the member should advise the client to make a repayment claim. The member should advise the client of the time limits to make a claim and have regard to any relevant time limits. The rest of this Help sheet deals with situations where tax may be due to HMRC.

4. Sometimes an error made by HMRC may mean that the client has not paid tax actually due or they have been incorrectly repaid tax. There may be fee costs as a result of correcting such mistakes. A member should bear in mind that, in some circumstances, clients or agents may be able to claim for additional professional costs incurred and compensation from HMRC.

5. A member should act correctly from the outset. A member should keep sufficient appropriate records of discussions and advice and when dealing with errors the member should:
   - give the client appropriate advice
   - if necessary, so long as they continue to act for the client, seek to persuade the client to behave correctly
   - take care not to appear to be assisting a client to plan or commit any criminal offence or to conceal any offence which has been committed
   - in appropriate situations, or where in doubt, discuss the client's situation with a colleague or an independent third party (having due regard to client confidentiality).

6. Once aware of a possible error, a member must bear in mind the legislation on money laundering and the obligations and duties which this places upon them.

7. Where the member may have made the error, the member should consider whether they need to notify their professional indemnity insurers.

8. In any situation where a member has concerns about their own position, they should consider taking specialist legal advice. For example, where a client appears to have used the member to assist in the commissioning of a criminal offence and people could question whether the member had acted honestly in in good faith. Note that The Criminal Finances Act 2017 has created new criminal offences of failure to prevent facilitation of tax evasion.

9. The flowchart below summarises the recommended steps a member should take where a possible error arises. It must be read in conjunction with the guidance and commentary that follow it.

Dealing with errors flowchart

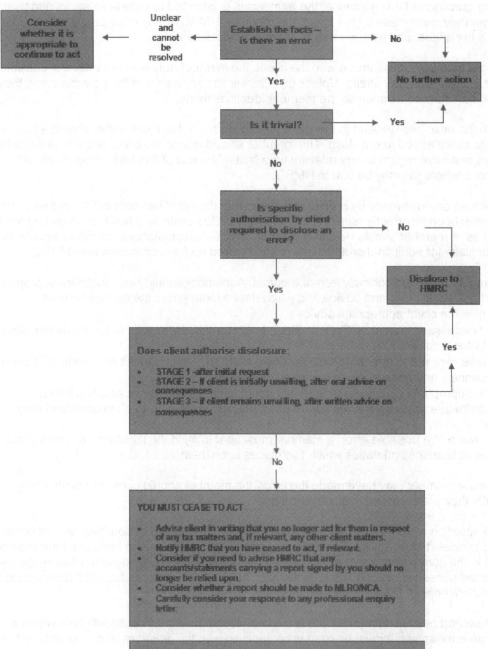

Establish the facts – is there an error

- Unclear and cannot be resolved → **Consider whether it is appropriate to continue to act**
- No → **No further action**
- Yes ↓

Is it trivial?
- Yes → No further action
- No ↓

Is specific authorisation by client required to disclose an error?
- No → **Disclose to HMRC**
- Yes ↓

Does client authorise disclosure:
- STAGE 1 –after initial request
- STAGE 2 – if client is initially unwilling, after oral advice on consequences
- STAGE 3 – if client remains unwilling, after written advice on consequences

- Yes → Disclose to HMRC
- No ↓

YOU MUST CEASE TO ACT
- Advise client in writing that you no longer act for them in respect of any tax matters and, if relevant, any other client matters.
- Notify HMRC that you have ceased to act, if relevant.
- Consider if you need to advise HMRC that any accounts/statements carrying a report signed by you should no longer be relied upon.
- Consider whether a report should be made to MLRO/NCA.
- Carefully consider your response to any professional enquiry letter.

At all times consider your obligations under anti money laundering legislation and whether you need to submit a Suspicious Activity Report.

6.   PCRT Help sheet D: Requests for data by HMRC

Introduction

1. For the purposes of this help sheet the term 'data' includes documents in whatever form (including electronic) and other information. While this guidance relates to HMRC requests, other government bodies or organisations may also approach the member for data. The same principles apply.

2. A distinction should be drawn between a request for data made informally ('informal requests') and those requests for data which are made in exercise of a power to require the provision of the data requested ('formal requests').

3. Similarly, requests addressed to a client and those addressed to a member require different handling.

4. Where a member no longer acts for a client, the member remains subject to the duty of confidentiality. In relation to informal requests, the member should refer the enquirer either to the former client or if authorised by the client to the new agent. In relation to formal requests addressed to the member, the termination of their professional relationship with the client does not affect the member's duty to comply with that request, where legally required to do so.

5. A member should comply with formal requests and should not seek to frustrate legitimate requests for information. Adopting a constructive approach may help to resolve issues promptly and minimise costs to all parties.

6. Whilst a member should be aware of HMRC's powers it may be appropriate to take specialist advice.

7. Devolved tax authorities have separate powers.

8. Two flowcharts are at the end of this help sheet:
    * requests for data addressed to the member
    * requests for data addressed to the client.

Informal requests addressed to the client

9. From time to time, HMRC chooses to communicate directly with clients rather than with the appointed agent.

10. HMRC has given reassurances that it is working to ensure that initial contact on compliance checks will normally be via the agent and only if the agent does not reply within an appropriate timescale will the contact be directly with the client.

11. When the member assists a client in dealing with such requests from HMRC, the member should advise the client that cooperation with informal requests can provide greater opportunities for the taxpayer to find a pragmatic way to work through the issue at hand with HMRC.

Informal requests addressed to the member

12. Disclosure in response to informal requests can only be made with the client's permission.

13. In many instances, the client will have authorised routine disclosure of relevant data, for example, through the engagement letter. However, if there is any doubt about whether the client has authorised disclosure, the member should ask the client to approve what is to be disclosed.

14. Where an oral enquiry is made by HMRC, a member should consider asking for it to be put in writing so that a response may be agreed with the client.

15. Although there is no obligation to comply with an informal request in whole or in part, a member should advise the client whether it is in the client's best interests to disclose such data, as lack of cooperation may have a direct impact on penalty negotiations post—enquiry.

16. Informal requests may be forerunners to formal requests compelling the disclosure of data. Consequently, it may be sensible to comply with such requests.

Formal requests addressed to the client

17. In advising their client a member should consider whether specialist advice may be needed, for example on such issues as whether the notice has been issued in accordance with the relevant tax legislation and whether the data request is valid.

18. The member should also advise the client about any relevant right of appeal against the formal request if appropriate and of the consequences of a failure to comply.

19. If the notice is legally effective the client is legally obliged to comply with the request.

20. The most common statutory notice issued to clients and third parties by HMRC is under Schedule 36 FA 2008.

Formal requests addressed to the member

21. The same principles apply to formal requests to the member as formal requests to clients.

22. If a formal request is valid it **overrides the member's duty of confidentiality** to their client. The member is therefore obliged to comply with the request. Failure to comply with their legal obligations can expose the member to civil or criminal penalties.

23. In cases where the member is not legally precluded by the terms of the notice from communicating with the client, the member should advise the client of the notice and keep the client informed of progress and developments.

24. The member should ensure that in complying with any notice they do not provide information or data outside the scope of the notice.

25. If a member is faced with a situation in which HMRC is seeking to enforce disclosure by the removal of data, or seeking entrance to inspect business premises occupied by a member in their capacity as an adviser, the member should consider seeking immediate professional advice, to ensure that this is the legally correct course of action.

Privileged data

26. Legal privilege arises under common law and may only be overridden if this is set out in legislation. It protects a party's right to communicate in confidence with a legal adviser. The privilege belongs to the client and not to the member.

27. If a document is privileged: The client cannot be required to make disclosure of that document to HMRC. Another party cannot disclose it (including the member), without the client's express permission.

28. There are two types of legal privilege under common law: legal advice privilege and litigation privilege.

(a) Legal advice privilege
Covers documents passing between a client and their legal adviser prepared for the purposes of obtaining or giving legal advice. However, communications from a tax adviser who is not a practising lawyer will not attract legal advice privilege even if such individuals are giving advice on legal matters such as tax law.

(b) Litigation privilege
Covers data created for the dominant purpose of litigation. Litigation privilege may arise where litigation has not begun, but is merely contemplated and may apply to data prepared by non-lawyer advisors (including tax advisors). There are two important limits on litigation privilege. First, it does not arise in respect of non- adversarial proceedings. Second, the documents must be produced for the 'dominant purpose' of litigation.

29. A privilege under Schedule 36 paragraphs 19, (documents relating to the conduct of a pending appeal), 24 and 25 (auditors, and tax advisors' documents) might exist by "quasi-privilege" and if this is the case a tax adviser does not have to provide those documents. Care should be taken as not all data may be privileged.

30. A member who receives a request for data, some of which the member believes may be subject to privilege or 'quasi-privilege', should take independent legal advice on the position, unless expert in this area.

Help sheet D: Flowchart regarding requests for data by HMRC to the Member

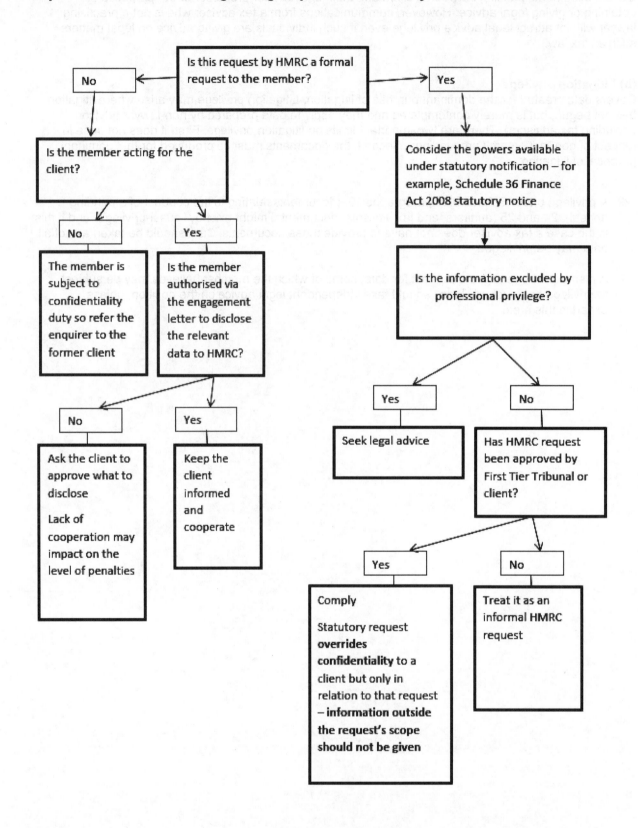

Is this request by HMRC a formal request to the member?

No → → **Yes**

No side:

Is the member acting for the client?

No → **The member is subject to confidentiality duty so refer the enquirer to the former client**

Yes → **Is the member authorised via the engagement letter to disclose the relevant data to HMRC?**

No → **Ask the client to approve what to disclose**

Lack of cooperation may impact on the level of penalties

Yes → **Keep the client informed and cooperate**

Yes side:

Consider the powers available under statutory notification – for example, Schedule 36 Finance Act 2008 statutory notice

Is the information excluded by professional privilege?

Yes → **Seek legal advice**

No → **Has HMRC request been approved by First Tier Tribunal or client?**

Yes → **Comply**

Statutory request overrides confidentiality to a client but only in relation to that request – information outside the request's scope should not be given

No → **Treat it as an informal HMRC request**

Help sheet D: Flowchart regarding requests for data by HMRC to the Client

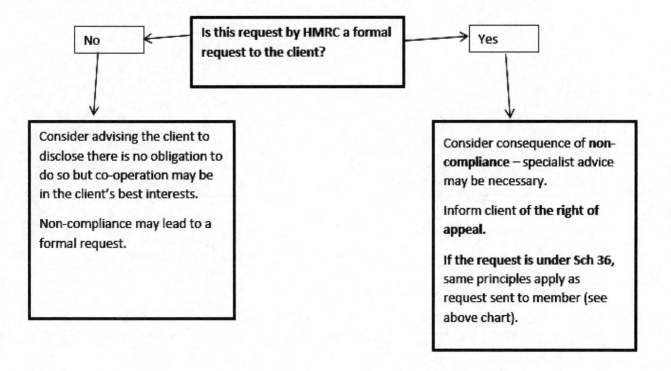

No

← **Is this request by HMRC a formal request to the client?** →

Yes

Consider advising the client to disclose there is no obligation to do so but co-operation may be in the client's best interests.

Non-compliance may lead to a formal request.

Consider consequence of **non-compliance** – specialist advice may be necessary.

Inform client of **the right of appeal.**

If the request is under Sch 36, same principles apply as request sent to member (see above chart).

The Association of Accounting Technicians
140 Aldersgate Street
London
EC1A 4HY
t: +44 (0)20 7397 3000
f: +44 (0)20 7397 3009
e: aat@aat.org.uk
aat.org.uk

Introduction to personal tax

1

Introduction

This chapter provides a context for the subsequent chapters in this text.

It outlines the features of a tax system and sets out the manner in which a professional tax adviser should behave when giving advice and dealing with clients.

It introduces the four taxes covered within personal tax and sets out the rules relating to residence and domicile.

<table>
<tr><td>

ASSESSMENT CRITERIA

Understand principles underpinning tax systems including neutrality, efficiency, certainty and simplicity, effectiveness and fairness, and flexibility (1.1)

Understand definitions of progressive, regressive and proportional tax (1.1)

Understand definitions of tax planning, tax avoidance and tax evasion (1.2)

Understand ethical implications of tax avoidance and tax evasion (1.2)

Understand requirements to report suspected tax evasion (1.2)

Understand AAT's expectations of its tax practitioners as set out in the AAT Professional Conduct in Relation to Taxation, particularly in dealing with clients and third parties (1.3)

Understand the ethical principle of confidentiality (1.3)

Understand the definition of residence and domicile (1.4)

Understand how to determine residence and domicile status (1.4)

Understand the impact of residence and domicile status on the taxation position of UK taxpayers (1.4)

</td><td>

CONTENTS

1   Features of tax systems

2   Duties and responsibilities of a tax adviser

3   Tax planning, avoidance and evasion

4   Taxes within the Personal Tax assessment

5   Tax residence

6   Tax domicile

7   Professional conduct in relation to taxation

</td></tr>
</table>

1 Features of tax systems

1.1 Tax system

The government needs tax revenues to finance expenditure such as the health service, retirement pensions, social benefits and government borrowing.

The government will use tax to stimulate one sector of the economy and control another. For example, allowances on capital expenditure may develop the manufacturing sector, while high taxes on tobacco and alcohol may discourage sales.

A tax system may have the following underlying principles:

- neutrality – tax should be neutral and equitable between all forms of business, rather than driving a particular economic choice

- efficiency – the costs to businesses of complying with the tax rules and the costs to governments of administering the tax should be as low as possible

- certainty and simplicity – the rules should be clear and simple for taxpayers to understand; complexity may encourage aggressive tax planning (see later in this chapter)

- effectiveness and fairness – the rules should give rise to the right amount of tax at the right time, without double taxation or no taxation through failure to enforce

- flexibility – the system should be flexible so that it can respond to technological and commercial developments

1.2 Tax rate structures

A particular tax falls into one of three categories depending on how rates are structured:

Progressive taxes

These take an increasing proportion of income as income rises. For example, income tax where tax is charged at 20%, then 40% and finally 45%.

Proportional taxes

These take the same proportion of income as income rises.

Regressive taxes

These take a decreasing proportion of income as income rises. For example, national insurance contributions which are charged at 12% and then at 2%.

Test your understanding 1

Tax systems

Read the following statements and state whether they are true or false.

1   The principle of flexibility requires tax systems to minimise the costs of administering tax.

2   A tax system with neutrality is equitable between forms of business activities.

3   Income tax is a regressive tax.

4   National insurance is a regressive tax.

---

2   Duties and responsibilities of a tax adviser

2.1   AAT expectations

A person advising either a company or an individual on taxation issues has duties and responsibilities towards both:

*   his or her client, and

*   HM Revenue and Customs (HMRC).

An adviser owes the greatest duty to his or her client.

AAT expects members to follow the guidance of the PCRT ('Professional conduct in relation to taxation') when dealing with clients and third parties such as HMRC.

2.2   Professional conduct in relation to taxation

Guidance on how tax advisers should conduct themselves has been published by the professional accountancy bodies in 'Professional conduct in relation to taxation' (PCRT).

The PCRT covers the five fundamental principles with which tax practitioners should comply. There are also additional help sheets which cover a practitioner's relationship with the client and HMRC specifically in terms of: submitting returns, tax advice, dealing with errors, and requests for data by HMRC. Later in this chapter there are several Test Your Understanding examples to help familiarise you with the PCRT in these areas.

Reference material

Extracts from PCRT are available for you to refer to in the assessment. These extracts are set out in the appendix to this chapter.

In the assessment you may be required to use this guidance to determine how a tax adviser should behave in a particular situation. Accordingly, you should ensure that you are very familiar with the matters covered in these extracts so that you are able to find the information you need.

2.3 Providing tax advice

When providing tax advice and preparing tax returns, a person should act in the best interests of the client.

However, he or she must ensure that services are consistent with the law and are carried out competently.

At all times an adviser must not in any way impair his or her:

- integrity, such that he or she is straightforward and honest in all professional and business relationships; or

- objectivity, such that he or she does not allow bias, conflict of interest or undue influence of others to override professional or business judgements.

2.4 Providing information to HMRC/other authorities

The 'Guidelines on Professional Ethics' require that a member should not be associated with any return or communication where there is reason to believe that it:

- contains a false or misleading statement

- contains statements or information furnished recklessly, or

- omits or obscures information required to be included and such omission or obscurity would mislead the tax authorities.

2.5   Confidentiality

A tax adviser has an overriding duty of confidentiality towards his or her client. Under normal circumstances a client's tax affairs should not be discussed with third parties. This duty remains even after the adviser no longer works for the client. It also applies in respect of prospective clients.

Confidential information obtained through professional and business relationships should not be used for personal advantage. Confidentiality should be maintained even in a social environment.

The duty of confidentiality also relates to dealings with HMRC.

However, the tax adviser must ensure that, whilst acting in the client's best interests, he or she consults with HMRC staff in an open and constructive manner (see below).

The exceptions to the rule to maintain confidentiality are where:

- authority has been given by the client, or

- there is a legal, regulatory or professional duty to disclose.

 Test your understanding 2

Which of the following statements is not correct?

A   Accountants need to follow the rules of confidentiality even in a social environment.

B   If there is a statutory requirement to disclose, accountants are allowed to break the rules of confidentiality.

C   Rules of confidentiality towards a client must be followed even after the business relationship has ended.

D   Accountants must follow the rules of confidentiality irrespective of the situation.

3 Tax planning, avoidance and evasion

3.1 Tax planning and tax avoidance

A tax adviser is required to act in the best interests of his or her client. This would include providing advice on how a client's affairs should be structured in order to minimise tax liabilities.

Tax planning is the use of legitimate means in order to reduce a tax liability such as making use of investment income generated by an ISA which would be exempt from income and capital gains tax.

Tax avoidance, although lawful, is where planning may not be deemed to comply with the spirit of the law i.e. to divert investments outside the UK to attract overseas tax rates which may be much lower than those in the UK.

Advice of this nature may subject the client and the adviser to scrutiny, investigation and possible public criticism. An adviser should therefore consider carefully when giving tax advice and factor in any potential negative impacts.

3.2 Tax evasion

Tax evasion is unlawful. A taxpayer who dishonestly withholds or falsifies information in order to evade tax may be subject to criminal proceedings or suffer civil penalties.

3.3 Dealing with problems

In spite of guidelines being available, there can be situations where the method of resolving an ethical issue is not straightforward.

In those situations additional advice should be sought from:

- a supervisor
- a professional body, or
- a legal adviser.

3.4 Dealing with errors and omissions in clients' tax returns

As seen above, tax evasion involves the deliberate withholding or falsifying of information. This means the relevant tax returns will be incorrect. Alternatively, a client, the tax adviser, or HMRC, may have made an error without this being deliberate. In all cases, the tax adviser needs to consider the PCRT guidance 'Dealing with errors' for what to do next.

Where a tax adviser realises that an error or omission has been made in a client's or employer's tax return he or she must recommend that the client/employer informs HMRC.

If the client/employer refuses to do so, the member must cease to act for the client.

Dishonestly retaining funds acquired as a result of an error or omission amounts to tax evasion.

More details regarding dealing with errors are given in relation to the PCRT later in this chapter.

 Test your understanding 3

When a taxpayer makes use a particular tax relief, what is this an example of?

A   Tax planning

B   Tax avoidance

C   Tax evasion

 4   **Taxes within the Personal Tax assessment**

4.1   The tax year

This study text is based on the tax year 2021/22.

The tax year 2021/22 runs from 6 April 2021 to 5 April 2022.

This study text will explain which items go into the tax computations for the tax year.

4.2   The taxes within personal tax

The four taxes within personal tax are:

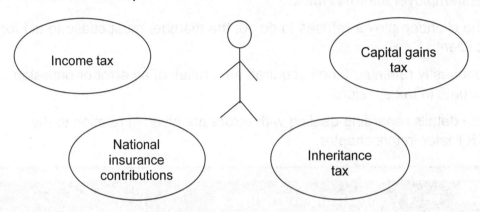

- income tax (Chapters 2 – 7)
- national insurance contributions (Chapter 8)
- capital gains tax (Chapters 9 – 11)
- inheritance tax (Chapter 12)

4.3   Income tax

Income tax applies mainly to:

- amounts earned in day to day work, and
- income generated from assets (for example dividend income on shares).

You will discover how to calculate an individual's income tax payable.

The ways in which the income tax payable by an individual can be reduced are also considered.

4.4   National insurance contributions (NICs)

The personal tax assessment requires knowledge of class 1 NICs, which are payable by employers and employees in respect of employment income as well as class 1A NICs, which are payable by employers in respect of taxable benefits received by the employees.

The NICs payable by the self-employed (class 2 and class 4) are covered in Business Tax.

You will discover how to calculate the class 1 NICs payable by both the employer and the employee and class 1A NICs payable by the employer.

4.5 Capital gains tax (CGT)

CGT applies mainly when assets are sold.

However, certain assets are exempt from CGT and there are other ways of reducing the gains.

You will discover how to calculate an individual's CGT payable.

4.6 Inheritance tax (IHT)

IHT applies mainly on the death of an individual in respect of the assets owned at death. It can also be payable in respect of gifts made by an individual during their lifetime.

Certain exemptions from IHT are available and there are other ways of reducing an individual's liability to IHT.

You will discover the tax rates applicable to lifetime transfers and on death, and how reliefs and exemptions can reduce an individual's IHT liability.

5 Tax residence

5.1 Tax residence status

An individual's residence is where they are deemed to be resident in a tax year for tax purposes. Residence status – whether they are UK resident or non-UK resident – is determined for each tax year under rules set out later in this section.

The residence status of an individual determines whether their overseas income is subject to income tax in the UK.

- Individuals who are resident in the UK are subject to UK income tax on both their UK and overseas income.

- Individuals who are not resident in the UK are subject to UK income tax on their UK income only.

5.2 Determination of residence

An individual is resident for the whole of a tax year if he:

- does not meet one of the automatic non-UK residence tests, and

- meets one of the automatic UK residence tests, or

- meets one or more of the sufficient ties tests.

In order to determine the tax residence status of an individual:

1 Check the automatic non-UK residence tests

   - if one test satisfied = non-UK resident
   - if not, go to step 2.

2 Check the automatic UK residence tests

   - if one test satisfied = UK resident
   - if not, go to step 3

3 Consider the number of ties the individual has with the UK

   - determine whether the individual has been UK resident in any of the last three tax years or has not
   - determine how many days the individual has spent in the UK
   - identify the relevant number of ties required for the individual to then be UK resident
   - determine how many ties the individual has with the UK
   - if the individual's ties are greater than or equal to the relevant number of ties = UK resident

5.3 Automatic non-UK residency tests

An individual is automatically not UK resident if he or she is 'in the UK' in the tax year for less than:

- 16 days, or
- 46 days, and he or she has not been UK resident in any of the previous three tax years, or
- 91 days with not more than 30 days working in the UK, and he or she works full-time overseas for an average of at least 35 hours per week.

Note that an individual is 'in the UK' if he or she is in the UK at midnight.

5.4 Automatic UK residency tests

An individual is automatically UK resident if:

- he or she is in the UK for at least 183 days in the tax year, or
- for a period of at least 91 consecutive days his or her only home is in the UK and he spends at least 30 days there in the tax year, or
- he or she works full-time in the UK (this aspect of the test will not be examined in the assessment).

If the individual does not satisfy any of the automatic tests, his or her residency status is determined by:

- how many of the five 'sufficient ties tests' are satisfied, and

- the number of days spent in the UK.

5.5 Sufficient ties tests

The number of days the individual has spent in the UK, together with his or her resident status in the three previous tax years determines the relevant number of ties required to be UK resident. This is set out in the table below:

Days in the UK	Previously resident in any of the last three tax years	Not previously resident in any of the last three tax years
Less than 16	Automatically not resident	Automatically not resident
16 to 45	Resident if 4 UK ties (or more)	Automatically not resident
46 to 90	Resident if 3 UK ties (or more)	Resident if 4 UK ties
91 to 120	Resident if 2 UK ties (or more)	Resident if 3 UK ties (or more)
121 to 182	Resident if 1 UK tie (or more)	Resident if 2 UK ties (or more)
183 or more	Automatically resident	Automatically resident

The ties include factors such as whether the individual has close family or accommodation in the UK, but you are not required to know details of ties in the assessment. Instead, you may be told the number of UK ties of an individual, and have to use this, with the number of days spent in the UK, to determine whether the individual is UK resident.

 Reference material

Some information about residence can be found in the 'Residence' section of your reference material provided in the real assessment, so you do not need to learn it.

Why not look up the correct part of the reference material in the introduction to this text book now?

Test your understanding 4

Residency status

Explain whether or not the following individuals are resident in the UK in the tax year 2021/22.

1   Dieter was born in Germany. He has lived in his home town in Germany until the tax year 2021/22 when he came to the UK to visit on 10 June 2021 until 18 January 2022.

2   Simone was born in France. She has lived in her home town in France until the tax year 2021/22 when she came to the UK to visit for a month.

3   Fred has always spent more than 300 days in the UK and has therefore been UK resident.

     He gave up work on 5 April 2021 and on 18 May 2021 he set off on a round the world holiday. He did not return until 6 April 2022.

     Initially he spent 5 weeks in his holiday home in Portugal and then stayed in hotels in various countries.

     He has four UK ties in 2021/22.

6   Tax domicile

The domicile status of an individual differs from the concepts of nationality and residence. It is based on the individual's permanent home. A person can only have one domicile at any one time.

- At birth an individual has the same domicile as his or her father. This is known as a domicile of origin.

- Until the individual is 16 years old, any change in his or her father's domicile also changes the domicile of the individual. This is known as a domicile of dependence.

- Once the individual is 16, it is possible to acquire a new country of domicile by severing all ties with the old country and establishing residence in the new country on a permanent basis. This is known as a domicile of choice.

On 6 April 2017 the government introduced a deemed domicile status for income tax and CGT. Different rules apply for IHT but these are not included in the PNTA assessment.

The impact of these rules means that even if an individual is non-domiciled he or she will be treated as UK domiciled for tax purposes if the rules under either condition A or condition B are met.

Condition A

- The individual was born in the UK **and**
- the individual had a UK domicile of origin, **and**
- the individual is resident in the UK for 2017/18 or later years.

Condition B

The individual has been UK resident for at least 15 out of the 20 tax years immediately before the current tax year.

 Reference material

Some information about deemed domicile can be found in the 'Deemed domicile' section of your reference material provided in the real assessment, so you do not need to learn it.

Why not look up the correct part of the reference material in the introduction to this text book now?

 Test your understanding 5

Domicile status

Explain whether the following individuals are domiciled or deemed domiciled in the UK in the tax year 2021/22.

1   Sunita was born in America. Her father has always been domiciled in the UK. Sunita occasionally visits the UK, and does not have a permanent home in any one country.

2   Francoise was born in the UK and his father was domiciled in the UK at his birth. Francoise moved to France when he was 20 years old and changed his domicile to France at that time. Francoise moved to the UK on 1 March 2020 and lived in the UK throughout the tax years 2020/21 and 2021/22.

3   Petra was born and is domiciled in Spain. She has lived in the UK since 6 April 2007.

7 Professional conduct in relation to taxation

In the assessment you will be able to consult the reference material relating to professional conduct in relation to taxation. This will be available through pop-up windows. The full document has been included in an appendix at the end of this chapter.

Use the following test your understanding questions to familiarise yourself with the content of the reference material.

 Test your understanding 6

PCRT familiarisation part 1

Answer the following questions by referring to PCRT Help sheet A: Submission of tax information and 'Tax filings', which will be available for you to refer to in the assessment. You should answer each question by writing a complete sentence.

1   What is meant by the term 'filing'?

2   What is the email address to which a member should forward suspicious emails?

3   Who has primary responsibility for submitting a correct tax return?

4   When acting as a tax agent, is a member required to verify information provided by the client?

5   Can the accounting concept of materiality be applied when completing tax filings?

6   When might it be advisable to consider fuller disclosure to HMRC than is strictly necessary?

7   When should attachments be included with a tax filing?

8   If HMRC guidance conflicts with the law, which will be applied by courts in the event of a dispute with HMRC?

9   What should a member bring a client's attention before the client approves a tax filing?

Test your understanding 7

PCRT familiarisation part 2

Answer the following questions by referring to PCRT Help sheet B: Tax advice, which will be available for you to refer to in the assessment. You should answer each question by writing a complete sentence.

1   What are the five standards for tax planning?

2   Is it acceptable for a member to act for a client who is trying to rectify their tax affairs having previously been involved in tax evasion?

3   What sort of tax planning must members refrain from promoting?

 Test your understanding 8

PCRT familiarisation part 3

Answer the following questions by referring to PCRT Help sheet C: Dealing with errors, which will be available for you to refer to in the assessment. You should answer each question by writing a complete sentence.

1   When should a member alert a client to a possible error in the client's tax affairs?

2   If a client is unwilling to disclose an error to HMRC and your firm has decided to cease to act for the client, how should the client be informed?

Test your understanding 9

PCRT familiarisation part 4

Answer the following questions by referring to PCRT Help sheet D: Requests for data by HMRC, which will be available for you to refer to in the assessment. You should answer each question by writing a complete sentence.

1   What is data in the context of PCRT?

2   Who will HMRC normally contact when initiating a compliance check?

3   Is a member obliged to comply with an informal request from HMRC?

4   What is the most common statutory notice issued to clients by HMRC?

5   Is a member obliged to comply with a formal request from HMRC?

6   What are the two types of legal privilege under common law?

 Test your understanding 10

Brenda

You work for a firm of accountants. One of your colleagues, Tim, has suggested that a particular tax planning idea may be suitable for Brenda, one of your clients. In fact, Tim claims that the idea works for all the firm's individual clients.

Tim has obtained a legal opinion that the idea does not break the law, although he admits HMRC take a different interpretation in their guidance on the particular technical area involved. However, he says that the legal opinion means clients do not need to be informed about this.

The idea, if implemented, would be fully disclosed in the client's relevant tax returns, and the rationale for the idea is fully documented.

Using the extracts from PCRT, which will be available for you to refer to in the assessment, explain why selling the idea to Brenda is likely to breach the Standards for Tax Planning.

Test your understanding 11

Qual Systems Ltd

You work for a firm of accountants. You have received a telephone call from HMRC requesting information in relation to Qual Systems Ltd. Qual Systems Ltd was a client of your firm until 31 October 2017.

Using the extracts from PCRT, which will be available for you to refer to in the assessment, explain your responsibilities in relation to this matter.

 Test your understanding 12

Golding Accounting Services

You work for Golding Accounting Services, a small firm of accountants. You have received information that one of your clients, Maya, has a number of rental properties. You have checked back through your records and no income from this has been included in her tax filings for recent years.

Using the extracts from PCRT, which will be available for you to refer to in the assessment, explain the action you should now take.

 Test your understanding 13

Clague and Co

You work for Clague and Co, a firm of accountants. A new starter at the firm has asked you about the difference between tax evasion and tax planning in relation to preparing client tax returns.

Explain what is meant by the terms 'tax evasion', 'tax avoidance' and 'tax planning'. Provide examples of each to illustrate your answer.

8 Summary

It is important that you do not neglect this chapter. Much of the information here could be tested in a written question, and such questions are, perhaps, more difficult to answer well than computational questions. So you should learn as much of this material as you can.

Test your understanding answers

Test your understanding 1

1   False

   The principle of flexibility is required to keep up with technological and commercial changes. The principle of **efficiency** requires costs of administration to be kept low.

2   True

3   False Income tax is a **progressive** tax.

4   True

Test your understanding 2

The answer is **D**.

The duty of confidentiality can be overridden if the client gives authority or if there is a legal, regulatory or professional duty to disclose.

Test your understanding 3

The answer is **A**.

Test your understanding 4

Residence status

1 Dieter has been in the UK for 222 days in the tax year 2021/22, which is more than 183 days.

Accordingly, he will automatically be treated as UK resident in the tax year 2021/22.

2 Simone has not been resident in the UK in any of the three previous tax years, and has been in the UK for less than 46 days.

Accordingly, she will automatically be treated as **not UK resident** in the tax year 2021/22.

3 Fred spent 42 days in the UK in the tax year 2021/22.

– He has spent too many days in the UK to be automatically not resident (i.e. > 16 days as previously resident in UK).

– He is not automatically resident as he has not been in the UK for sufficient days and has an overseas home during the tax year 2021/22.

Fred has been UK resident and is now leaving the UK.

He was in the UK in the tax year 2021/22 for between 16 and 45 days and will be UK resident if he meets at least four of the UK ties tests, which he does.

He is therefore UK resident in the tax year 2021/22.

Test your understanding 5

Domicile status

1. Sunita has a domicile of origin in the UK (her domicile of origin follows the domicile of her father). She does not appear to have made a domicile of choice and therefore is still domiciled in the UK. As Sunita has an actual domicile in the UK, the concept of deemed domicile would not be relevant here.

2. Francoise was born in the UK and had a domicile of origin in the UK. Although he has a domicile of choice in France, he was UK resident in both of the tax years 2020/21 and 2021/22, therefore he is treated as deemed domiciled in the UK under Condition A.

3. Petra has been resident in the UK for 14 tax years immediately prior to the tax year 2021/22 (the tax years 2007/08 to 2020/21). She is not deemed domiciled in the tax year 2021/22 but will become so in the following tax year under Condition B.

 Test your understanding 6

PCRT familiarisation part 1

The answers are in the following paragraphs of PCRT Help sheet A: Submission of tax information and 'Tax filings':

1. **Definition of filing of tax information and tax filings**

   Paragraph 1 – The term 'filing' includes any online submission of data, online filing or other filing that is prepared on behalf of the client for the purposes of disclosing to any taxing authority (such as HMRC) details that are to be used in the calculation of tax due by a client or a refund of tax due to the client or for other official purposes.

2. **Making Tax Digital and filing**

   Paragraph 6 – A member is recommended to forward suspicious emails to phishing@hmrc.gsi.gov.uk and then delete them.

3. **Taxpayer's responsibility**

   Paragraph 8 – The taxpayer has primary responsibility to submit correct and complete filings to the best of their knowledge and belief.

4   **Member's responsibility**

Paragraph 13 – Where acting as a tax agent, a member is not required to audit the figures in the books and records provided or verify information provided by a client or by a third party.

5   **Materiality**

Paragraph 17 – The accounting concept of materiality cannot be applied when completing tax filings.

6   **Disclosure**

Paragraph 21 – It might be advisable to consider fuller disclosure to HMRC than is strictly necessary if, for example, a filing relies on a valuation.

7   **Supporting documents**

Paragraph 26 – Attachments should be included with a tax filing where the taxpayer feels it is crucial to provide additional information to support the filing but for some reason cannot utilise the white space provided on the return.

8   **Reliance on HMRC published guidance**

Paragraph 27 – If HMRC guidance conflicts with the law, the law will be applied by courts in the event of a dispute with HMRC.

9   **Approval of tax filings**

Paragraph 30 – Before a client approves a tax filing the member should draw the client's attention to the responsibility which the client is taking in approving the filing as correct and complete. Attention should be drawn to any judgmental areas or positions reflected in the filing to ensure that the client is aware of these and their implications.

KAPLAN PUBLISHING

Test your understanding 7

PCRT familiarisation part 2

The answers are in the following paragraphs of PCRT Help sheet B: Tax advice:

1   **The Standards for Tax Planning**

Paragraph 1 – The five standards for tax planning are: client specific; lawful; disclosure and transparency; tax planning arrangements; professional judgement and appropriate documentation.

2   **Tax evasion**

Paragraph 3 – It is acceptable for a member to act for a client who is trying to rectify their tax affairs having previously been involved in tax evasion.

3   **Tax planning and advice**

Paragraph 4 – Members must refrain from promoting tax planning arrangements that either sets out to achieve results that are contrary to the clear intention of Parliament in enacting relevant legislation and/or are highly artificial or highly contrived and seek to exploit shortcomings within the relevant legislation.

Test your understanding 8

PCRT familiarisation part 3

The answers are in the following parts of PCRT Help sheet C: Dealing with errors:

1   **Introduction**

Paragraph 2 – A member should alert a client to a possible error in the client's tax affairs as soon as the member identifies such a possibility

2   **Flowchart**

Box 'YOU MUST CEASE TO ACT' – If a client is unwilling to disclose an error to HMRC and your firm has decided to cease to act for the client, the client should be informed in writing.

Test your understanding 9

PCRT familiarisation part 4

The answers are in the following parts of PCRT Help sheet D: Requests for data by HMRC:

1   **Introduction**

Paragraph 1 – in the context of PCRT, data includes documents in whatever form (including electronic) and other information.

2   **Informal requests addressed to the client**

Paragraph 10 – HMRC normally contact a client's appointed agent when initiating a compliance check.

3   **Informal requests addressed to the member**

Paragraph 15 – A member is not obliged to comply with an informal request from HMRC, but a member should advise the client whether it is in the client's best interests to disclose data requested in this way, as lack of cooperation may have a direct impact on penalty negotiations after the enquiry.

4   **Formal requests addressed to the client**

Paragraph 20 – The most common statutory notice issued to clients and third parties by HMRC is under Schedule 36 FA 2008.

5   **Formal requests addressed to the member**

Paragraph 22 – A member is obliged to comply with a valid formal request from HMRC and this overrides the professional duty of confidentiality.

6   **Privileged data**

Paragraph 28 – The two types of legal privilege under common law are legal advice privilege and litigation privilege.

Test your understanding 10

Brenda

The proposal may not comply with the Standards for Tax Planning set out in 'Professional conduct in relation to taxation'.

– Tax planning must be client specific, tailored to Brenda's facts and circumstances. This is not the case here if the idea can be used by all individual clients.

– Even though the idea is considered lawful under the legal opinion, the Standards require us to draw Brenda's attention to the fact that the law is uncertain, and specifically that HMRC take a different view.

– We must not create, encourage or promote tax planning arrangements that are contrary to the intention of Parliament when the law was enacted and/or are highly artificial or contrived and exploit shortcomings in the law. This may be the case if HMRC clearly take a different view in respect of the law.

Therefore, selling the tax planning idea is likely to breach these Standards.

Test your understanding 11

Qual Systems Ltd

In order to comply with the fundamental principles set out in 'Professional conduct in relation to taxation' we must:

– be straightforward and honest in our professional and business relationships (the principle of integrity)

– respect the confidentiality of information acquired as a result of professional and business relationships and, therefore, not disclose any such information to third parties without proper and specific authority, unless there is a legal or professional right or duty to disclose (the principle of confidentiality); and

– comply with relevant laws and regulations and avoid any action that discredits the profession (the principle of professional behaviour).

The duty to respect the confidentiality of information still applies in relation to Qual Systems Ltd even though it is no longer a client.

A telephone call is an informal request for information as opposed to one that is statutory. Accordingly, we should refer HMRC either to Qual Systems Ltd or, if authorised by Qual Systems Ltd, to their new agent.

 Test your understanding 12

Golding Services

In order to comply with the fundamental principles set out in 'Professional conduct in relation to taxation' we must:

– be straightforward and honest in our professional and business relationships (the principle of integrity); and

– comply with relevant laws and regulations and avoid any action that discredits the profession (the principle of professional behaviour).

It appears that there is an error in Maya's tax return as she is likely to have income that has not been declared.

Our first step should be to contact Maya and confirm that an error does exist.

If there is an error the next step would be to ascertain whether this error is trivial. As we can see that she owns a number of rental properties it appears unlikely that this is the case.

We would then check the engagement letter to determine whether disclosure is authorised within this. If such authority exists we would contact HMRC at this point.

If no authority exists we should ask Maya to provide this. If she refuses we would contact her again, this time informing her of the consequences of non-disclosure including increased penalties.

Finally, if she still refuses we would confirm this advice in writing.

If Maya still refuses to disclose we would advise her in writing that we can no longer act for her in respect of tax matters and any other relevant matters. We would also notify HMRC that we no longer act for her but not the reason why.

If it is felt that this is a matter of tax evasion we must consider whether a report needs to be made under Money Laundering.

 Test your understanding 13

Clague and Co

Tax evasion is the use of illegal methods to reduce the tax liability. This would include deliberately understating income or overstating expenses.

Tax avoidance is legal methods of reducing the tax liability but does not follow the spirit of tax legislation. This would usually involve exploiting loopholes in the law.

Tax planning means using the tax legislation in the manner it was legitimately intended to ensure that taxpayers pay the right amount of tax, but no more than is necessary. This could involve for example, investing in an ISA whereby income earned is free from tax.

Appendix

Professional conduct in relation to taxation

Extracts relevant for Personal Tax unit

Introduction

This document comprises data that you may need to consult during your Personal Tax computer-based assessment. The material can be consulted during the sample and live assessments through pop-up windows. It is made available here so you can familiarise yourself with the content before the test.

Do not take a print of this document into the exam room with you. Unless you need a printed version as part of reasonable adjustments for particular needs, in which case you must discuss this with your tutor at least six weeks before the assessment date.

This document may be changed to reflect periodical updates in the computer-based assessment, so please check you have the most recent version while studying. This version is based on Finance Act 2021 and is for use in AAT assessments from February 2022.

We are grateful to the Association of Accounting Technicians for permission to reproduce this reference material. The page numbering shown below refers to the pages where the content can be found within the paper version of the reference material on the AAT website.

Contents	Page

1 Interpretation and abbreviations

Context

Tax advisers operate in a complex business and financial environment. The increasing public focus on the role of taxation in wider society means a greater interest in the actions of tax advisers and their clients.

This guidance, written by the professional bodies for their members working in tax, sets out the hallmarks of a good tax adviser, and in particular the fundamental principles of behaviour that members are expected to follow.

Interpretation

1.1 In this guidance:

- 'Client' includes, where the context requires, 'former client'.

- 'Member' (and 'members') includes 'firm' or 'practice' and the staff thereof.

- Words in the singular include the plural and words in the plural include the singular.

Abbreviations

1.2 The following abbreviations have been used:

AML	Anti-Money Laundering
CCAB	Consultative Committee of Accountancy Bodies
DOTAS	Disclosure of Tax Avoidance Schemes
GAAP	Generally Accepted Accounting Principles
GAAR	General Anti-Abuse Rule in Finance Act 2013
GDPR	General Data Protection Regulation
HMRC	Her Majesty's Revenue and Customs
MTD	Making Tax Digital
MLRO	Money Laundering Reporting Officer
NCA	National Crime Agency (previously the Serious Organised Crime Agency, SOCA)
POTAS	Promoters of Tax Avoidance Schemes
PCRT	Professional Conduct in Relation to Taxation
SRN	Scheme Reference Number

2 Fundamental principles

Overview of the fundamental principles

1 Ethical behaviour in the tax profession is critical. The work carried out by a member needs to be trusted by society at large as well as by clients and other stakeholders. What a member does reflects not just on themselves but on the profession as a whole.

2 A member must comply with the following fundamental principles:

Integrity

To be straightforward and honest in all professional and business relationships.

Objectivity

To not allow bias, conflict of interest or undue influence of others to override professional or business judgements.

Professional competence and due care

To maintain professional knowledge and skill at the level required to ensure that a client or employer receives competent professional service based on current developments in practice, legislation and techniques and act diligently and in accordance with applicable technical and professional standards.

Confidentiality

To respect the confidentiality of information acquired as a result of professional and business relationships and, therefore, not disclose any such information to third parties without proper and specific authority, unless there is a legal or professional right or duty to disclose, nor use the information for the personal advantage of the member or third parties.

Professional behaviour

To comply with relevant laws and regulations and avoid any action that discredits the profession.

3 PCRT Help sheet A: Submission of tax information and 'Tax filings'

Definition of filing of tax information and tax filings (filing)

1 For the purposes of this guidance, the term 'filing' includes any online submission of data, online filing or other filing that is prepared on behalf of the client for the purposes of disclosing to any taxing authority details that are to be used in the calculation of tax due by a client or a refund of tax due to the client or for other official purposes. It includes all taxes, NIC and duties.

2 A letter, or online notification, giving details in respect of a filing or as an amendment to a filing including, for example, any voluntary disclosure of an error should be dealt with as if it was a filing.

Making Tax Digital and filing

3 Tax administration systems, including the UK's, are increasingly moving to mandatory digital filing of tax information and returns.

4 Except in exceptional circumstances, a member will explicitly file in their capacity as agent. A member is advised to use the facilities provided for agents and to avoid knowing or using the client's personal access credentials.

5 A member should keep their access credentials safe from unauthorised use and consider periodic change of passwords.

6 A member is recommended to forward suspicious emails to phishing@hmrc.gsi.gov.uk and then delete them. It is also important to avoid clicking on websites or links in suspicious emails, or opening attachments.

7 Firms should have policies on cyber security, AML and GDPR.

Taxpayer's responsibility

8 The taxpayer has primary responsibility to submit correct and complete filings to the best of their knowledge and belief. The final decision as to whether to disclose any issue is that of the client but in relation to your responsibilities see paragraph 12 below.

9 In annual self-assessment returns or returns with short filing periods the filing may include reasonable estimates where necessary.

Member's responsibility

10 A member who prepares a filing on behalf of a client is responsible to the client for the accuracy of the filing based on the information provided.

11 In dealing with HMRC in relation to a client's tax affairs a member should bear in mind their duty of confidentiality to the client and that they are acting as the agent of their client. They have a duty to act in the best interests of their client.

12 A member should act in good faith in dealings with HMRC in accordance with the fundamental principle of integrity. In particular the member should take reasonable care and exercise appropriate professional scepticism when making statements or asserting facts on behalf of a client.

13 Where acting as a tax agent, a member is not required to audit the figures in the books and records provided or verify information provided by a client or by a third party. However, a member should take care not to be associated with the presentation of facts they know or believe to be incorrect or misleading, not to assert tax positions in a tax filing which they consider to have no sustainable basis.

14 When a member is communicating with HMRC, they should consider whether they need to make it clear to what extent they are relying on information which has been supplied by the client or a third party.

Materiality

15 Whether an amount is to be regarded as material depends upon the facts and circumstances of each case.

16 The profits of a trade, profession, vocation or property business should be computed in accordance with GAAP subject to any adjustment required or authorised by law in computing profits for those purposes. This permits a trade, profession, vocation or property business to disregard non-material adjustments in computing its accounting profits.

17 The application of GAAP, and therefore materiality does not extend beyond the accounting profits. Thus, the accounting concept of materiality cannot be applied when completing tax filings.

18 It should be noted that for certain small businesses an election may be made to use the cash basis instead; for small property businesses the default position is the cash basis. Where the cash basis is used, materiality is not relevant.

Disclosure

19 If a client is unwilling to include in a tax filing the minimum information required by law, the member should follow the guidance in Help sheet C: Dealing with Errors. The paragraphs below (paras 20 – 24) give guidance on some of the more common areas of uncertainty over disclosure.

20 In general, it is likely to be in a client's own interests to ensure that factors relevant to their tax liability are adequately disclosed to HMRC because:

- Their relationship with HMRC is more likely to be on a satisfactory footing if they can demonstrate good faith in their dealings with them. HMRC notes in 'Your Charter' that 'We want to give you a service that is fair, accurate and based on mutual trust and respect'; and

- They will reduce the risk of a discovery or further assessment and may reduce exposure to interest and penalties.

21 It may be advisable to consider fuller disclosure than is strictly necessary. Reference to 'The Standards for Tax Planning' in PCRT may be relevant. The factors involved in making this decision include:

- A filing relies on a valuation;

- The terms of the applicable law;

- The view taken by the member;

- The extent of any doubt that exists;

- The manner in which disclosure is to be made; and

- The size and gravity of the item in question.

22 When advocating fuller disclosure than is necessary a member should ensure that their client is adequately aware of the issues involved and their potential implications. Fuller disclosure should only be made with the client's consent.

23 Cases will arise where there is doubt as to the correct treatment of an item of income or expenditure, or the computation of a gain or allowance. In such cases a member ought to consider what additional disclosure, if any, might be necessary. For example, additional disclosure should be considered where:

- There is inherent doubt as to the correct treatment of an item, for example, expenditure on repairs which might be regarded as capital in whole or part, or the VAT liability of a particular transaction; or

- HMRC has published its interpretation or has indicated its practice on a point, but the client proposes to adopt a different view, whether or not supported by Counsel's opinion. The member should refer to the guidance on the Veltema case and the paragraph below. See also HMRC guidance.

24 A member who is uncertain whether their client should disclose a particular item or of its treatment should consider taking further advice before reaching a decision. They should use their best endeavours to ensure that the client understands the issues, implications and the proposed course of action. Such a decision may have to be justified at a later date, so the member's files should contain sufficient evidence to support the position taken, including timely notes of discussions with the client and/or with other advisers, copies of any second opinion obtained and the client's final decision. A failure to take reasonable care may result in HMRC imposing a penalty if an error is identified after an enquiry.

Supporting documents

25 For the most part, HMRC does not consider that it is necessary for a taxpayer to provide supporting documentation in order to satisfy the taxpayer's overriding need to make a correct filing. HMRC's view is that, where it is necessary for that purpose, explanatory information should be entered in the 'white space' provided on the filing. However, HMRC does recognise that the taxpayer may wish to supply further details of a particular computation or transaction in order to minimise the risk of a discovery assessment being raised at a later time. Following the uncertainty created by the decision in Veltema, HMRC's guidance can be found in SP1/06 – Self Assessment: Finality and Discovery.

26 Further HMRC guidance says that sending attachments with a tax filing is intended for those cases where the taxpayer 'feels it is crucial to provide additional information to support the filing but for some reason cannot utilise the white space'.

Reliance on HMRC published guidance

27 Whilst it is reasonable in most circumstances to rely on HMRC published guidance, a member should be aware that the Tribunal and the courts will apply the law even if this conflicts with HMRC guidance.

28 Notwithstanding this, if a client has relied on HMRC guidance which is clear and unequivocal and HMRC resiles from any of the terms of the guidance, a Judicial Review claim is a possible route to pursue.

Approval of tax filings

29 The member should advise the client to review their tax filing before it is submitted.

30 The member should draw the client's attention to the responsibility which the client is taking in approving the filing as correct and complete. Attention should be drawn to any judgmental areas or positions reflected in the filing to ensure that the client is aware of these and their implications before they approve the filing.

31 A member should obtain evidence of the client's approval of the filing in electronic or non-electronic form.

4   PCRT Help sheet B: Tax advice

The Standards for Tax Planning

1   The Standards for Tax Planning are critical to any planning undertaken by members. They are:

- Client Specific

    Tax planning must be specific to the particular client's facts and circumstances. Clients must be alerted to the wider risks and implications of any courses of action.

- Lawful

    At all times members must act lawfully and with integrity and expect the same from their clients. Tax planning should be based on a realistic assessment of the facts and on a credible view of the law.

    Members should draw their client's attention to where the law is materially uncertain, for example because HMRC is known to take a different view of the law. Members should consider taking further advice appropriate to the risks and circumstances of the particular case, for example where litigation is likely.

- Disclosure and transparency

    Tax advice must not rely for its effectiveness on HMRC having less than the relevant facts. Any disclosure must fairly represent all relevant facts.

- Tax planning arrangements

    Members must not create, encourage or promote tax planning arrangements or structures that i) set out to achieve results that are contrary to the clear intention of Parliament in enacting relevant legislation and/or ii) are highly artificial or highly contrived and seek to exploit shortcomings within the relevant legislation.

- Professional judgement and appropriate documentation

  Applying these requirements to particular client advisory situations requires members to exercise professional judgement on a number of matters. Members should keep notes on a timely basis of the rationale for the judgements exercised in seeking to adhere to these requirements

Guidance

2 The paragraphs below provide guidance for members when considering whether advice complies with the Fundamental Principles and Standards for Tax Planning.

Tax evasion

3 A member should never be knowingly involved in tax evasion, although, of course, it is appropriate to act for a client who is rectifying their affairs.

Tax planning and advice

4 In contrast to tax evasion, tax planning is legal. However, under the Standard members 'must not create, encourage or promote tax planning arrangements that (i) set out to achieve results that are contrary to the clear intention of Parliament in enacting relevant legislation and/or (ii) are highly artificial or highly contrived and seek to exploit shortcomings within the relevant legislation'.

5 Things to consider:

- Have you checked that your engagement letter fully covers the scope of the planning advice?

- Have you taken the Standards for Tax Planning and the Fundamental Principles into account? Is it client specific? Is it lawful? Will all relevant facts be disclosed to HMRC? Is it creating, encouraging or promoting tax planning contrary to the 4th Standard for Tax Planning.

- How tax sophisticated is the client?

- Has the client made clear what they wish to achieve by the planning?

- What are the issues involved with the implementation of the planning?

- What are the risks associated with the planning and have you warned the client of them? For example:

  - The strength of the legal interpretation relied upon.

  - The potential application of the GAAR.

    – The implications for the client, including the obligations of the client in relation to their tax return, if the planning requires disclosure under DOTAS or DASVOIT and the potential for an accelerated payment notice or partner payment notice?

    – The reputational risk to the client and the member of the planning in the public arena.

    – The stress, cost and wider personal or business implications to the client in the event of a prolonged dispute with HMRC. This may involve unwelcomed publicity, costs, expenses and loss of management time over a significant period.

    – If the client tenders for government contracts, the potential impact of the proposed tax planning on tendering for and retaining public sector contracts.

    – The risk of counteraction. This may occur before the planning is completed or potentially there may be retrospective counteraction at a later date.

    – The risk of challenge by HMRC. Such challenge may relate to the legal interpretation relied upon, but may alternatively relate to the construction of the facts, including the implementation of the planning.

    – The risk and inherent uncertainty of litigation. The probability of the planning being overturned by the courts if litigated and the potential ultimate downside should the client be unsuccessful.

    – Is a second opinion necessary/advisable?

- Are the arrangements in line with any applicable code of conduct or ethical guidelines or stances for example the Banking Code, and fit and proper tests for charity trustees and pension administrators?

- Are you satisfied that the client understands the planning proposed?

- Have you documented the advice given and the reasoning behind it?

5   PCRT Help sheet C: Dealing with errors

Introduction

1   For the purposes of this guidance, the term 'error' is intended to include all errors and mistakes whether they were made by the client, the member, HMRC or any other party involved in a client's tax affairs, and whether made innocently or deliberately.

2   During a member's relationship with the client, the member may become aware of possible errors in the client's tax affairs. Unless the client is already aware of the possible error, they should be informed as soon as the member identifies them.

3   Where the error has resulted in the client paying too much tax the member should advise the client to make a repayment claim. The member should advise the client of the time limits to make a claim and have regard to any relevant time limits. The rest of this Help sheet deals with situations where tax may be due to HMRC.

4   Sometimes an error made by HMRC may mean that the client has not paid tax actually due or they have been incorrectly repaid tax. There may be fee costs as a result of correcting such mistakes. A member should bear in mind that, in some circumstances, clients or agents may be able to claim for additional professional costs incurred and compensation from HMRC.

5   A member should act correctly from the outset. A member should keep sufficient appropriate records of discussions and advice and when dealing with errors the member should:

- give the client appropriate advice';

- if necessary, so long as they continue to act for the client, seek to persuade the client to behave correctly;

- take care not to appear to be assisting a client to plan or commit any criminal offence or to conceal any offence which has been committed; and

- in appropriate situations, or where in doubt, discuss the client's situation with a colleague or an independent third party (having due regard to client confidentiality).

6   Once aware of a possible error, a member must bear in mind the legislation on money laundering and the obligations and duties which this places upon them.

7   Where the member may have made the error, the member should consider whether they need to notify their professional indemnity insurers.

8   In any situation where a member has concerns about their own position, they should consider taking specialist legal advice. For example, where a client appears to have used the member to assist in the commissioning of a criminal offence and people could question whether the member had acted honestly in in good faith. Note that The Criminal Finances Act 2017 has created new criminal offences of failure to prevent facilitation of tax evasion.

9   The flowchart below summarises the recommended steps a member should take where a possible error arises. It must be read in conjunction with the guidance and commentary that follow it.

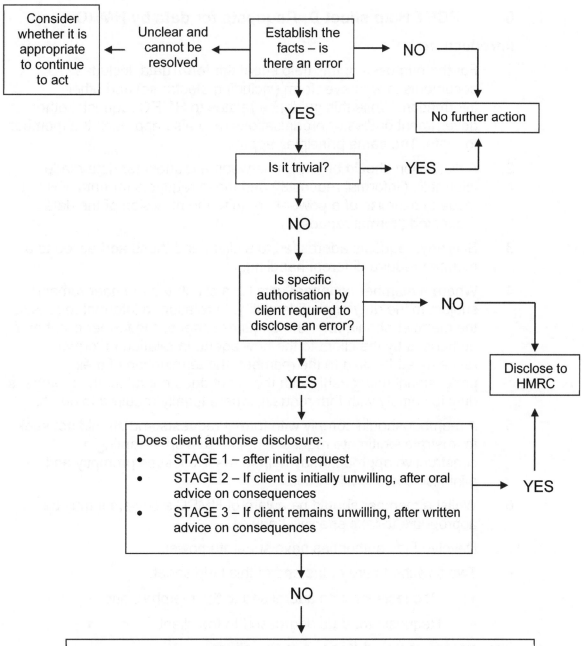

Consider whether it is appropriate to continue to act

Unclear and cannot be resolved

Establish the facts – is there an error

NO

No further action

YES

Is it trivial? → **YES**

NO

Is specific authorisation by client required to disclose an error? → **NO** → **Disclose to HMRC**

YES

Does client authorise disclosure:
- STAGE 1 – after initial request
- STAGE 2 – If client is initially unwilling, after oral advice on consequences
- STAGE 3 – If client remains unwilling, after written advice on consequences

YES

NO

YOU MUST CEASE TO ACT
- Advise client in writing that you no longer act for them in respect of any tax matters and, if relevant, any other client matters.
- Notify HMRC that you have ceased to act, if relevant.
- Consider if you need to advise HMRC that any accounts/statements carrying a report signed by you should no longer be relied upon.
- Consider whether a report should be made to MLRO/NCA.
- Carefully consider your response to any professional enquiry letter.

At all times consider your obligations under anti money laundering legislation and whether you need to submit a Suspicious Activity Report.

6 PCRT Help sheet D: Requests for data by HMRC

Introduction

1 For the purposes of this help sheet the term 'data' includes documents in whatever form (including electronic) and other information. While this guidance relates to HMRC requests, other government bodies or organisations may also approach the member for data. The same principles apply.

2 A distinction should be drawn between a request for data made informally ('informal requests') and those requests for data which are made in exercise of a power to require the provision of the data requested ('formal requests').

3 Similarly, requests addressed to a client and those addressed to a member require different handling.

4 Where a member no longer acts for a client, the member remains subject to the duty of confidentiality. In relation to informal requests, the member should refer the enquirer either to the former client or if authorised by the client to the new agent. In relation to formal requests addressed to the member, the termination of their professional relationship with the client does not affect the member's duty to comply with that request, where legally required to do so.

5 A member should comply with formal requests and should not seek to frustrate legitimate requests for information. Adopting a constructive approach may help to resolve issues promptly and minimise costs to all parties.

6 Whilst a member should be aware of HMRC's powers it may be appropriate to take specialist advice.

7 Devolved tax authorities have separate powers.

8 Two flowcharts are at the end of this help sheet;

- Requests for data addressed to the member, and

- Requests for data addressed to the client.

Informal requests addressed to the client

9 From time to time HMRC chooses to communicate directly with clients rather than with the appointed agent.

10 HMRC has given reassurances that it is working to ensure that initial contact on compliance checks will normally be via the agent and only if the agent does not reply within an appropriate timescale will the contact be directly with the client.

11 When the member assists a client in dealing with such requests from HMRC, the member should advise the client that cooperation with informal requests can provide greater opportunities for the taxpayer to find a pragmatic way to work through the issue at hand with HMRC.

Informal requests addressed to the member

12   Disclosure in response to informal requests can only be made with the client's permission.

13   In many instances, the client will have authorised routine disclosure of relevant data, for example, through the engagement letter. However, if there is any doubt about whether the client has authorised disclosure, the member should ask the client to approve what is to be disclosed.

14   Where an oral enquiry is made by HMRC, a member should consider asking for it to be put in writing so that a response may be agreed with the client.

15   Although there is no obligation to comply with an informal request in whole or in part, a member should advise the client whether it is in the client's best interests to disclose such data, as lack of cooperation may have a direct impact on penalty negotiations post – enquiry.

16   Informal requests may be forerunners to formal requests compelling the disclosure of data. Consequently, it may be sensible to comply with such requests.

Formal requests addressed to the client

17   In advising their client a member should consider whether specialist advice may be needed, for example on such issues as whether the notice has been issued in accordance with the relevant tax legislation and whether the data request is valid.

18   The member should also advise the client about any relevant right of appeal against the formal request if appropriate and of the consequences of a failure to comply.

19   If the notice is legally effective the client is legally obliged to comply with the request.

20   The most common statutory notice issued to clients and third parties by HMRC is under Schedule 36 FA 2008.

Formal requests addressed to the member

21   The same principles apply to formal requests to the member as formal requests to clients.

22   If a formal request is valid it **overrides the member's duty of confidentiality** to their client. The member is therefore obliged to comply with the request. Failure to comply with their legal obligations can expose the member to civil or criminal penalties.

23   In cases where the member is not legally precluded by the terms of the notice from communicating with the client, the member should advise the client of the notice and keep the client informed of progress and developments.

24   The member should ensure that in complying with any notice they do not provide information or data outside the scope of the notice.

25   If a member is faced with a situation in which HMRC is seeking to enforce disclosure by the removal of data, or seeking entrance to inspect business premises occupied by a member in their capacity as an adviser, the member should consider seeking immediate professional advice, to ensure that this is the legally correct course of action.

Privileged data

26   Legal privilege arises under common law and may only be overridden if this is set out in legislation. It protects a party's right to communicate in confidence with a legal adviser. The privilege belongs to the client and not to the member.

27   If a document is privileged: The client cannot be required to make disclosure of that document to HMRC. Another party cannot disclose it (including the member), without the client's express permission.

28   There are two types of legal privilege under common law: legal advice privilege and litigation privilege.

   (a)   Legal advice privilege

          Covers documents passing between a client and their legal adviser prepared for the purposes of obtaining or giving legal advice. However, communications from a tax adviser who is not a practising lawyer will not attract legal advice privilege even if such individuals are giving advice on legal matters such as tax law.

   (b)   Litigation privilege

          Covers data created for the dominant purpose of litigation. Litigation privilege may arise where litigation has not begun, but is merely contemplated and may apply to data prepared by non-lawyer advisers (including tax advisers). There are two important limits on litigation privilege. First, it does not arise in respect of non-adversarial proceedings. Second, the documents must be produced for the 'dominant purpose' of litigation.

29   A privilege under Schedule 36 paragraphs 19, (documents relating to the conduct of a pending appeal), 24 and 25 (auditors, and tax advisers' documents) might exist by "quasi-privilege" and if this is the case a tax adviser does not have to provide those documents. Care should be taken as not all data may be privileged.

30   A member who receives a request for data, some of which the member believes may be subject to privilege or 'quasi-privilege', should take independent legal advice on the position, unless expert in this area.

Help sheet D: Flowchart regarding requests for data by HMRC to the Member.

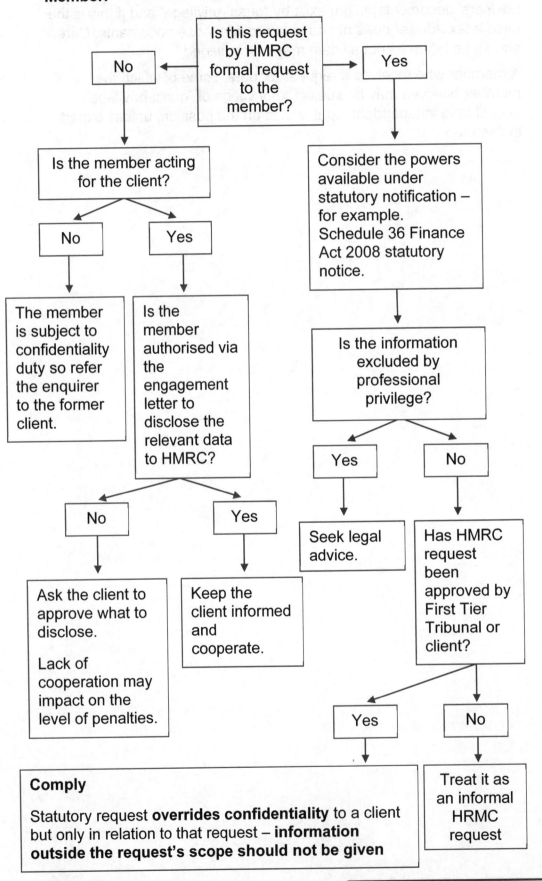

Help sheet D: Flowchart regarding requests for data by HMRC to the Client.

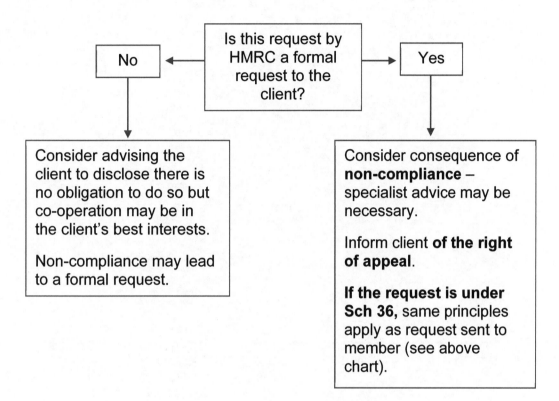

No ← Is this request by HMRC a formal request to the client? → **Yes**

Consider advising the client to disclose there is no obligation to do so but co-operation may be in the client's best interests.

Non-compliance may lead to a formal request.

Consider consequence of **non-compliance** – specialist advice may be necessary.

Inform client **of the right of appeal**.

If the request is under Sch 36, same principles apply as request sent to member (see above chart).

Principles of income tax

2

Introduction

In the assessment you will have to calculate the taxable income of an individual and the individual's income tax payable.

In this chapter we look at the basic pro forma income tax computation with a view to building this up over the next few chapters.

ASSESSMENT CRITERIA	CONTENTS
Calculate taxable income (3.1)	1 Sources of income
	2 Pro forma income tax computation

1   Sources of income

1.1   Main sources

Individuals essentially obtain income from two main sources.

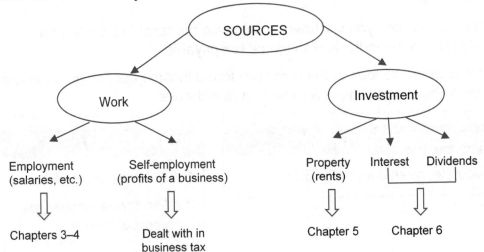

1.2   Classification of income

Income can either be classified as:

- **taxable income** – which is shown on the income tax computation (section 2 below), or

- **exempt income** – which is not shown on the income tax computation (1.5 below).

1.3   Taxable income

Each type of taxable income has a slightly different tax treatment.

The types of taxable income, which are each considered in detail in the following chapters, are:

Taxable income	Includes
Employment income	Salaries, wages, bonuses, benefits
Property income	Rents received less expenses of renting
Interest	Interest received from, for example, building societies, banks, etc.
Dividends	Dividends received from UK companies

The computation of income from self-employment is not considered in this study text as it is outside the scope of Personal Tax (it is covered in Business Tax).

Income from self-employment does, however, form part of an individual's taxable income. In an assessment question you will be told the amount of taxable self-employment income to include if necessary.

1.4 Deduction of tax at source

Income is always shown 'gross' in the income tax computation.

However, sometimes individuals receive income 'net' of tax. This means that the person paying the income has deducted tax before making the payment, and has paid the tax to HM Revenue and Customs (HMRC) on the individual's behalf.

These sources of income need to be 'grossed up' and the gross amount included in the income tax computation.

The common source of income received net of tax is salary from employment.

 Example

Amy's salary is £3,000 per month. The amount credited to her bank account each month, after deduction of PAYE, is £2,500, such that Amy receives £30,000 (£2,500 × 12) each year.

Amy's income tax computation must include her gross salary for the year of £36,000 (£3,000 × 12).

1.5 Exempt income

Exempt income, as stated earlier, does **not** go in the income tax computation.

Exempt income includes the following.

- Interest on NS&I Savings Certificates.

- Interest on Save As You Earn (SAYE) sharesave accounts.

- Interest on delayed income tax repayments.

- Interest, dividends and capital gains arising in respect of ISAs (individual savings accounts).

- Damages for personal injury or death.

- Scholarships and educational grants.

- Prizes, lottery winnings and gambling winnings.

- Statutory redundancy pay. This is the minimum amount an employer must pay on termination of employment. You will be told in the assessment if an amount paid on loss of office is the statutory amount.

- Some social security benefits, including housing benefit, universal credit, working tax credit and child tax credit. Child benefit is also exempt but it triggers a tax charge for high income individuals. Calculation of this charge is not in the syllabus.

This is not a complete listing of exempt income, but does cover the main examples that appear in assessments.

Test your understanding 1

Mark the following statements as true or false.

		True	False
1	Income tax is payable on lottery winnings.		
2	Interest received in respect of a repayment of income tax from HM Revenue and Customs is taxable.		
3	Statutory redundancy pay of £5,000 is exempt from income tax.		

---

2 Pro forma income tax computation

2.1 The main tax rates

For the tax year 2021/22 an individual must pay income tax on total taxable income at the basic, higher and additional rates.

Total taxable income is found by adding up the amounts of taxable income from all the different sources and deducting any available reliefs and allowances.

Reference material

Some information about tax rates can be found in the 'Tax rates and bands' section of your reference material provided in the real assessment, so you do not need to learn them.

Why not look up the correct part of the reference material in the introduction to this text book now?

The basic rate of 20% is charged on the first £37,700 of taxable income.

The higher rate of 40% is charged on taxable income between £37,700 and £150,000.

The additional rate of 45% is charged on taxable income in excess of £150,000.

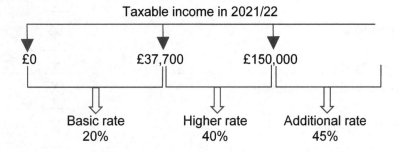

Special tax rates may apply to savings income and dividend income, as explained in the chapter on investment income, but other income is taxed at the above rates.

 Example

An individual has taxable earned income of £150,400.

Calculate the income tax liability for the tax year 2021/22.

Solution

£		£
37,700	× 20%	7,540
112,300	× 40%	44,920
400	× 45%	180
———		———
150,400		52,640
———		———

2.2   Pro forma income tax computation – overview

The following is an overview of the construction of a personal income tax computation.

It is essential to focus your attention on the key headings within the pro forma. They will be explained in more detail in the following chapters.

	£
A Person	
Income tax computation – 2021/22	
Earned income	X
Investment income	X
Net income	X
Less: Personal allowance	(X)
Taxable income	X
Income tax liability	X
Less: Tax deducted at source	(X)
Income tax payable	X

Note: A full pro forma is included in the chapter on calculating income tax payable.

Test your understanding 2

Mark the following statements as true or false.

		True	False
1	Interest from a building society account is exempt from tax.		
2	Income from an ISA account is exempt.		
3	Income from employment is excluded from the income tax computation because it has been taxed under PAYE.		
4	The basic rate of income tax is 40%.		

Test your understanding 3

Karim has taxable earned income of £39,060.

What is his income tax liability for the tax year 2021/22?

3 Summary

The chapter has prepared the foundations to gradually build up a full income tax computation by looking at:

- taxable income

- exempt income

- the pro forma income tax computation.

Test your understanding answers

Test your understanding 1

1 **False** – Lottery winnings are exempt.

2 **False** – Interest in respect of a tax repayment is exempt.

3 **True** – Statutory redundancy pay is exempt from income tax.

Test your understanding 2

1 **False** – Interest from a building society account is taxable.

2 **True** – Income from an ISA is exempt from tax.

3 **False** – The gross amount of the employment income should be included in the income tax computation.

4 **False** – The basic rate of income tax is 20%; 40% is the higher rate.

Test your understanding 3

The correct answer is **£8,084**

	£		£
37,700 × 20%			7,540
1,360 × 40%			544
	39,060		8,084

Introduction to employment income 3

Introduction

The assessment will test the different elements of an individual's employment income.

This will include some or all of the following:

	£
Cash income	X
Benefits (Chapter 4)	X
Less: Allowable expenses	(X)
Employment income	X

We will first cover the taxation of cash income and the deduction of expenses. We will then cover benefits in Chapter 4.

ASSESSMENT CRITERIA
Identify allowable and disallowable expenses (2.1)
Calculate employment income and allowable expenses (2.1)

CONTENTS
1 Employment status
2 Earnings
3 Allowable expenses and deductions
4 The PAYE system

1 Employment status

1.1 Introduction

An individual who works may be either an employee or self-employed (including business partners).

It is important to distinguish between the two because an employee is liable for tax on his/her employment income whilst a self-employed individual is liable for tax on his/her trading profits. The rules for the two types of income are different.

This text is concerned only with the calculation of employment income; the calculation of trading income is dealt with in the Business Tax unit.

1.2 Contract of service

In many instances it will be a straightforward matter to decide whether an individual is an employee or is self-employed. If it is not clear, there are various matters to take into account.

HM Revenue and Customs (HMRC) may be asked to give a status ruling to ensure that there is no doubt. The HMRC online service 'Check employment status for tax' can also be used to determine the status of an individual.

The basic distinction is that an employee has a **contract of service,** whereas a self-employed person will have a **contract for services.**

Some of the features of a contract of service are:

- The employer is under an obligation to offer work and the employee is under an obligation to carry it out.

- The employer will control how the work is carried out.

- The employee will be committed to work a specified number of hours at fixed times and places.

- The employee must do the work himself or herself; he or she cannot arrange for someone else to do it.

- The employee does not take any financial risk.

- An employee does not usually have to provide their own equipment.

- Employees are entitled to paid holidays and sickness benefits.

Test your understanding 1

For each statement, tick either employment or self-employment:

	Employment	Self-employment
Contract of service is for:		
Contract for services is for:		
A high level of control by another over the work performed would indicate what type of relationship?		

2 Earnings

2.1 Types of income

Employment income covers all earnings received from an employment. Such income includes salaries, wages, bonuses, commissions, directors' fees, tips, certain expense allowances and reimbursed expenses, and benefits.

Benefits are dealt with in Chapter 4.

Any pension income resulting from an employment is also taxable non-savings income.

2.2 Basis of assessment

The expression 'basis of assessment' means which income we should tax in which tax year.

The basis of assessment for employment income is the **receipts basis**.

This means that income is taxed in the tax year in which an employee receives it or becomes entitled to the payment, if earlier.

Example

Bertha receives her salary on the last day of the calendar month.

In the year to 31 December 2021 her salary is £1,000 per month. In the year to 31 December 2022 her salary is £1,100 per month.

(a) What is her taxable employment income for the tax year 2021/22?

(b) Would this be different if her salary was paid in advance on the first day of the month?

Solution

(a) **2021/22 – taxable employment income**

	£
In year ended 31 December 2021	
30 April 2021 to 31 December 2021 (9 months)	
(£1,000 × 9)	9,000
In year ended 31 December 2022	
31 January 2022 to 31 March 2022 (3 months)	
(£1,100 × 3)	3,300
	12,300

(b) **2021/22 – taxable employment income**

	£
In year ended 31 December 2021	
1 May 2021 to 1 December 2021 (8 months)	
(£1,000 × 8)	8,000
In year ended 31 December 2022	
1 January 2022 to 1 April 2022 (4 months)	
(£1,100 × 4)	4,400
	12,400

2.3 Expenses

Broadly speaking, expense allowances and reimbursed expenses are taxable income.

A deduction is available for allowable expenses incurred by the employee as set out in section 3 below. Where allowable expenses are incurred by the employee and reimbursed by the employer, the reimbursed income is exempt (rather than included in taxable income but then also deducted), as set out in section 3.4.

2.4 Bonuses

One of the main areas that can cause problems is bonuses.

Many individuals receive bonuses (e.g. sales representatives). The bonus may be based on the employer's accounting period (e.g. sales made in that period). However, the employee may not be entitled to payment until after the end of the period.

Remember that employees are taxed on the receipts basis, which is deemed to be the earlier of:

- the date of receipt

- the date the employee became entitled to receipt

There are special rules for directors' earnings, which are treated as received on the earlier of:

- the date of receipt

- the date the director became entitled to receipt

- the date the amount is credited to the accounting records of the company

- the last day of the company's period of account (if the amount has been determined before then)

- the date the amount is determined (if determined after the end of the company's period of account).

Example

Gordon is a salesman working for Jones Ltd. He is entitled to a bonus each year based on the sales he has made in the company's accounting period ended 31 December.

His recent bonuses have been as follows:

For the year ended	Date of payment/entitlement	£
31 December 2019	10 April 2020	8,000
31 December 2020	8 April 2021	10,000
31 December 2021	4 April 2022	9,500
31 December 2022	8 April 2023	7,500

What is the amount of taxable bonus in the tax year 2021/22?

Solution

The taxable amount is the amount received by Gordon in the tax year 2021/22.

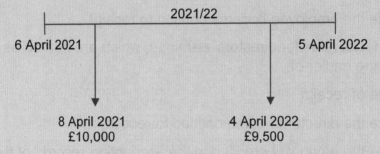

Hence the total taxable bonus in the tax year 2021/22 is £19,500.

Note that no bonus will be taxable in the following tax year.

3 Allowable expenses and deductions

3.1 Principle of allowable expenses

Allowable expenses are those that can be deducted from earnings to arrive at the taxable employment income.

3.2 Wholly, exclusively and necessarily

The general rule for an expense to be deducted from earnings is that it must be incurred 'wholly, exclusively and necessarily' in the performance of the duties of employment.

If in doubt about an expense in the assessment, return to this rule to seek guidance.

The expense **cannot** be deducted **just** because it makes the job easier.

 Example

A bank manager joined a golf club with a view to taking potential clients there. In his or her opinion it would make his or her job easier because in the relaxed atmosphere the potential clients would be more likely to put business his or her way.

Are the membership fees an allowable expense?

Solution

No.

The expense is not wholly, exclusively and necessarily incurred in the performance of the duties of employment.

NECESSARY – No, he or she could try to win business at his or her office. It is not necessary to play golf to be a bank manager!

EXCLUSIVELY – No, he or she could also go to the golf club in his or her own private time.

3.3 Other specific allowable expenses

Set out below are specific expenses that are allowable.

- **Costs of business travel and subsistence.**

    Business travel includes journeys made in the performance of an employee's duties. It does not include travel between home and the permanent workplace (i.e. ordinary commuting).

    However, special rules apply if an employee uses his own vehicle for business travel.

    Under the 'Approved Mileage Allowance Payments' (AMAP) system, only amounts paid in excess of the approved rates are taxable.

    If the amounts paid are lower, the employee can claim the shortfall as an allowable expense.

    Cars

First 10,000 business miles per tax year	45p per mile
Additional business mileage	25p per mile
Additional passengers (per passenger)	5p per mile
Motorcycles	24p per mile
Bicycles	20p per mile

Reference material

Some information about AMAP is included in the reference material in the 'Approved mileage allowance payments' section, so you do not need to learn it.

Why not look up the correct part of the reference material in the introduction to this text book now?

Example

Mariam has travelled 12,000 business miles in the tax year 2021/22 in her own car. Her employer pays 42p per mile.

(a)   How much of the mileage allowance is taxable?

(b)   How would your answer differ if Mariam's employer paid 38p per mile?

Solution

(a)   Taxable mileage allowance

	£	£
Income (12,000 × 42p)		5,040
Less: Allowable expense		
10,000 × 45p	4,500	
2,000 × 25p	500	
	───	(5,000)
Taxable amount		40

(b)   If Mariam's employer paid 38p per mile, the total amount received by Mariam would be 12,000 × 38p = £4,560.

Mariam could deduct the shortfall of £440 (£5,000 – £4,560) as an allowable expense.

Test your understanding 2

Charles

Charles has the following income for the tax year 2021/22:

		£
(a)	Salary as a sales representative paid on the last day of the month: year ending 31 December 2021 year ending 31 December 2022	16,000 18,000
(b)	Bonus based on the company profits for the accounting year to: 30 September 2021 (paid 1 December 2021) 30 September 2022 (paid 1 December 2022)	600 900
(c)	Mileage allowance paid (8,000 miles at 50p) The allowance was only paid for business mileage.	4,000

Based on the information above, answer the following questions:

1　What is his taxable salary for the tax year 2021/22?

2　What is his taxable bonus for the tax year 2021/22?

3　What is his taxable/allowable mileage allowance for the tax year 2021/22?

- **Professional subscriptions**

   Professional subscriptions (e.g. annual subscriptions to AAT, subscriptions to trade associations, etc.) are allowable expenses. Compare this to golf club subscriptions mentioned earlier.

- **Amounts donated under the payroll deduction scheme**

   Under this scheme employees can have sums deducted from their salaries on a weekly/monthly basis by their employer and paid directly to charity. This is also referred to as payroll giving or Give As You Earn.

- **Contributions to company pension schemes**

  Where an individual contributes to the employer's own company pension scheme (also known as an 'occupational pension scheme'), the amount contributed is deducted directly from wages/salaries.

  The amount deducted is an allowable expense (see more on pensions in Chapter 7).

  Contributions to the pension scheme by the employer are an exempt benefit (see Chapter 4).

- **Entertaining**

  Where an employee incurs entertaining costs (e.g. for taking clients out for a meal), he or she will usually reclaim the costs from the employer. This reimbursement of allowable expenses is not taxable income (see section 3.4 below).

  Alternatively, he or she may have a regular specific 'entertaining allowance' which is always spent in its entirety on entertaining (e.g. £100 each month). Again, there will be no taxable income.

  However, if the employee pays for entertaining costs out of a general round sum allowance, the employee cannot claim a deduction for the entertaining expenses that he or she has incurred. The employee can claim deductions for any part of the round sum allowance used to pay for other, tax deductible, expenses, such as business travel.

3.4 Reimbursement of employee's expenses by employer

Where an employer pays expenses on behalf of an employee or reimburses expenses to an employee the amounts concerned are taxable income for the employee unless the following exemption is available.

The exemption is available where the employee would be able to claim a tax deduction for the business related expenses under the rules set out above (e.g. business travel, professional subscriptions, expenses which fall within the wholly, exclusively and necessarily provisions).

Where an expense is partly allowable and partly disallowable, the exemption can be applied to the allowable part. For example, where an employee's home telephone bill is fully reimbursed, the exemption can be applied to the business calls, but not to the private calls and the line rental.

Reimbursed expenses which are not exempt must be included in taxable income.

Test your understanding 3

Egbert

Egbert is the sales director of Pinafores Limited.

The company paid the following expenses in relation to Egbert in the year ended 5 April 2022:

	£
Sums reimbursed to Egbert:	
Business entertainment	46
Travelling and subsistence (all business related) – fares, hotels, meals etc.	938
General expenses allowance paid to Egbert	500

Egbert advises you that 35% of the general expenses allowance was used in entertaining customers and the balance was spent on business travelling.

How will each of these amounts be treated when calculating Egbert's income tax liability for the tax year 2021/22?

3.5 Flat rate payments

An employer can apply to HMRC for approval to reimburse tax free expenses at a flat rate or use HMRC tax-free benchmark rates (e.g. £5 subsistence allowance whilst travelling on company business, see Chapter 4).

The employer must have a system in place to check that the employee is actually incurring the expenses covered by the flat rate allowance.

3.6 Pro forma employment income computation – 2021/22

	£
Salary/fees/commission/bonus etc.	X
Expense allowances and reimbursed expenses (not covered by exemptions)	X
Benefits (see Chapter 4)	X
	——
	X
Less: Professional subscriptions	(X)
Donations under payroll giving schemes	(X)
Occupational pension scheme contributions	(X)
Expenses incurred wholly, exclusively and necessarily in the performance of duties	(X)
	——
Taxable employment income	X
	——

✳ Test your understanding 4

Kosuke

Kosuke is employed as an insurance salesman at a monthly salary of £1,450.

In addition to his basic salary he receives a bonus which is paid in May each year and which is related to the sales achieved by Kosuke in the year to the previous 31 October.

His bonuses are as follows:

Bonus for year to	Paid during	£
31 October 2019	May 2020	1,920
31 October 2020	May 2021	1,260
31 October 2021	May 2022	2,700

Kosuke made the following payments in respect of his employment in the tax year 2021/22.

	£
Contribution to occupational pension scheme	342
Subscription to Chartered Insurance Institute	100
Payroll giving scheme (in favour of Oxfam)	200
Gym membership – often meets clients at the gym	150

Using the following pro forma calculate Kosuke's taxable employment income for 2021/22.

	£
Salary	
Bonus	
	————
Less: Allowable expenses	
	————
Taxable employment income	
	————

 Test your understanding 5

Bartholomew

Bartholomew has been employed by Telnet TV Ltd in central London for several years as a television producer.

The following information is available for the year 2021/22:

(1)   His annual salary is £52,000.

(2)   On 31 May 2021 he received a bonus of £7,644 in respect of the company's year ended 31 March 2021.

  The bonus for the company's year ended 31 March 2022, paid on 31 May 2022, was £10,400.

(3)   Telnet TV Ltd has a registered occupational pension scheme to which it contributes 10% of employees' basic salary. Bartholomew is required to contribute 5% of his basic salary.

Calculate the amount of employment income taxable on Bartholomew for the tax year 2021/22 using the following pro forma.

	£
Salary	
Bonus	
	———
Less: Pension contributions	
	———
Taxable employment income	
	———

4 The PAYE system

4.1 Principle of the PAYE system

The PAYE system collects income tax at source from the earnings of employees. Employers deduct the income tax liabilities of their employees before paying them their salaries. The tax deducted is then paid to HMRC.

The aim of the PAYE system is to remove the requirement to submit a tax return from as many people as possible (i.e. all of their tax is deducted at source by their employer and paid to HMRC on their behalf).

The PAYE system will not be examined in the Personal Tax assessment.

Test your understanding 6

Mark each of the following statements as true or false.

		True	False
1	Sally is paid her bonus for the year ended 31 December 2020 in May 2021. Her bonus will be taxed partly in the tax year 2020/21 and partly in the tax year 2021/22.		
2	If Chen is paid 50p a mile by his employer for business mileage, there will be no tax consequences.		
3	Yana is employed as an electrician. Her subscription for the Financial Times is an allowable employment expense.		

5 Summary

The important aspects of this chapter are:

- **Basis of assessment** – when employment income is taxed.

  Bonuses are often tested here. Remember that all employment income, including bonuses, is taxable on the earlier of the date of receipt or entitlement to receipt.

- **Allowable expenses** – these are often included in an assessment.

  Remember that for an expense to be allowable it must be incurred 'wholly, exclusively and necessarily' in the performance of the duties of the employment.

Test your understanding answers

 ### Test your understanding 1

Contract of service is for **employment**.

Contract for services is for **self-employment**.

A high level of control would indicate **employment**.

 ### Test your understanding 2

1   The answer is £16,500 (9/12 × £16,000 + 3/12 × £18,000)

2   The answer is £600 which is the bonus received in the tax year

3   The answer is £400 taxable
      = 8,000 × (50p received − 45p allowed)

 ### Test your understanding 3

Egbert

Treatment of expenses

Amounts paid to or on behalf of Egbert in respect of expenses are taxable and should be included in his employment income unless they are also allowable deductions from employment income.

Business entertainment expenses are allowable deductions from employment income unless they are paid out of a general expense allowance.

Business related travel and subsistence expenses are also allowable deductions from employment income.

Accordingly, the only taxable amount is the 35% of the general expenses allowance spent on entertaining.

Egbert will have taxable employment income of £175 (£500 × 35%).

✱ Test your understanding 4

Kosuke

Kosuke's taxable employment income is as follows:

	£	£
Basic salary (£1,450 × 12)		17,400
Bonus paid in May 2021		1,260
		─────
		18,660
Less: Allowable expenses		
Pension scheme	342	
Subscription	100	
Payroll giving scheme	200	
	─────	
		(642)
		─────
Taxable employment income		18,018
		─────

✱ Test your understanding 5

Bartholomew

Taxable employment income

	£
Salary	52,000
Bonus (received) – May 2021	7,644
	─────
	59,644
Pension contributions (5% paid by employee)	
(employer's contribution is not taxable)	(2,600)
	─────
Taxable employment income	57,044
	─────

Test your understanding 6

1   **False** – The bonus will be taxed in full in the tax 2021/22.

2   **False** – A mileage allowance of 50p per mile would result in an excess amount taxable on Chen.

3   **False** – It is not wholly, exclusively and necessarily incurred in the performance of the duties of the employment.

Employment income – benefits

Introduction

In this chapter we look at the different types of benefits received by employees and how they are taxed.

This is an important area of the syllabus and is always likely to be tested in the assessment.

ASSESSMENT CRITERIA	CONTENTS
Identify exempt benefits in kind (2.1)	1 General rules
Calculate taxable benefits in kind (2.1)	2 Exempt benefits
Calculate the impact on tax liabilities of the following in order to make them more tax efficient: different benefits in kind (3.3)	3 Taxable benefits

1 General rules

1.1 Introduction

Taxable benefits are added to an employee's salary and bonus when calculating employment income (section 3 below).

Certain benefits are specifically exempt from income tax (section 2 below).

It is to be expected that benefits will be tested in every assessment.

1.2 General points

Before we consider the specific benefits, here are some general points which are likely to be tested frequently.

- If an employee makes a payment to his/her employer in respect of a benefit, the taxable amount is reduced by the payment.

	£
Value of benefit	X
Less: Contribution by employee towards the benefit	(X)
Taxable benefit	X

The only exception to this rule is that partial payments for private fuel cannot be deducted (covered later).

- An employee may be able to claim that a benefit (or part of it) was provided wholly, exclusively and necessarily for the purposes of the employment. Such benefits are not subject to income tax.

- For most benefits, **time apportion** the taxable amount if the benefit was only available for part of the tax year.

- This adjustment should be calculated in **months** and is likely to be a popular adjustment in assessment questions.

2 Exempt benefits

2.1 Types of exempt benefit

Reference material

Some information about exempt benefits can be found in the 'Other benefits in kind' section of your reference material provided in the real assessment, so you do not need to learn it.

Why not look up the correct part of the reference material in the introduction to this text book now?

- The provision of an annual private medical and/or a health screening.

- Personal expenses (e.g. telephone calls home, newspapers, laundry) paid by the employer whilst the employee is required to stay away on business. The payment limits are up to £5 per night in the UK and £10 per night for overseas. The payments can be averaged over a single trip, e.g. an employee incurs costs of £14 for a three night trip, which is under £15 (5 × 3), therefore the whole amount is exempt, even if the employee spent more than £5 on one night. If the total payments for a trip exceed these limits then the whole amount is taxable, e.g. if an employer reimburses expenses of £22 for a four night trip then the whole £22 is taxable.

- Job related accommodation (see 3.3 below).

- Low-rate or interest free loans, provided the total loans to an employee do not exceed £10,000 at any time during the tax year (see section 3.7).

- The provision of one mobile telephone per employee (including smartphones). Tablets and computers used to make telephone calls are not exempt because they use the internet to make the calls.

- Non-cash gifts received from someone other than the employer and costing no more than £250 per donor per tax year. The gift must not be in recognition of particular services by the employee in the course of employment.

- A long service award of £50 for each year of service provided service is at least 20 years. The award must not be in cash and the recipient must not have had an award within the previous 10 years.

- An employee who attends a full time course can receive tax free pay of up to £15,480 each academic year.

- Provision of eye care tests and/or corrective glasses for visual display units (VDU) use.

- Provision of parking spaces at or near place of work – for cars, bicycles or motorcycles.

- Provision of workplace nurseries (crèches) either at the workplace or in other premises that the employer manages and finances.

- Provision of sport and recreational facilities available to all staff but not to the public generally. The facilities can also be used by former employees and employees' families.

- Removal expenses up to £8,000 for a new employment or if an employee's job is relocated. This can include hotel costs whilst looking for somewhere to live, legal and estate agents' fees and any other costs related to the removal. There is a time limit such that if an employee needs to move in the tax year 2021/22 then expenses must be incurred or benefits provided by the end of the tax year 2022/23. If removal expenses exceed £8,000 then only the excess is taxable on the employee.

- The funding of an annual party or similar event (e.g. Christmas office party or staff summer outing) up to £150 per attendee per tax year. If the event costs more than £150 per head none of the amount is exempt. If employees attend two events with total costs more than £150 then only one of the events (with a cost below £150) can be exempt. The more expensive of the two events should be chosen for the exemption.

- Awards in accordance with a staff suggestion scheme. These reward employees for suggestions that improve the employer's business and which are not made as part of the employee's normal job. Awards up to a maximum of £5,000 can be exempt.

- Subsidised canteen provided it is available to all staff.

- Contributions by an employer towards the additional household costs incurred by an employee working from home instead of at the employer's premises of up to £6 per week or £26 per month. Only payments above the limit require supporting evidence.

There are other benefits which are also exempt from income tax, but no information in respect of these benefits is provided in the assessment.

In particular, remember from Chapter 3 that contributions by an employer to a registered pension scheme are not taxable.

3 Taxable benefits

3.1 General rule for taxable benefits

The general rule is that the taxable amount of a benefit is:

Cost to the employer of providing the benefit less any amount contributed towards the cost by the employee

These rules apply where, for example, an employer pays for private health insurance, for membership of a sports club for an employee, or for an employee's liabilities (e.g. telephone bill).

This rule applies even if, thanks to the employer's buying power, the employer's cost is less than the price an employee would have to pay.

 Test your understanding 1

Jutta

Jutta gives you the following information about her employment.

- She belongs to a private medical insurance scheme and her employer paid the required premium of £1,270 (including £650 for her family).

- Jutta took meals in the fully subsidised staff canteen, the cost for the year being £335.

- Jutta was paid a round sum expense allowance of £1,870, out of which she paid £800 on entertaining customers and £550 on business travel.

On what amount will Jutta be taxed in respect of these items?

3.2 Specific rules

There are specific rules in respect of the following:

Type of benefit	Amount taxable
Cash vouchers	Cash receivable when cashed in
Non-cash vouchers (includes transport vouchers, cheque vouchers)	Cost of voucher to the employer

Type of benefit	Amount taxable
Credit cards	Whatever private expenses the employee charges to the card but does not reimburse (but not interest and annual fee)
Accommodation	Section 3.3 below
Company cars	Section 3.4 below
Fuel provided for company cars	Section 3.5 below
Vans	Section 3.6 below
Beneficial loans	Section 3.7 below
Use of assets	Section 3.8 below
Gifts of assets	Section 3.9 below

3.3 Accommodation

The taxable benefit amount depends on whether or not the accommodation is 'job-related'.

Accommodation is 'job-related':

(a)   if it is **necessary** for the proper performance of employment duties

(b)   if it is provided for the **better performance** of duties and it is **customary** to provide accommodation in such circumstances

(c)   if there is a **special security** threat and the accommodation is part of the arrangements to counter the threat.

'Job-related' therefore includes accommodation provided for caretakers, hotel staff, clergy and certain members of the government.

A director can only claim exemption under (a) or (b) if:

•   the director has no material interest in the company, and

•   the director is a full time working director or the company is a non-profit making organisation.

◑ Test your understanding 2

Would the following situations be treated as being job-related, such that no accommodation benefit arises?

1	Accommodation provided for a caretaker of a school	YES/NO
2	Accommodation provided for a hotel worker	YES/NO
3	Accommodation provided for security reasons	YES/NO

The calculation of the taxable benefit is split into three parts.

3.3.1 Part 1 – Basic charge

The basic charge for being provided with accommodation is:

Not job-related	Job-related
Higher of (i) Annual value of the property (also known as gross rateable value or market rental value), which will be provided in the question, and (ii) rent paid by employer (where the property is rented rather than owned by the employer).	Exempt benefit

---

Example

Harry is provided with a flat to live in by his employer throughout the tax year 2021/22 (it is not job-related accommodation).

The flat has an annual value of £2,000 and the employer pays rent of £200 each month.

Harry contributes £50 each month towards the private use of the flat.

What is his taxable benefit in the tax year 2021/22?

Solution

	£	£
Basic charge		
Higher of (i) annual value; and	2,000	
(ii) rent paid by employer (£200 × 12)	2,400	
	———	2,400
Less: Contribution by employee (as mentioned in 1.2 above) (£50 × 12)		(600)
		———
Taxable benefit		1,800
		———

Test your understanding 3

Leona

Leona was provided with a house to live in by her employer. The employer rented the house from a local resident and paid rent of £32,000 per year. Leona paid rent of £12,000 per year to her employer. The property has an annual value of £9,750.

What is the taxable value of this benefit, assuming the accommodation is not job-related?

3.3.2 Part 2 – Expensive accommodation charge

If the accommodation provided is purchased by the company and cost more than £75,000, it is deemed to be 'expensive'. An additional benefit may apply as follows:

Not job-related	Job-related
(Cost – £75,000) × Official rate of interest	Exempt benefit

The official rate of interest is set annually by HMRC and is 2% in the tax year 2021/22.

 Reference material

The official rate of interest can be found in the 'HMRC official rate' section of your reference material provided in the real assessment, so you do not need to learn it.

Why not look up the correct part of the reference material in the introduction to this text book now?

The cost used to calculate the benefit includes any improvements made to the property before 6 April in the tax year for which the benefit is being calculated. So if the benefit is being calculated for the tax year 2021/22, then all improvement costs incurred up to 5 April 2021 must be included in the 'cost' figure.

Example

Jack is provided with a house to live in by his employer throughout the tax year 2021/22 (it is not job-related accommodation).

It cost his employer £150,000 in June 2016. An extension was added in May 2019 costing £50,000. The house has an annual value of £3,000.

What is the taxable benefit for the tax year 2021/22?

Solution

	£	£
Basic charge		
Higher of (i) annual value; and	3,000	
(ii) rent paid by employer (owned)	Nil	
		3,000
Expensive accommodation		
((£150,000 + £50,000) – £75,000) × 2%		2,500
Taxable benefit		5,500

If the accommodation was purchased by the company more than 6 years before the employee moves in, then a different rule applies.

Cost is replaced by the market value of the property at the date the employee moves in, plus the cost of any improvements made after the employee moves in but before the 6 April in the tax year of calculation.

 Example

Sanjay is provided with a house to live in by his employer throughout the tax year 2021/22 (it is not job-related accommodation).

The house cost £100,000 when the company bought it in December 2010.

Sanjay moved in during March 2019 when the property was worth £210,000. In July 2021 an extension was built on the house costing £32,000.

What is the 'expensive' accommodation charge in Sanjay's benefit calculation for the tax year 2021/22?

Solution

The answer is (£210,000 – £75,000) × 2% = £2,700.

Since the employer bought the house more than 6 years before Sanjay moved in, the cost is replaced by market value at March 2019.

The cost of the extension in July 2021 is ignored for the tax year 2021/22. It will be included in the 'expensive' accommodation benefit calculation for the next tax year and thereafter.

3.3.3 Part 3 – Provision of services

Not job-related	Job-related
Use of furniture – 20% per annum of market value when first provided (usually cost) Household expenses (e.g. heating, maintenance, decorating, but not capital improvements) – cost to employer	The same as not job-related – but restricted to: 10% of employee's net earnings (employment income other than any amounts included as a benefit from household expenses)

Reference material

Some information about expensive accommodation and provision of services can be found in the 'Other benefits in kind' section of your reference material provided in the real assessment, so you do not need to learn it.

Why not look up the correct part of the reference material in the introduction to this text book now?

Example

Amy is a hotel manager and is provided with job-related accommodation on the site of the hotel. Her annual salary is £25,000. She has other benefits of £500 and makes payments into her employer's registered occupational pension scheme of £2,000 per annum.

The accommodation has an annual value of £1,500 and cost her employer £90,000 four years ago. The accommodation contains furniture which cost her employer £10,000 four years ago (when she first moved into the accommodation). The employer pays all of her household bills totalling £1,000.

Calculate the taxable accommodation benefit for the tax year 2021/22.

Solution

	£
Basic charge (exempt)	Nil
Expensive accommodation charge (exempt)	Nil
Provision of services – furniture (£10,000 × 20%)	2,000
– household bills	1,000
Total	3,000
Restricted to (£23,500 (W) × 10%)	2,350

Working: Net earnings

	£
Salary	25,000
Other benefits	500
Less: Allowable expenses	(2,000)
Net earnings	23,500

There are many places to go wrong in calculating an accommodation benefit. Before starting to calculate consider all the factors that can impact it (e.g. does it cost more than £75,000, is it owned or rented by the employer, is it job-related, and was it bought by the employer more than 6 years before the employee moved in?).

Test your understanding 4

Usain

Usain has a salary of £30,000 and lives in a furnished company flat that cost his employers £105,000 in June 2016.

The annual value of the flat is £2,400 and Usain pays his employer rent of £100 a month. The accommodation is not job-related. Furniture costing £6,500 was first provided in June 2016.

Which is the correct figure for Usain's taxable benefit for the tax year 2021/22?

 Test your understanding 5

Read the following statements which relate to the provision of accommodation for an employee which is not job-related.

Mark each statement as true or false.

		True	False
1	Furniture provided by an employer for use by an employee is taxed each year on 20% of the market value when first made available.		
2	Furniture provided by an employer for use by an employee is taxed each year on 20% of the cost to the employer in the year of purchase.		
3	The running costs of the accommodation which are paid for by the employer are taxed on the employee on 20% of their total cost.		
4	The running costs of the accommodation which are paid for by the employer are taxed on the employee on their total cost.		

Test your understanding 6

Marianne

Marianne was employed by Logistics Ltd at an annual salary of £52,000.

Throughout the tax year 2021/22 she was provided with a rent-free furnished flat which had an annual value of £1,500. Logistics Ltd paid £150,000 for the flat in 2020.

The furniture in the flat was paid for by Logistics Ltd in 2020 and had cost £20,000.

Logistics Ltd paid heating and lighting bills for the flat amounting to £3,000 during the tax year 2021/22.

Other benefits for the tax year 2021/22 amounted to £3,600.

Calculate the amount of employment income chargeable on Marianne for the tax year 2021/22 assuming:

(a)   the occupation of the flat was job-related

(b)   the occupation of the flat was not job-related.

 Test your understanding 7

Joseph

Joseph has been employed by Rock Radio in central London for several years as a producer.

On 1 January 2020 he was provided with a company flat which has an annual value of £5,000 and was let at an annual rent of £8,500 paid for by Rock Radio on a five year tenancy from the same date. The occupation of the flat was not 'job-related'.

The furniture in the flat had cost £40,000 when first provided by Rock Radio.

Rock Radio paid £7,000 for utility services, decorating and repairs for the flat.

What is the amount of Joseph's taxable accommodation benefit for the tax year 2021/22?

3.4 Company cars

It is likely that this benefit will be tested in the assessment.

When a car is made available by an employer for **private** use, a taxable benefit arises as a result of the private use of the car.

The benefit is calculated as a percentage of the list price of the car when first registered.

$$\text{Benefit} = (\% \times \text{List price when new})$$

List price

The list price may be different from the price paid for the car by the employer. Take care to select the correct figure.

The cost of any extra accessories provided with the car must be added to the list price. In addition, the cost of any accessories acquired subsequently must also be added to the list price, but only if the accessory cost £100 or more.

The list price can be reduced by any capital contribution made by the employee towards the purchase of the car, subject to a maximum deduction of £5,000. This maximum is not provided in the rates and allowances available in the assessment.

Determining the percentage

The base percentage for petrol cars is 15% and the maximum is 37%.

The percentage depends on the rate at which the car emits carbon dioxide (CO_2). This is usually recorded on the car's registration document (and is supplied in the assessment).

If the emission rate is 55 grams per kilometre travelled (for the tax year 2021/22), the percentage of 15% applies to petrol cars if the petrol car was registered on or after 6 April 2020.

This is increased by 1% for every extra complete 5 grams emitted.

For petrol cars registered before 6 April 2020 an extra 1% is added.

Diesel engine vehicles are subject to a surcharge of an extra 4% to reflect the additional pollutants compared to petrol engines for the same carbon dioxide level of emission. However, the maximum percentage for diesel cars is still 37%.

The additional 4% does not apply to diesel cars which are registered after 1 September 2017 and meet the Real Driving Emissions Step 2 (RDE2) standards. You will be told in the assessment if the car meets these standards.

Reference material

Some information about car benefit percentages can be found in the 'Car benefit percentages' section of your reference material provided in the real assessment, so you do not need to learn it.

Why not look up the correct part of the reference material in the introduction to this text book now?

Example

Louise is provided with a company car with a carbon dioxide emission rate of 107g/km.

What percentage is to be applied assuming the car runs on:

(a) petrol (registered on 6 April 2021)

(b) diesel (not meeting RDE2 standards and registered on 6 April 2021)?

Solution

Ignore the extra 2g/km (always round down to the next 0 or 5).

∴ 105g/km

(a)	**107g/km petrol**	
	55g/km	15%
	105g/km = extra 50g/km	
	Therefore 50 × $^1/_5$	10%
		———
	Appropriate percentage	25%
		———
(b)	**107g/km diesel**	
	As above	25%
	Diesel supplement	4%
		———
	Appropriate percentage	29%
		———

Always look out for the type of fuel.

There are lower percentages for cars with low carbon dioxide emissions. These could be petrol, diesel, hybrid or electric cars.

Emissions	Electric range in miles	Petrol cars first registered from 6 April 2020
Nil		1%
1g/km to 50g/km	130 or more	1%
1g/km to 50g/km	70 – 129	4%
1g/km to 50g/km	40 – 69	7%
1g/km to 50g/km	30 – 39	11%
1g/km to 50g/km	Less than 30	13%
51g/km to 54g/km		14%
55g/km or more		15% + 1% for every extra 5g/km above 55g/km

An additional 1% should be added to these percentages for cars registered before 6 April 2020.

In the assessment the drive range will be provided for hybrid cars.

 Test your understanding 8

What percentage would be applied for petrol cars registered on 6 April 2021 with the following CO_2 emissions?

1   48g/km (hybrid car with an electric range of 100 miles)

2   72g/km

3   123g/km

4   228g/km

Non-availability

Where a car is unavailable to the employee for 30 consecutive days or more during any part of the tax year, the benefit is reduced proportionately.

Temporary non-availability of less than 30 days is ignored.

Where a car is unavailable for part of the tax year, the benefit should be calculated on a daily basis. However, in the assessment you should prepare calculations to the nearest month unless you are told otherwise.

Running costs

Running expenses (for example servicing and insurance) are deemed to be included in the benefit figure and **do not** produce an additional benefit.

However, the provision of a **chauffeur** is counted as an additional benefit valued at the **private use portion** of the chauffeur's employment costs.

Contributions for private use

Employees are commonly required to make a monthly payment towards the cost of **private use**. Such contributions made by the employee are deducted from the taxable benefit.

Remember that where the employee contributes towards the **cost of purchasing** the car, the treatment is different; such a contribution reduces the list price used in calculating the benefit.

Cars used only for business

Where an employee is specifically forbidden from using the company car for private purposes and, as a matter of fact, does not so use it, there will be no taxable car benefit.

There is also no benefit where there is provision of a company car (and associated services) which is a 'pool' car.

A pool car is one which is not exclusively used by any one employee, and which is not available for travel from home to work, being garaged at company premises, and is only used for business travel.

Test your understanding 9

1 Kerron is provided with petrol driven car by her employer that cost £15,400. The car was first registered before 6 April 2020. The emission rate shown on the registration document is 142g/km and the list price of the car when new was £16,000.

   During the tax year 2021/22 Kerron drove 3,000 business miles and paid her employer £2,000 in respect of her private use of the car.

   What is the benefit taxable on Kerron for the tax year 2021/22?

2 Valeriy is provided with a diesel car by his employer that cost £34,000. The car was registered on 6 April 2021 but does not meet RDE2 standards. The list price of the car when new was £39,000. Valeriy paid £3,000 towards the purchase of the car.

   During the tax year 2021/22 Valeriy drove 28,000 business miles. The emission rating of the car is 182g/km.

   What is the benefit taxable on Valeriy for the tax year 2021/22?

3.5 Fuel provided for private purposes

The provision of petrol or diesel in a company car for **private use** is the subject of a benefit charge which is in addition to the charge for the provision of the car itself.

The benefit is calculated as £24,600 multiplied by the same percentage used for calculating the car benefit.

Reference material

Some information about the fuel benefit can be found in the 'Car fuel benefit' section of your reference material provided in the real assessment, so you do not need to learn it.

Why not look up the correct part of the reference material in the introduction to this text book now?

The fuel benefit is £Nil if either:

- the employee has to repay the employer for all fuel provided for private use; or

- the fuel is only provided by the employer for business use.

There is no reduction in the fuel benefit if the employee only **partially** reimburses his/her employer for private fuel. This is a common source of error in questions.

As for the car benefit, where the car is unavailable to the employee for 30 consecutive days or more during any part of the tax year the fuel benefit is reduced proportionately (work to the nearest month).

If private use fuel is withdrawn during the year, the fuel benefit figure is reduced pro rata. However, this only applies if the withdrawal is permanent (e.g. if the car is provided throughout the year but the provision of private use fuel is only suspended between 1 October and 31 December, a full year's charge will still apply).

Example

From 1 November 2021 Joan's employer provided her with a car. The car was first registered on 6 April 2021. The car had a list price of £15,000 and an emission rate of 117g/km. Up to 5 April 2022 Joan drove 6,000 miles of which 4,500 were private. The company paid for all running expenses.

Between 1 November 2021 and 31 January 2022 the company paid for all petrol usage including private use. Joan made a contribution to her employer of £15 each month towards the provision of the petrol for her private use. From 1 February 2022 her employer only paid for business use petrol.

Calculate Joan's taxable benefits for the tax year 2021/22.

Solution

	£
Car benefit (£15,000 × 27% × $^5/_{12}$)	1,688
Fuel benefit (£24,600 × 27% × $^3/_{12}$)	1,661
	———
Taxable benefits	3,349
	———

The percentage is 27% = 15% + (115 − 55) × $^1/_5$.

The car was available for five months (1 November 2021 to 5 April 2022).

Fuel for private use was only available for three months (1 November 2021 to 31 January 2022). Fuel was permanently withdrawn from 1 February 2022.

The contribution towards the cost of private petrol does not reduce the fuel benefit, as the cost of the private petrol was not reimbursed in full.

Test your understanding 10

Rhadi

1   Rhadi is employed by Coliseum Ltd.

When at the company's premises Rhadi has use of a petrol driven car owned by the company for business journeys only. It had a list price of £62,000 and an emission rating of 208g/km. The car was first registered before 6 April 2020. It costs £4,800 a year to run and the chauffeur's salary is £17,500. It is garaged at the company's head office and is also used by all the directors.

What is Rhadi's taxable benefit in respect of this arrangement?

2   Rhadi is also provided with a Rover car which was first registered in April 2018. Coliseum Ltd paid £16,100 for the car, which had a list price of £17,000. However, Rhadi prefers to use his own car, a Lotus, and therefore lets his wife use the Rover.

The company pays for all of the running costs of the Rover car, including petrol for private use.

The carbon dioxide emission rate of the Rover is 192g/km. Rhadi's business mileage in his own car is 12,000 miles. Both cars run on petrol.

What is the total taxable employment income in respect of these two vehicles?

 Test your understanding 11

Ethelred

Ethelred is the finance director of Buttercup Ltd. The company provided him with benefits in the year ended 5 April 2022 as follows:

	£
Season travel ticket from home to office	292
Car owned by the company:	
Citroen CX 2000	
List price when new	13,800
First registered on 1 October 2016	
Emission rating: 112g/km	
Private medical insurance	1,628

Ethelred advises you that during the year his car did 16,800 miles, of which 3,360 miles represented private use, and that the company paid £1,848 in respect of all of the petrol for the car.

Ethelred paid £800 towards the cost of purchasing the car.

He also paid £1,000 to Buttercup Ltd for his wife and family to be included on the private medical insurance.

1   What is the taxable benefit in respect of the season travel ticket?

2   What is the total taxable benefit in respect of the car?

3   What is the taxable benefit in respect of the private medical insurance?

3.6   Company vans

In the case of a company van with private use the taxable benefits are:

- £3,500 per annum for unrestricted private use of the van

- £669 per annum if private fuel is provided by the employer.

- There is no charge for zero emissions vans

 Reference material

Some information about company vans can be found in the 'Van benefit charge' section of your reference material provided in the real assessment, so you do not need to learn it.

Why not look up the correct part of the reference material in the introduction to this text book now?

Taking the van home at night is not treated as private use.

Incidental private use, such as the occasional trip to the rubbish tip, is ignored. However, this would not extend to regular shopping trips.

These benefits are time apportioned if the van is unavailable to the employee for 30 consecutive days or more during any part of the tax year.

Test your understanding 12

Ghada is the sales director of a large manufacturing company. She receives the following benefits in addition to her salary.

The company supplied Ghada with a mobile telephone which she used for making private and business calls. The phone cost £250.

Throughout the tax year 2021/22, the company provided Ghada with a van, which Ghada uses for both business and private purposes. The van is electric and does not emit any carbon dioxide.

The company paid £1,420 in January 2022 as the annual premium for private medical insurance cover for Ghada and her family. She contributed £750 to her employer to include her husband in the scheme.

Show the total taxable benefit in respect of each of the above items for the tax year 2021/22.

3.7 Beneficial loans

Where by reason of employment an employee or a relative is provided with an interest free or cheap loan, the benefit derived from such an arrangement is taxable.

There is no taxable benefit where:

- the total loans to an employee do not exceed £10,000 at any time during the tax year; or

- the loan is used by the employee to purchase equipment required for the purposes of his/her employment; or

- the loan is used by the employee to pay for expenditure incurred wholly, exclusively and necessarily in the performance of the duties of the employment.

The taxable benefit is calculated as follows:

	£
Loan outstanding × the official rate of interest (ORI)	X
Less: Interest actually paid by the employee	(X)
Taxable benefit	X

Reference material

Some information about beneficial loans can be found in the 'Other benefits in kind' section of your reference material provided in the real assessment, so you do not need to learn it.

Why not look up the correct part of the reference material in the introduction to this text book now?

Where the loan is provided or repaid part way through the year, the benefit is calculated using either the average or the precise method.

- *Precise method*

  Interest is calculated on the balance of the loan on a daily basis.

- *Average method*

	£
½ × (Balance outstanding at beginning of year + Balance outstanding at the end of the year) × ORI	X
Less: Interest actually paid by the employee (Note)	(X)
Taxable benefit	X

Usually, the average method will be used for simplicity.

Note: although the interest actually paid by the employee should be deducted, in the assessment this can also be calculated on an average basis.

If the loan was provided or repaid during the tax year, the amount of the loan on those dates is used instead of the balance at the beginning or end of the tax year and the benefit is multiplied by the proportion of the year that the loan was available.

A taxable benefit arises in respect of any amount of loan written off by the employer, even if the loan was for less than £10,000.

Example

Brahim was loaned £15,000 by his employer on 6 August 2020. He repaid £2,000 on 6 November 2021. During the year Brahim paid interest on the loan of £105.

Calculate the amount taxable on Brahim in the tax year 2021/22.

Solution

The taxable benefit using the average method is:

	£
½ × (£15,000 + £13,000) × 2%	280
Less interest paid: given	(105)
	———
Taxable benefit	175
	———

 Example

Flora was loaned £15,000, interest free, by her employer on 6 August 2021 and repaid £2,000 on 6 September 2021.

Calculate the amount taxable on Flora in the tax year 2021/22 using the average method.

Solution

The taxable benefit using the average method is:

	£
½ × (£15,000 + £13,000) × 8/12 × 2%	187
Less: Interest paid by employee	(Nil)
	———
Taxable benefit	187
	———

Test your understanding 13

Kate

On 6 July 2021, Kate was provided with a company loan of £25,000 on which she pays interest of 0.15% per annum.

What is the taxable benefit for the tax year 2021/22?

 Test your understanding 14

Marina

Worf Limited provided Marina with the following benefits.

A loan of £32,300 on 6 April 2021 on which annual interest of 0.25% was payable.

Marina attended a staff party costing the company £140 per employee in December 2021.

Worf Limited provided group membership of a nearby gymnasium. The cost to the company of Marina's membership was £350 per annum although the normal annual membership fee was £750.

1   What is the amount of the loan benefit taxable on Marina for the tax year 2021/22?

2   What is the total of the taxable benefits for the party and the gym membership?

Test your understanding 15

Merlin

Merlin's annual salary from Shalot Limited is £50,000. He was relocated by Shalot Limited on 6 April 2021 and was reimbursed relevant relocation expenditure incurred of £10,000.

Shalot Limited provided Merlin with a loan of £30,000 on 6 April 2020 on which annual interest of 0.5% was payable.

What is the amount of employment income taxable on Merlin for the tax year 2021/22?

 Test your understanding 16

William

William has the following employment income for the tax year 2021/22:

(a) William has the use of a company car throughout the year, all the costs being met by his employer.

The details for the year ended 5 April 2022 are:

	£
List price of car when first registered on 6 April 2021	8,000
Cost of car on 6 April 2021	7,800
Emission rating: 111g/km	
Contribution made by William for:	
Private use of car	600
Private use petrol	480

The total mileage for the year was 20,000 miles of which 15,000 miles were for private motoring.

During the year, however, William had two accidents and the car was incapable of being used for 12 days in July 2021 and for all of November and December 2021, whilst repairs were being carried out.

No replacement car was provided during these periods.

(b) William had a loan of £50,000 from his employer throughout the year on which he paid interest of 0.25%. The loan had been used to purchase a yacht.

1   What is William's taxable car benefit for the tax year 2021/22?

2   What is William's fuel benefit for the tax year 2021/22?

3   What is William's loan benefit for the tax year 2021/22?

3.8   Use of assets

If an asset (for example, a television) is owned by the employer but the employee is allowed to use it privately, the taxable benefit is calculated as:

20% of the open market value when the asset was first made available (usually 20% of the cost).

This has been seen already as part of the accommodation benefit.

 Reference material

Some information about use of assets can be found in the 'Other benefits in kind' section of your reference material provided in the real assessment, so you do not need to learn it.

Why not look up the correct part of the reference material in the introduction to this text book now?

If the employer does not own the asset, but rents it, the benefit is the greater of 20% of the value of the asset and the rent paid by the employer.

 Test your understanding 17

Wang

Wang was provided with a computer for private use on 1 October 2021. The market value of the computer when first provided was £4,300 and at 5 April 2022 the market value was £3,000.

What is the value of the benefit in respect of this computer for the tax year 2021/22?

Test your understanding 18

Julius

Julius is the managing director of a large manufacturing company. He receives the following benefits in addition to his salary.

School fees totalling £10,000 are paid direct to a school in respect of his two children.

Julius is provided with a hybrid petrol engine car (list price £25,000 when registered on 6 April 2021) with an emission rating of 43g/km and an electric range of 22 miles.

Julius paid £1,300 towards the cost of purchasing the car. He also paid £150 per month towards the cost of his private use of the car. He is not provided with fuel for private use.

A car parking space is provided for him in a multi-storey car park near his office at a cost to his employer of £600 per annum.

He was provided with a laptop computer for personal use which cost £750 on 6 September 2021. Ownership of the laptop is retained by the company.

1   The school fees are not a taxable benefit. TRUE or FALSE?

2   What is Julius' car benefit?

   A   £1,281

   B   £3,081

   C   £150

   D   £1,450

3   What is the benefit in respect of the car parking space?

   A   £600

   B   £Nil

4   What is the benefit in respect of the laptop computer?

   A   £150

   B   £87

   C   £75

   D   £62

3.9 Gifts of assets

If an asset which is **new** is gifted to the employee, the benefit will be the **cost to the company**.

If an asset has been **used** and is then subsequently gifted to an employee, the benefit is the **higher of:**

- market value (MV) at the date of the gift (less the amount paid by the employee), or

- original market value less amounts assessed as benefits to date (less the amount paid by the employee)

- This rule does not apply for cars or bicycles, the gift of these assets will just be the market value (MV) at the date of the gift (less the amount paid by employee).

 Example

A suit costing £300 was purchased for Bill's use by his employer on 6 April 2020. One year later Bill purchased the suit for £20. Its market value at that time is estimated to be £30.

Calculate the amounts taxable on Bill in the tax years 2020/21 and 2021/22.

Solution

The taxable benefits are computed as follows:

	£
2020/21 – Use of suit	
Annual value (20% × £300)	60
	——
2021/22 – Purchase of suit	
Suit's current market value	30
Less: Price paid by employee	(20)
	——
	10
	——

	£
Suit's original market value	300
Less: Taxed in 2020/21 in respect of use	(60)
Less: Price paid by employee	(20)
	——
	220
	——

Thus the taxable benefit in the tax year 2021/22 is £220, being the greater of £10 and £220.

Test your understanding 19

Read the following statements and mark each one as true or false.

		True	False
1	Howie is loaned a new computer costing £1,000 by his employer on 6 April 2021. The taxable benefit for 2021/22 is £200.		
2	If the computer had been given to Howie on 6 April 2021 there would be no taxable benefit.		
3	Dale is a housemaster at a boarding school and is required to live on the premises. This is an example of job related accommodation.		
4	Ken drives a company van. He is required to take it home every night ready for work in the morning as he frequently drives from home straight to the customer's premises. He does not use it for any other private purposes. The taxable benefit is £3,500.		

3.10 Changing benefits to make them more tax efficient

It may be possible for an employee to choose a different benefit in order to reduce their taxable employment income. For example, choosing a car with lower CO_2 emissions will reduce the car and fuel benefit.

Alternatively they may be able to substitute a taxable benefit with one that is exempt, such as the provision of a mobile phone or workplace parking.

4 Summary

You should be prepared for any/all of the taxable benefits to be tested.

Company cars

Employees are taxed on a percentage of the vehicle's list price.

The percentage used is dependent upon the level of CO_2 emissions normally ranging from 15% to 37% moving up in increments of 1% for every 5g/km in excess of the base figure of 55g/km.

There is also a 4% supplement for diesel engines, unless the car meets RDE2 standards (although the maximum percentage is still 37%).

Do not forget the lower rates for cars with low emissions.

The fuel benefit uses the same percentage as calculated for the car, applied to a figure of £24,600.

Accommodation

Employees are taxed in three areas in relation to non-job related accommodation provided by the employer:

- Basic charge:

  Annual value (always given in the assessment).

- Expensive accommodation charge:

  For accommodation costing more than £75,000, an additional benefit of ((Cost – £75,000) × 2% (ORI)) is also charged.

- Provision of services:

  – Use of furniture:

    Furniture is treated in the same way as an employee using an employer's assets (i.e. MV when provided × 20%).

  – Household expenses:

    Cost to employer.

Beneficial loan

Employees are taxed on the interest they would normally pay on a loan, when provided by an employer at below market rates of interest.

The calculation is: (Loan amount × 2% (ORI)) – interest paid

Exempt benefits

These are very likely to be tested.

Test your understanding answers

Test your understanding 1

Jutta

The correct answer is £2,590.

	£
Private medical insurance	1,270
Canteen	Exempt
Round sum expense allowance	1,870
Less: Business travel	(550)
	———
Taxable amount	2,590
	———

Test your understanding 2

1　**Yes**
2　**Yes**
3　**Yes**

Test your understanding 3

The correct answer is £20,000 (£32,000 – £12,000).

The basic charge is the higher of the annual value or rent paid by the employer, which is £32,000, less the rent of £12,000 paid by Leona.

Test your understanding 4

Usain

The correct answer is £3,100.

	£
Basic charge – annual value (no rent paid by employer)	2,400
Expensive property charge	
(£105,000 – £75,000) = £30,000 × 2%	600
Use of furniture (£6,500 × 20%)	1,300
	4,300
Less: Contribution by employee (£100 × 12)	(1,200)
Taxable benefit	3,100

Test your understanding 5

1 **True**

2 **False** – Although often the MV when first made available is the same as the cost to the employer.

3 **False**

4 **True**

Test your understanding 6

Marianne

Employment income – 2021/22

(a)   Job-related accommodation

	£	£
Salary		52,000
Other benefits		3,600
		─────
		55,600
Living accommodation		Exempt
Other benefits in respect of accommodation		
Heating and lighting	3,000	
Furniture (£20,000 × 20%)	4,000	
	─────	
	7,000	
	─────	
Restricted to (£55,600 × 10%)		5,560
		─────
Employment income		61,160
		─────

(b)   Not job-related accommodation

	£	£
Salary		52,000
Other benefits		3,600
		─────
		55,600
Living accommodation:		
Basic charge	1,500	
Expensive charge		
(£150,000 – £75,000) × 2%	1,500	
	─────	
		3,000
Heating and lighting		3,000
Furniture (£20,000 × 20%)		4,000
		─────
Employment income		65,600
		─────

Test your understanding 7

Joseph

The correct answer is £23,500.

	£
Accommodation	
(rent paid by employer higher than annual value)	8,500
Utility services, decorating and repairs	7,000
Use of furniture (£40,000 × 20%)	8,000
	————
Taxable benefits	23,500
	————

Test your understanding 8

1   4% (Emissions between 1g/km and 50g/km with an electric range between 70 – 129 miles)

2   18% (15% + (70 – 55) × $^1/_5$)
    Round down emissions to 70g/km

3   28% (15% + (120 – 55) × $^1/_5$)
    Round down emissions to 120g/km

4   37% (15% + (225 – 55g/km) × $^1/_5$ = 49%), but maximum is 37%
    Round down emissions to 225g/km

Test your understanding 9

Kerron and Valeriy

1   The correct answer is £3,280.

The amount of the benefit arising is as follows:

	£
£16,000 (the list price) × 33%	5,280
Less: Contribution	(2,000)
Benefit	3,280

The benefit is calculated at the rate of 33% being

15% + 1% + ((140 − 55) × $^1/_5$.)

2   The correct answer is £13,320.

The amount of the benefit arising is as follows:

(£39,000 − £3,000) × 37% = £13,320

The benefit is calculated at the maximum rate of 37%
(15% + (180 − 55) × $^1/_5$ + 4% (diesel) = 44%).

Note that the business mileage driven is of no relevance to the calculations.

Test your understanding 10

Rhadi

1   There is no taxable benefit in respect of this arrangement because the car satisfies the conditions to be classified as a pool car.

2   The correct answer is £10,392.

The amount of the benefit arising is as follows:	£
Car benefit (£17,000 × 37%)	6,290
Fuel benefit (£24,600 × 37%)	9,102
	———
	15,392
Less: Mileage allowance claim for own car	(5,000)
	———
	10,392
	———

The benefit is calculated at the maximum rate of 37%
(15% + (190 – 55) × 1/5 + 1% = 43% so use maximum)

The business mileage claim is £5,000
((10,000 × 45p) + (2,000 × 25p))

Rhadi can claim relief for the business miles he does in his own car using the AMAP rates.

Test your understanding 11

Ethelred

		£
1	Season travel ticket	292
2	Motor car = (£13,800 – £800) × 27% (W)	3,510
	Petrol = £24,600 × 27% (W)	6,642
		10,152
3	Private medical insurance (£1,628 – £1,000)	628

Working

Appropriate percentage: 15% + (110 – 55) × $\frac{1}{5}$ + 1% = 27%

Test your understanding 12

Ghada

Benefits taxable as employment income – 2021/22

	£	£
Mobile telephone		
One phone per employee = exempt		Nil
Van – zero emission		Nil
Medical insurance cover		
Premium paid by employer	1,420	
Less: Contribution by Ghada	(750)	
		670
Total taxable benefits		670

Test your understanding 13

The correct answer is £347.

£25,000 × (2% – 0.15%) × 9/12	£347

Test your understanding 14

1   The correct answer is £565.

£32,300 × (2% − 0.25%)   £565

2   The answer is £350.

The staff party is an exempt benefit as the cost to the employer did not exceed £150 per head.

Gym membership is taxable on the cost to the   £350
employer.

Test your understanding 15

Merlin

The correct answer is £52,450.

	£
Salary	50,000
Relocation (W1)	2,000
Beneficial loan (W2)	450
Employment income	52,450

Workings

(W1) The first £8,000 of relocation expenses are tax-free provided they are reimbursed expenditure or paid direct to a third party (i.e. you cannot give an £8,000 round sum tax free to the employee).

(£10,000 − £8,000) = £2,000

(W2) Beneficial loan:

£30,000 × (2% − 0.50%) = £450

Test your understanding 16

William

		£	£
1	The correct answer is £1,133.		
	Car £8,000 × 26% × $\frac{10}{12}$ (Note)	1,733	
	Less: Contribution	(600)	
			1,133
2	The correct answer is £5,330.		
	Fuel charge £24,600 × 26% × $\frac{10}{12}$		5,330
3	The correct answer is £875.		
	Cheap loan £50,000 × (2% − 0.25%)		875

Note

The car benefit percentage is 26% (15% + (110 − 55) × $^1/_5$). The car and petrol benefits are time apportioned as the car was unavailable for use for more than 30 consecutive days during November and December 2021. No reduction is made for the 12 day period in July 2021. No deduction is made for the contribution towards private use petrol as it did not cover the full cost.

Test your understanding 17

The correct answer is £430 (£4,300 × 20% × 6/12).

The computer was not made available until 1 October 2021 so the benefit must be time apportioned.

Test your understanding 18

Julius

1   **False** – School fees are taxable on the cost to the employer.

		£	£
2	The correct answer is **A**.		
	Basic car benefit		
	((£25,000 – £1,300) × 13%) (W1)	3,081	
	Contribution towards private use		
	(£150 × 12)	(1,800)	
		—————	1,281

3   The correct answer is **B** – Parking place is exempt

4   The correct answer is **B**.
    Provision of asset (computer)
    (£750 × 20% × 7/12) (W2)   87
                                                                        ————

Workings

(W1) Appropriate percentage:

   13% (1g/km – 50g/km and less than 30 miles of electric range).

(W2) The computer was only available from 6 September 2021 and therefore the benefit is time apportioned for 7 months.

 Test your understanding 19

1   **True** – The benefit is (£1,000 × 20%).

2   **False** – The benefit would be £1,000, the market value of the asset.

3   **True**.

4   **False** – There is no benefit. Taking the van home at night is not treated as private use.

Property income

5

Introduction

This chapter explains how taxable property income is calculated and how losses can be relieved.

ASSESSMENT CRITERIA
Understand when claiming the property allowance is appropriate (2.3)
Identify allowable and disallowable expenses (2.3)
Understand how losses on property may be relieved (2.3)
Understand the difference between the cash basis and accruals basis (2.3)
Calculate profits and losses from property using cash basis and accruals basis (2.3)

CONTENTS

1　Property income

2　Allowable expenditure

3　Losses

4　Property allowance

1 Property income

1.1 Property letting

All income from letting property in the UK is added together.

It includes:

- rental income from land
- rental income from commercial property
- rental income from residential property.

1.2 Basis of assessment

It is critical to ensure that the correct amount of property income is taxed in a tax year. There are two possible ways to work out property income for a landlord.

(i) The default assumption is that a landlord will use the cash basis to work out their profit for the tax year. This means income is taxable when received and expenses are deducted when paid. This is similar to what you saw with employment income and is illustrated below.

	£
Rental income received	X
Less: Allowable expenses paid (section 2)	(X)
Taxable property income	X

In the assessment, where there is more than one property being let out, you may be asked to calculate the profit on each property separately, or the total from all properties together. You may be asked to calculate income and allowable expenses separately.

(ii) Alternatively a landlord can elect to use the accruals basis. The accruals basis **must** also be used if the gross annual rents exceed £150,000. The accruals basis means that we deal with income and expenses that **relate to the tax year**, not necessarily those paid and received in the year.

If a landlord wishes to elect to use the accruals basis they must do so within 12 months of 31 January following the relevant tax year – for the tax year 2021/22 the deadline is 31 January 2024.

You will be told in the assessment if a landlord has elected to use the accruals basis.

Any apportionment of income and expenses should be carried out to the nearest month.

	£
Net rental income receivable (less any non-recoverable amounts)	X
Less: Allowable expenses (section 2)	(X)
Taxable property income	X

The same basis (i.e. cash or accruals) must be used for all properties in a single property business.

 Example

In the tax year 2021/22, Jelena let out a property, beginning on 6 October 2021, at £2,000 per month. Rent for the first 5 months was received on time. However, rent for the last month was not received until 20 April 2022.

What is the rental income taxable in the tax year 2021/22?

Solution

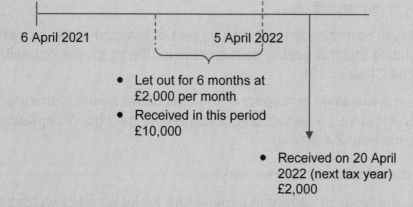

Under the cash basis (the default as his or her gross rents are under £150,000) we only consider the rents actually received from 6 October 2021 to the 5 April 2022. This would be £10,000 (£2,000 × 5).

Note

Under the accruals basis, we would ignore the dates the amounts were received and instead tax what is due in the tax year. The amounts relating to the tax year 2021/22 are the months from 6 October 2021 to 5 April 2022 which is six months and therefore the rental income would be £12,000 (£2,000 × 6). As this is higher than under the cash basis, Jelena would not elect for the accruals basis.

2 Allowable expenditure

2.1 'Wholly and exclusively'

Expenditure which may be deducted in computing the profit from property income is that which is incurred 'wholly and exclusively' for the purposes of letting.

Note: This rule is similar to that for allowable expenditure for employment income, but omits the 'necessarily' condition.

2.2 Capital expenditure

The capital cost of the property is not an allowable deduction in calculating property income. Similarly, the cost of improving or enhancing the value of the property is not deductible.

These costs will normally be dealt with as part of the cost of the property when calculating the chargeable gain on sale for the purposes of capital gains tax (see Chapter 10).

No deduction is available in respect of the cost of the original furniture in the property. However, a deduction is available for the cost of **replacing** domestic items (see 2.4 below).

2.3 Items of allowable expenditure

Specifically, the types of allowable expenditure for let property will include:

(a) internal and external repairs and redecoration provided that they relate to the making good of current dilapidations. This would include the replacement of a broken boiler or the replacement of single glaze windows with double glazed ones.

Note that the cost of initial repairs necessary in order to make a property usable are not deductible (e.g. repairs to a roof which had been damaged prior to the purchase of the property).

(b)   gardening

(c)   cleaning

(d)   agent's commission

(e)   costs of collecting rents (legal costs), including unpaid rents

(f)   advertising for new tenants

(g)   insurance premiums against damage to the structure of the property

(h)   legal and accountancy costs for preparing claims, accounts and tax computations in respect of the property

(i)   maintenance of common parts of blocks, offices and flats

(j)   interest on loans taken out to buy or improve the property (tested regarding non-residential properties only)

(k)   council tax and water rates

(l)   irrecoverable rents

(m)   the cost of replacing domestic items (see 2.4 below).

A landlord can also claim a deduction for business mileage when using their own car using the approved mileage allowance payments (AMAP) rates as set out in Chapter 3.

Expenses do not have to be incurred whilst the property is let, as long as they are incurred on a property that is available for letting.

Reference material

Some information about AMAP can be found in the 'Approved mileage allowance payments' section of your reference material provided in the real assessment, so you do not need to learn it.

Why not look up the correct part of the reference material in the introduction to this text book now?

Cars

First 10,000 business miles per tax year	45p per mile
Additional business mileage	25p per mile
Motorcycles	24p per mile
Bicycles	20p per mile

 Example

Sileshi has one property, which he lets on a commercial basis.

The property is let for £2,000 per month paid in advance at the start of each month. The rent is increased to £2,500 from 1 January 2022.

During the tax year 2021/22 Sileshi has the following expenditure:

Roof repair	£5,000
Agent's commission paid	£750
Buildings insurance	
y/e 31 December 2021	£480
y/e 31 December 2022	£520

Sileshi always pays his insurance in advance on 1 January.

Calculate Sileshi's taxable property income for the tax year 2021/22 using the cash basis and the accruals basis.

Solution – cash basis

	£
Rentals (£2,000 × 8) + (£2,500 × 4)	26,000
Expenses: Roof repair	(5,000)
Agent's commission	(750)
Buildings insurance (paid on 1 January 2022)	(520)
	———
Taxable property income	19,730
	———

Under the cash basis Sileshi will receive eight months of rent in 2021 from 1 May to 1 December. He will then receive four payments in 2022 from 1 January to 1 April.

Solution – accruals basis

	£
Rentals (£2,000 × 9) + (£2,500 × 3)	25,500
Expenses: Roof repair	(5,000)
Agent's commission	(750)
Buildings insurance (£480 × 9/12) + (£520 × 3/12)	(490)
	———
Taxable property income	19,260
	———

Under the accruals basis Sileshi will ignore the cash payments and accrue nine months of insurance costs to 31 December 2021 and then three months to 31 March 2022. Although he receives £2,500 of rent on 1 April 2022 this relates to the tax year 2022/23 and so is not recognised in the tax year 2021/22.

Test your understanding 1

Jane lets out two properties at an annual rental of £5,000 each. She incurs agent's fees of £1,200 on property 1 and £700 on property 2. She also incurs expenses of £6,000 repairing and redecorating property 2 during the year.

Required:

What is her taxable property income?

2.4 Replacement of domestic items

The cost of **replacing** domestic items in a residential property is an allowable deduction when calculating taxable property income. The cost of acquiring the original domestic items in the property is not allowable.

If the replacement item is substantially different from the original item the deduction is restricted to the cost which would have been incurred if the item had been replaced by a similar item (e.g. if a fridge is replaced with a fridge-freezer only the cost of a fridge similar to the original one is allowable).

The allowable deduction is reduced by any proceeds from the disposal of the original asset.

Domestic items are those items acquired for domestic use, e.g. furniture, furnishings, household appliances and kitchenware. However, 'fixtures' i.e. any plant and machinery that is fixed to a dwelling, including boilers and radiators are specifically excluded.

Although the replacement of fixtures and fittings such as boilers is specifically excluded from the replacement of domestic items rules, the replacement of such an item will generally be allowed as a repair to the property itself (see section 2.3 above). It is treated as if the fixture is a part of the house that has broken and is being repaired. Therefore, such a replacement will be an allowable deduction, although not under the replacement domestic items relief rules.

 Example

During the tax year 2021/22 Jerome lets out a furnished property at an annual rent of £10,000. The expenses incurred for the year are as follows:

	£
Repairs and maintenance (no capital items)	2,000
Council tax and water rates	500
Gardening and cleaning	250
Buildings insurance	300
New hall table	200
Replacement bed	800
Replacement chairs for kitchen	300

Jerome is raising the standard of the property's furnishings in order to be able to increase the rent charged. There was no table in the hall prior to the purchase. A bed of a similar standard to the old bed would have cost £450. Similarly, the new chairs cost £80 more than ones similar to those which were replaced.

The old chairs were sold for £40 but Jerome was unable to sell the bed.

What is Jerome's taxable property income for the tax year 2021/22?

Solution

	£	£
Rental income		10,000
Less: Allowable expenditure		
Repairs and maintenance	2,000	
Council tax and water rates	500	
Gardening and cleaning	250	
Buildings insurance	300	
Hall table (capital)	–	
Replacement of bed (note)	450	
Replacement of chairs (note)	180	
		(3,680)
Taxable property income		6,320

Note:

The allowable deduction in respect of the bed is restricted to £450, being the cost of a bed similar to the one replaced.

Similarly, the allowable deduction in respect of the chairs is £220 (£300 – £80) less the proceeds of £40 received in respect of the old chairs.

Test your understanding 2

Raoul

On 1 December 2020, Raoul purchased a freehold block of flats for £200,000. All the flats were let unfurnished on monthly tenancies. In the year to 5 April 2022, his receipts and payments were as follows:

	Year ended 5 April 2022 £
Receipts	
Rents collected (see (a))	26,280
Payments	
Repairs and maintenance (see (b))	1,480
Caretaker's wages	5,800
Insurance and incidentals (all allowable)	269
	7,549

(a) Rents

	£
Rents owing at beginning of period	240
Rents due	26,850
	27,090
Less: Rent owing at end of period	(810)
Cash received for rents	26,280

(b) Repairs and maintenance

	£
Garden maintenance	500
Lift maintenance	180
Normal decorations and incidental repairs	800
	1,480

Compute the taxable property income for the tax year 2021/22.

Test your understanding 3

James

In October 2020, James purchased a freehold flat for £150,000. The flat was let furnished for a monthly rent of £700 until 31 July 2021. Unfortunately, the tenant disappeared still owing the July rent.

The property was re-let from 1 October 2021 for a monthly rent of £750. Outgoings for the year to 5 April 2022 were:

	£
Agent's commission	1,163
Redecoration between tenants	1,745
Installation of central heating	1,980
Purchase of furniture (see (a))	800
Insurance and incidentals (all allowable)	547
Professional charges (see (b))	730
	─────
	6,965
	─────

(a) James purchased a dining table and chairs at the request of the tenant who moved in on 1 October 2021.

(b) Professional charges

Accountancy	420
Valuation for insurance purposes	310
	─────
	730
	─────

James has a significant property portfolio with gross rental income of over £200,000.

Compute James's property income in relation to the flat for the tax year 2021/22.

Test your understanding 4

Bernard

Bernard has presented you with a statement of income and expenditure on the three furnished properties that he lets out.

Property number	1	2	3
	£	£	£
Rental income received	3,000	3,500	2,500
Less: Expenses paid			
Agent's commission	(300)	(350)	(250)
Buildings insurance	(120)	(120)	(120)
Repairs and maintenance (Note)	(560)	(1,000)	(1,060)
Council tax	(400)	(450)	(380)
Accountancy fees	(50)	(50)	(50)
	———	———	———
Net income for year = £3,740	1,570	1,530	640
	———	———	———

Note

Repairs and maintenance is as follows:

	£	£	£
Gardening	260	260	260
General repairs (allowable)	300	400	800
Replacement furniture		340	
	———	———	———
	560	1,000	1,060
	———	———	———

The furniture in house 2 replaced furniture of a similar standard, which was sold for £35.

Calculate Bernard's taxable property income for the tax year 2021/22.

3 Losses

3.1 Treatment of a loss

A loss arises if allowable expenses are more than the rental income. For example in the tax year 2021/22:

	£
Rental income	10,000
Less: Allowable expenses	(10,500)
	———
Loss	(500)
	———

If this happens:

(i) the tax computation will show property income = £NIL: never show a negative figure in the tax computation; and

(ii) the loss is carried forward and set off against the next available profit from property letting only in future years (e.g. the £500 above is carried forward to the computation for the tax year 2022/23). This treatment is automatic.

Test your understanding 5

Are the following statements true or false?

1   Income from property is always taxed on a receipts basis.

2   The deduction allowed in respect of the replacement of a domestic item is restricted to the cost of an item similar to the one replaced.

3   Where the allowable expenses exceed the rental income, the loss arising can be deducted from the individual's other taxable income.

Test your understanding 6

Arthur

Arthur has two shops which he lets.

Shop 1

The annual rent was £3,000 on a lease which expired on 30 June 2021. Arthur took advantage of the shop being empty to carry out repairs and decorating. The shop was let to another tenant on a five year lease at £4,000 per annum from 1 October 2021.

Shop 2

The shop was purchased on 10 April 2021 and required treatment for dry-rot. Arthur also undertook some normal re-decorating work before the shop was let on 1 October 2021 on a seven year lease at an annual rental of £6,000.

The rent for both shops was due in advance on the first day of each month.

The following expenditure was incurred in the tax year 2021/22:

	Shop 1		Shop 2	
	£		£	
Insurance	190		300	
Ground rent	10		40	
Repairs and decorating	3,900	(Note 1)	5,000	(Note 2)
Accountancy	50		50	
Advertising for tenant	100		100	

Notes:

(1) Includes £2,500 for re-roofing the shop following gale damage in February 2022. As the roof had been badly maintained the insurance company refused to pay for the repair work.

(2) Includes £3,000 for dry rot remedial treatment. The dry rot was present when the shop was bought in April 2021.

Using the following pro forma calculate the property income or loss made on each property for the tax year 2021/22 using the accruals basis. Calculate Arthur's total property income or loss for 2021/22.

	Shop 1 £	Shop 2 £
Income		
Expenses		
	_____	_____
Net profit/loss	_____	_____

4 Property allowance

The property allowance is £1,000 and can be deducted from the gross rental income instead of deducting the allowable expenses. This would clearly be advantageous to a landlord who has a small amount of expenditure. For other landlords, with greater expenditure, deducting their actual expenditure from their rental receipts will give them a lower profit figure.

If property income is below £1,000 the allowance will apply automatically, giving the landlord assessable property income of £Nil. The taxpayer will not have to declare or pay tax on the income. If the taxpayer has actual expenditure in excess of their income they can elect to not use the allowance so as to generate a loss.

If property income is above £1,000 the landlord will deduct allowable expenses, unless they want to elect to use the property allowance, which can then be used in place of the actual expenditure. This would only be a preferable option if the actual expenditure was below £1,000.

The time limits for any elections with respect to the property allowance is within 12 months of 31 January following the relevant tax year – for the tax year 2021/22 the deadline is 31 January 2024.

Reference material

Some information about the property allowance can be found in the 'Property income allowance' section of your reference material provided in the real assessment, so you do not need to learn it.

Why not look up the correct part of the reference material in the introduction to this text book now?

Test your understanding 7

Four landlords have provided you with details of their income and expenditure for the tax year 2021/22 below.

Landlord	Eden	Dave	Jane	Freddy
	£	£	£	£
Rental income received	500	600	3,800	6,500
Less: Expenses paid				
Agent's commission	(100)	(500)	(150)	(900)
Buildings insurance		(220)	(240)	(360)
Accountancy fees	(150)	(160)	(400)	(150)

Required:

Calculate their respective taxable property income for the tax year 2021/22 taking advantage of any elections that may be available.

5 Summary

Property income is an important aspect of preparing an income tax computation. The main issues to beware of are:

- Income and expenses
  – cash basis but can elect for the accruals basis.

- Capital items
  – usually disallow but the replacement cost of domestic items is allowable.

- Losses
  – carry forward to the next tax year.

Test your understanding answers

Test your understanding 1

The correct answer is £2,100

	£
Rental income (£5,000 × 2)	10,000
Less: Expenses	
Agents fees (£1,200 + £700)	(1,900)
Repairs and redecoration	(6,000)
	———
Taxable property income	2,100
	———

Test your understanding 2

Raoul

Computation of taxable property income – 2021/22

	£	£
Rents received for 2021/22		26,280
Less: Garden maintenance	500	
Lift maintenance	180	
Normal decorations	800	
Caretaker's wages	5,800	
Insurance etc.	269	
	———	(7,549)
		———
Taxable property income		18,731
		———

As Raoul's gross rents for the year do not exceed £150,000 he is automatically assessed on the cash basis. This basis of assessment will apply unless he makes an election to use the accruals basis.

Test your understanding 3

James

Computation of property income – 2021/22

	£	£
Rents		
(4 × £700) + (6 × £750) – £700 (Note 2)		6,600
Less: Agent's commission	1,163	
Normal redecorations	1,745	
Installation of central heating (Note 3)	–	
Purchase of furniture (Note 4)	–	
Insurance etc.	547	
Professional charges	730	
		(4,185)
Profit		2,415

Notes

(1) As James' gross rental income exceeds £150,000 he will have to use the accruals basis to calculate his property income.

(2) Relief is available for irrecoverable rent.

(3) The cost of installing the central heating is not allowable as it represents an improvement rather than ongoing maintenance and is therefore capital in nature.

(4) The purchase of the dining furniture was not a replacement of domestic items and therefore the cost is not allowable.

Test your understanding 4

Bernard Taxable property income – 2021/22

The cash basis automatically applies

Property number	1	2	3	Total
	£	£	£	£
Rental income	3,000	3,500	2,500	9,000
Less: Allowable expenses				
Agent's commission	(300)	(350)	(250)	(900)
Building insurance	(120)	(120)	(120)	(360)
Repairs and maintenance	(560)	(660)	(1,060)	(2,280)
Council tax	(400)	(450)	(380)	(1,230)
Accountancy fees	(50)	(50)	(50)	(150)
Furniture (£340 – £35)		(305)		(305)
	———	———	———	———
Taxable property income	1,570	1,565	640	3,775
	———	———	———	———

Test your understanding 5

1 **False** – The accruals basis is used if the gross annual rents exceed £150,000 or if the landlord elects to use it.

2 **True**

3 **False** – The loss must be carried forward and set off against the next available profit from property letting in future years. It cannot be carried back or offset against any other income earned by the taxpayer.

Test your understanding 6

Arthur

Property income – 2021/22

	Shop 1 £	Shop 2 £
Income		
Rents accrued		
($\frac{3}{12} \times$ £3,000 + $\frac{6}{12} \times$ £4,000)	2,750	
(£6,000 × $\frac{6}{12}$)		3,000
	2,750	3,000
Expenses		
Less: Insurance	190	300
Ground rent	10	40
Repairs and decorating	3,900	2,000
Accountancy	50	50
Advertising for tenant	100	100
	4,250	2,490
Net profit/(loss)	(1,500)	510

Arthur's property loss for 2021/22 is £990 (£510 – £1,500).

Note: Repairs relating to conditions present when the building is purchased are not generally allowable as they represent capital expenditure (e.g. dry rot in Shop 2).

Test your understanding 7

Taxable property income – 2021/22

Landlord	Eden £	Dave £	Jane £	Freddy £
Without property allowance				
Rental income	500	600	3,800	6,500
Less: Expenses paid				
Agent's commission	(100)	(500)	(150)	(900)
Building insurance		(220)	(240)	(360)
Accountancy fees	(150)	(160)	(400)	(150)
Profit/(Loss)	250	(280)	3,010	5,090
With property allowance				
Rental income	500	600	3,800	6,500
Less: Property allowance	(500)	(600)	(1,000)	(1,000)
Property income	0	0	2,800	5,500
Optimal position				
Taxable property income	0	(280)	2,800	5,090

Eden has rental income below £1,000 so will automatically receive the property allowance and will not have to declare any property income on her tax return.

Dave is also automatically entitled to the property allowance but would prefer to elect not to use it as this will give him a loss of £280 which he could set off against future property income.

Jane has rental income in excess of £1,000 and so will not get the property allowance automatically. However as her total expenses are below £1,000 at £790 (£150 + £240 + £400) she will elect to use the property allowance to ensure her property income is as low as possible at £2,800 rather than £3,010 under the normal basis.

For Freddy the property allowance is also not applied automatically and he will not want to elect to use it as his total expenses of £1,410 are above £1,000 and thus he would be better off using the normal basis.

Calculating income tax payable

Introduction

This chapter brings together all the types of income considered in the earlier chapters and also introduces investment income. It then works towards calculating income tax payable.

This is an important chapter as calculation of taxable income and the income tax liability should always be tested.

ASSESSMENT CRITERIA

Understand the amount of personal savings allowance available for all taxpayers (2.2)

Understand the amount of dividend allowance available for all taxpayers (2.2)

Understand how to identify exempt income (2.2)

Calculate taxable investment income for all taxpayers (2.2)

Calculate the personal allowance for all taxpayers (3.1)

Apply all tax rates and bands (3.1)

Calculate total tax liability and net income tax payable/repayable (3.1)

Understand the impact of choices made on net tax liabilities (3.3)

Understand how to advise clients on legally minimising their tax liability (3.3)

Calculate the impact on tax liabilities of the following in order to make them more tax efficient: different investments, maximising relevance and exemptions and reliefs (3.3)

CONTENTS

1   The income tax computation

2   Calculation of taxable income

3   Income from self-employment

4   Investment income

5   Savings income

6   Dividend income

7   Personal allowance (PA)

8   Calculation of income tax payable

9   Approach to computations in the assessment

10 Tax planning

1 The income tax computation

The income tax computation is completed in two stages:

(i)   calculation of taxable income

(ii) calculation of income tax payable.

Each of these is looked at in turn in this chapter.

2 Calculation of taxable income

2.1   Overview of the calculation of taxable income

In Chapter 2 there was a pro forma income tax computation. The first part of the pro forma calculates taxable income. It is repeated here with more detail added. This pro forma should be learned.

A Person Income tax computation – 2021/22	£	£
Earned income		
Employment income		X
Pension income		X
Income from self-employment		X
		___
		X
Savings income		
Building society interest	X	
Bank interest	X	
Quoted loan note interest	X	
Treasury stock interest	X	
NS&I interest	X	
	___	X
Dividend income		X
Property income		X
		___
Net income		X
Less: Personal allowance (PA)		(X)
		___
Taxable income		X
		___

Some of the entries in the pro forma have been considered in detail in Chapters 3 to 5. The remaining entries are:

- income from self-employment,
- investment income (savings and dividend income) and
- personal allowance.

These are covered in sections 3 to 7 of this chapter.

2.2 Expanded pro forma income tax computation

The pro forma is expanded as set out below in order to assist in the calculation of the income tax liability.

As we have seen earlier, non-savings income is all income apart from savings income (interest) and dividends. Accordingly, it includes employment income, property income and income from self-employment. Non-savings income is sometimes referred to as 'other' income.

A Person

Income tax computation – 2021/22

	Non-savings	Savings	Dividends	Total
	£	£	£	£
Earned income	X			X
Savings income		X		X
Dividend income			X	X
Property income	X			X
Net income	X	X	X	X
Less: Personal allowance	(X)*			(X)
Taxable income	X	X	X	X

* The personal allowance is deducted primarily from non-savings income. If the non-savings income is reduced to nil, any remaining deduction is then made from savings income and finally dividend income.

3 Income from self-employment

The computation of income from self-employment is covered in Business Tax, and is outside the scope of Personal Tax.

It does, however, form part of an individual's total income.

If a task in the assessment includes income from self-employment, you simply need to include the figure given to you for taxable trading profit in the income tax computation as earned income.

4 Investment income

4.1 Types of investment income

Investment income can generally be separated into two categories.

4.2 Basis of assessment

All investment income is taxed on **receipts basis** (i.e. when the cash is received).

The period in respect of which the income has been paid is not relevant.

 Example

Bank interest of £1,000 for the year to 30 June 2021 was received on 30 June 2021.

In which tax year is the income taxed?

Solution

The interest was **received** on 30 June 2021 which is in the tax year 2021/22. Hence, it is all taxed in the tax year 2021/22.

5 Savings income

5.1 Types of savings income

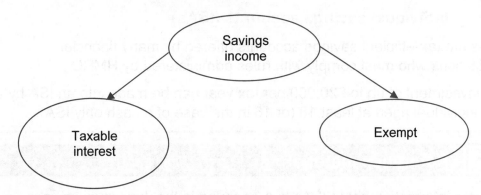

There are two possible treatments of savings income (interest).

- If taxable: include the amount received in the income tax computation.

- If exempt: do not include in the income tax computation, but make a note in your answer to state that it is exempt.

5.2 Interest received gross

In the assessment all interest is received gross, including interest in respect of:

- Bank accounts

- Building society accounts

- Quoted loan notes (debentures) of companies

- Gilts (for example, Treasury stock or Exchequer stock)

- NS&I accounts and bonds unless exempt (see below).

5.3 Exempt interest

The following types of interest are exempt. They should not be included in the income tax computation.

- Interest on NS&I Savings Certificates.

- Interest on Save As You Earn (SAYE) sharesave accounts.

- Interest on delayed repayments of income tax.

- Interest on ISAs (see 5.4 below).

These types of exempt interest were considered in Chapter 2, but are repeated here to reinforce that they are likely to be included amongst a list of other (taxable) interest received.

Interest on individual savings accounts (ISAs) is an example of exempt income which very frequently appears in the assessment.

5.4 Individual savings accounts (ISAs)

ISAs are tax-efficient savings accounts offered by many financial institutions who must comply with rules administered by HMRC.

An investment of up to £20,000 per tax year can be made into an ISA by a UK individual aged at least 18 (or 16 in the case of a cash only ISA).

> ### Reference material
>
> Some information about ISAs can be found in the 'Individual savings accounts' section of your reference material provided in the real assessment, so you do not need to learn it.
>
> Why not look up the correct part of the reference material in the introduction to this text book now?

The funds in an ISA can be held as cash, or invested in securities or stocks and shares.

- Interest arising on cash deposits is exempt from income tax.

- Dividends arising in respect of investments in shares are exempt from income tax.

- Gains arising on the sale of investments are exempt from capital gains tax.

5.5 Tax rates to apply to taxable savings income

The normal tax rates (as previously considered in Chapter 2) are:

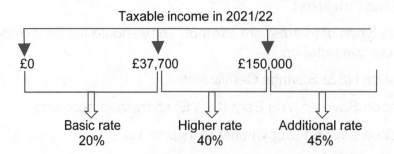

Taxable income in 2021/22

£0	£37,700	£150,000
Basic rate 20%	Higher rate 40%	Additional rate 45%

These are the rates of tax to apply to non-savings income (e.g. employment income and property income).

In addition, basic rate and higher rate taxpayers are entitled to a **savings allowance**.

The savings allowance is:

–	Basic rate taxpayer	£1,000 of savings income
–	Higher rate taxpayer	£500 of savings income
–	Additional rate taxpayer	£Nil

To determine if the taxpayer is a basic rate taxpayer or higher rate taxpayer we must identify his or her total taxable income and compare to the relevant basic and higher rate bands. The savings allowance operates like a nil rate band, i.e. the amount of the allowance is taxable income, however the tax rate applied to the income covered by the allowance is 0%.

 Reference material

Some information about rates, bands and allowances can be found in the 'Tax rates and bands' and 'Allowances' sections of your reference material provided in the real assessment, so you do not need to learn it.

Why not look up the correct part of the reference material in the introduction to this text book now?

 Test your understanding 1

Joseph has taxable non-savings income of £13,000 and taxable savings income of £9,000 for the tax year 2021/22. He has no other income.

What is Joseph's income tax liability in respect of his savings income for the tax year 2021/22?

Where an individual has non-savings and savings income, the non-savings income is taxed first and then the savings income, to work through the different rate bands.

Example

Patrice has taxable income in the tax year 2021/22 of:

(i) £11,500

(ii) £39,500

(iii) £45,500

This includes £6,500 of savings income.

What is his income tax liability for the tax year?

Solution

(i) £11,500 taxable income (£5,000 non-savings (N-S) and £6,500 savings (S)).

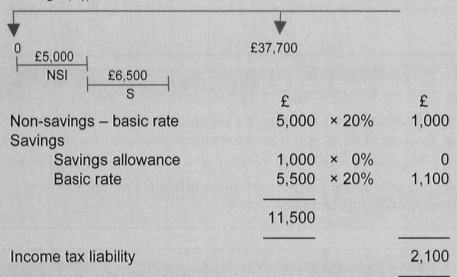

	£		£
Non-savings – basic rate	5,000	× 20%	1,000
Savings			
Savings allowance	1,000	× 0%	0
Basic rate	5,500	× 20%	1,100
	11,500		
Income tax liability			2,100

Note: As Patrice is a basic rate taxpayer the savings allowance is £1,000.

(ii) £39,500 taxable income (£33,000 non-savings and £6,500 savings).

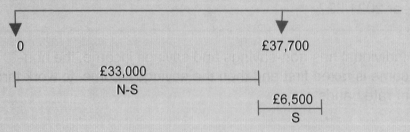

	£		£
Non-savings – basic rate	33,000	× 20%	6,600
Savings			
Savings allowance	500	× 0%	0
Basic rate	4,200	× 20%	840
	_____		
	37,700		
Savings – higher rate	1,800	× 40%	720
	_____		
	39,500		
	_____		
Income tax liability			8,160
			_____

Note: Patrice is a higher rate taxpayer as his taxable income falls between £37,700 and £150,000. This means he is entitled to a savings allowance of £500. The savings allowance uses £500 of the basic rate band. Accordingly, only £4,200 of the savings income is taxed at 20%.

(iii) £45,500 taxable income (£39,000 non-savings and £6,500 savings).

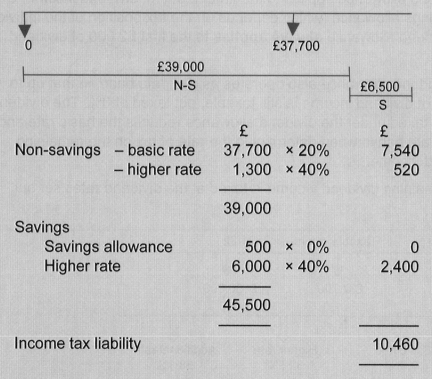

		£		£
Non-savings	– basic rate	37,700	× 20%	7,540
	– higher rate	1,300	× 40%	520
		_____		
		39,000		
Savings				
Savings allowance		500	× 0%	0
Higher rate		6,000	× 40%	2,400
		_____		
		45,500		
		_____		
Income tax liability				10,460
				_____

Note: As Patrice is a higher rate taxpayer he is entitled to a savings allowance of £500.

6 Dividend income

6.1 Types of dividend income

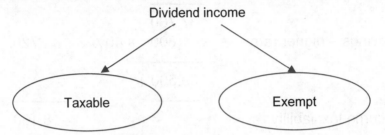

Dividend income

Taxable   Exempt

Dividend income is usually taxable (only dividends from ISA investments are exempt).

Dividends may be paid by:

- companies, or
- unit trusts and open-ended investment companies.

6.2 Tax rates

A dividend allowance applies to the first £2,000 of dividend income. Unlike the savings allowance (which depends on the tax position of the individual) the dividend allowance **always applies** to the first £2,000 of dividend income.

The dividend allowance also operates as a nil rate band, in that up to £2,000 of dividend income is still taxable, but taxed at 0%. The dividend income taxed under the dividend allowance reduces the basic rate and higher rate bands when determining the rate of tax on the remaining dividend income.

Any remaining dividend income is taxed at the dividend rates set out below.

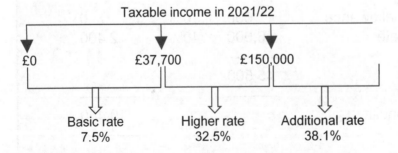

Taxable income in 2021/22

£0   £37,700   £150,000

Basic rate	Higher rate	Additional rate
7.5%	32.5%	38.1%

Reference material

Some information about rates and bands and allowances can be found in the 'Tax rates and bands' and 'Allowances' sections of your reference material provided in the real assessment, so you do not need to learn it.

Why not look up the correct part of the reference material in the introduction to this text book now?

Where an individual has a mixture of all different types of income, we work through the different rate bands in the order:

(i) non-savings income

(ii) savings income

(iii) dividend income.

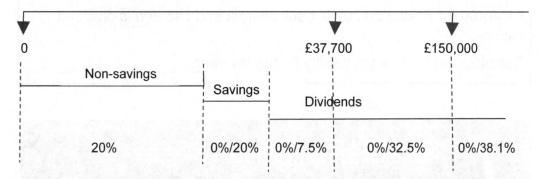

 Test your understanding 2

Emily

Emily has taxable income in the tax year 2021/22 as follows:

£39,610, of which £2,000 is bank interest and £8,000 is dividend income.

Calculate her income tax liability for the tax year.

Test your understanding 3

Ralph

Ralph has taxable income in the tax year 2021/22 of £75,600.

This consists of non-savings income of £10,800, savings income of £14,700 and dividend income of £50,100.

Calculate Ralph's income tax liability for the tax year.

 Test your understanding 4

Lara

Lara has taxable income in the tax year 2021/22 as follows:

£158,400, of which £26,300 is bank interest and £46,200 is dividend income.

Calculate her income tax liability for the tax year.

7 Personal allowance (PA)

7.1 Availability

All individuals are entitled to a personal allowance of £12,570 for the tax year 2021/22.

 Reference material

Some information about personal allowance can be found in the 'Allowances' section of your reference material provided in the real assessment, so you do not need to learn it.

Why not look up the correct part of the reference material in the introduction to this text book now?

The personal allowance is deducted from net income in arriving at taxable income.

The personal allowance can only be relieved against income of the current tax year. Any unused amount cannot be carried forward or carried back, nor can it be offset against capital gains.

 Example

Mavis has a salary of £23,000 in the tax year 2021/22 which is her only source of income.

Calculate her taxable income and income tax liability for the tax year 2021/22.

Solution

	£
Net income	23,000
Less: Personal allowance	(12,570)
Taxable income	10,430
Mavis' income tax liability is:	
(£10,430 × 20%)	£2,086

7.2 Restricted personal allowance

The personal allowance is restricted if an individual's net income exceeds £100,000.

The reduction is half of the amount by which the individual's net income exceeds £100,000. The allowance remaining is rounded up to the next whole pound.

 Reference material

Some information about restricted personal allowance can be found in the 'Allowances' section of your reference material provided in the real assessment, so you do not need to learn it.

Why not look up the correct part of the reference material in the introduction to this text book now?

Once an individual's net income exceeds £125,140 (£100,000 + (2 × £12,570)) they will not receive a personal allowance.

The personal allowance is never a negative number.

Example

Emilia has net income in the tax year 2021/22 of £111,475.

Calculate Emilia's personal allowance for the tax year 2021/22.

Solution

	£
Personal allowance	12,570
Less: Restriction	
(£111,475 – £100,000) × 50%	(5,738)
	―――――
	6,832
	―――――

 Test your understanding 5

Leon

Leon has income for the tax year 2021/22 as follows:

	£
Employment income	93,000
Dividends received	15,000

Compute Leon's taxable income for the tax year 2021/22.

8 Calculation of income tax payable

8.1 Tax rates

 Reference material

Information about tax rates summarised below can be found in the 'Tax rates and bands' section of your reference material provided in the real assessment, so you do not need to learn it.

Why not look up the correct part of the reference material in the introduction to this text book now?

	Allowance	Basic rate band	Higher rate band	Additional rate band
Non-savings	N/A	20%	40%	45%
Savings*	£1,000 or £500 or Nil	20%	40%	45%
Dividends	£2,000	7.5%	32.5%	38.1%

* There is a starting rate band of 0% that is sometimes available on savings income but this is not examinable.

Calculations should be performed to the nearest £.

However, in your assessment you must follow the instructions you are given for a particular task.

8.2   Pro forma calculation of income tax payable

A Person

Income tax payable – 2021/22

	Non-savings	Savings	Dividends	Total
	£	£	£	£
Taxable income (from first part of pro forma)	A	B	C	X
Income tax				£
Non-savings income A × 20%/40%/45%				X
Savings income B × 0%/20%/40%/45%				X
Dividend income C × 0%/7.5%/32.5%/38.1%				X
Income tax liability				X
Less: Tax deducted at source				(X)
Income tax payable				X

It is important to be able to distinguish between:

- income tax liability

  which is the total income tax due in respect of the taxpayer's income

and

- income tax payable (sometimes referred to as **net income tax liability**)

  which is the total income tax still to be paid after taking off any tax deducted at source.

8.3   Tax deducted at source

The income tax **liability** is the total amount of income tax that an individual must pay to HM Revenue and Customs (HMRC) for a tax year.

Many individuals will have already paid some tax at source (known as tax credits). The most common example is that salaries have tax deducted under the PAYE system at all relevant rates (20%, 40% and 45%). The employer then pays the withheld tax to HMRC on behalf of the taxpayer.

PAYE can also be deducted from occupational pension income.

Tax credits can reduce the tax liability leaving a smaller amount of tax still owed to HMRC (or possibly a tax repayment). This is the income tax **payable** (or repayable).

Example

From the example in section 7.1, Mavis had PAYE deducted from her salary.

What is her income tax payable/repayable if the PAYE deducted was:

(a)   £1,950, or

(b)   £2,750?

Solution

	(a)	(b)
From section 7 solution		
Income tax liability	2,086	2,086
Less: Tax deducted at source		
PAYE	(1,950)	(2,750)
Income tax payable	136	
Income tax repayable		(664)

Example

Stephanie

Stephanie was paid a gross salary in the tax year 2021/22 of £29,305. Her employer deducted income tax under PAYE of £3,581.

Stephanie also receives the following amounts of investment income in the tax year 2021/22:

	£
Dividends	20,300
Bank interest	1,300

Calculate Stephanie's income tax payable for the tax year 2021/22.

Solution

Stephanie – Income tax computation – 2021/22

	Non-savings	Savings	Dividends	Total
	£	£	£	£
Employment income	29,305			29,305
Bank interest		1,300		1,300
Dividends			20,300	20,300
Net income	29,305	1,300	20,300	50,905
Less: PA	(12,570)			(12,570)
Taxable income	16,735	1,300	20,300	38,335

Income tax

£			£
16,735	× 20%	(non-savings – basic rate)	3,347
500	× 0%	(savings allowance)	0
800	× 20%	(savings – basic rate)	160
2,000	× 0%	(dividends allowance)	0
17,665	× 7.5%	(dividends – basic rate)	1,325
37,700			
635	× 32.5%	(dividends – higher rate)	206
38,335			

Income tax liability		5,038
Less:	Tax deducted at source (PAYE)	(3,581)
		―――――
Income tax payable		1,457
		―――――

Note: the savings allowance is £500 because Stephanie is a higher rate taxpayer (her total taxable income is more than £37,700).

Test your understanding 6

Mark the following statements as true or false.

		True	False
1	The first £2,000 of dividend income is always taxed at 0%.		
2	The first £1,000 of savings income is always taxed at 0%.		
3	The tax credit in respect of PAYE can never be repaid but can be used to reduce the tax liability to nil.		
4	If a taxpayer has no taxable income for the tax year 2021/22 the benefit of the unused personal allowance for that tax year can be carried forward to the tax year 2022/23.		

Test your understanding 7

Stanley

Stanley's tax return for the tax year 2021/22 shows the following income:

	£
Gross salary from Dee Ltd	102,485
Dividends received	29,000
Building society interest received	3,500

Dee Ltd paid Stanley a performance related bonus. On 9 September 2020 he was paid his first bonus of £43,280 relating to the year ended 30 June 2020 and on 17 September 2021 he was paid £38,480 relating to the year ended 30 June 2021.

Stanley has travelled 11,500 business miles in his own car in the tax year 2021/22, for which Dee Ltd paid him 47p per mile.

During the tax year 2021/22 PAYE of £49,098 was deducted from Stanley's salary.

Compute Stanley's income tax payable for the tax year 2021/22.

Approach to this question

The first step is to draw up an income tax computation pro forma.

In this case, you will have to be careful when slotting in the figure for the bonus, as information is given for two tax years.

The income tax liability can then be calculated, but as this question requires the calculation of tax payable you must deduct the PAYE from the income tax liability.

KAPLAN PUBLISHING

Test your understanding 8

Briony

Until 31 December 2021 Briony was employed by JJ Gyms Ltd as a fitness consultant. Her taxable employment income for the tax year 2021/22 was £39,295, from which PAYE of £5,359 was deducted.

On 1 January 2022 Briony commenced in self-employment running a music recording studio. Her taxable trading profit for the tax year 2021/22 is £15,415.

During the tax year 2021/22, Briony received rental income from an investment property of £8,000 (after utilising the property allowance) and dividend income of £6,710.

Briony had a brought forward property loss from 2020/21 of £1,500.

Calculate Briony's income tax payable for the tax year 2021/22.

 Test your understanding 9

Sally

Sally has net income from employment and self-employment for the tax year 2021/22 of £51,615. She suffered PAYE on her employment income of £4,500.

What is Sally's income tax liability for the tax year 2021/22?

Test your understanding 10

Jon

Jon informs you of the following matters so that you can prepare his income tax computation.

- His salary for the tax year 2021/22 is £46,830, with tax deducted of £6,866.

- During June 2021 he cashed in his holding of NS&I Savings Certificates for £2,340. These had been purchased in 2016 for £2,000 and had earned 4% per annum compound for five years.

- Jon has been very lucky with his bets on the horses this year, winning £500 on the Derby in June 2021 but he tells you that most years he loses more than he wins.

- He received building society interest of £900 in the year to 5 April 2022.

- He received dividends of £3,100 in the year to 5 April 2022.

Calculate Jon's income tax payable for the tax year 2021/22.

 Test your understanding 11

Marcel

Marcel's income for the tax year 2021/22 was as follows:

	£
Occupational pension (gross)	17,630
Interest on NS&I Savings Certificates	1,250
Dividends	6,200
Interest on British Government stocks	9,410
Bank interest	2,480

PAYE of £1,026 was deducted from the occupational pension.

Calculate the income tax payable by Marcel for the tax year 2021/22.

Test your understanding 12

Galina

Galina gives you the following information for the tax year 2021/22:

	£
Salary (PAYE deducted £7,820)	50,800
Dividends received	330
Bank interest received	728

What is the income tax payable by Galina for the tax year 2021/22?

9 Approach to computations in the assessment

There may be at least two tasks in the assessment which require you to prepare all or part of an income tax computation. Additionally, you may need to apply your knowledge of tax rates and bands to calculate tax savings in a tax planning task (see later in this chapter).

In one task regarding investment income, you may be asked to calculate the income tax on a specific item of savings or dividend income. In such a task, you would be told the taxpayer's level of other income to work out the tax rates to apply. If there is doubt as to the source of other income, always assume it is 'non-savings income'.

In another large task, it is likely that you will be asked to complete a full computation of income tax liability or income tax payable for one or more taxpayers with a range of different types of income.

A grid is provided in the assessment to assist you when preparing full income tax computations. This may have between three and five columns.

A five column grid will allow you to enter a full computation following the pro forma in this chapter. The example below shows a suggested approach.

Example

Aage has an annual pension of £18,250 from his former employer. In the tax year 2021/22 he received a state pension of £5,200 and dividends of £6,500.

Calculate Aage's income tax liability using the grid below.

Approach

Step 1

Use the paper provided in your assessment to draw up a standard income tax computation. This need not be particularly neat as it will be thrown away at the end of the assessment!

	Non-savings	Dividends	Total
	£	£	£
Employment pension	18,250		18,250
State pension	5,200		5,200
Dividends		6,500	6,500
	———	———	———
Net income	23,450	6,500	29,950
Less: PA	(12,570)		(12,570)
	———	———	———
Taxable income	10,880	6,500	17,380
	———	———	———

£			
10,880	× 20%	(non-savings – basic rate)	2,176
2,000	× 0%	(dividends allowance)	0
4,500	× 7.5%	(dividends allowance – basic rate)	338
———			
17,380			
———			———
Income tax liability			2,514
			———

Step 2

Enter the figures into the assessment grid.

You cannot insert lines marking totals and subtotals. Remember to check you have enough space before you start – if not abbreviate.

		NSI	DI	Total
		£	£	£
Employment pension		18,250		18,250
State pension		5,200		5,200
Dividends			6,500	6,500
Total = Net income		23,450	6,500	29,950
Less: PA		(12,570)		(12,570)
Taxable income		10,880	6,500	17,380
£10,880 × 20%	2,176			
£2,000 × 0%	0			
£4,500 × 7.5%	338			
Income tax liability	2,514			

This will be manually marked so you need to include your workings.

In some questions you may need to calculate a restricted personal allowance as part of completing the full computation, using the net income figure.

Sometimes the space provided in the assessment will only have three columns, in which case it will not be possible to separate out the income into different types in your on-screen answer. It is still best to do this on paper first, however, when you input your answer you should show the workings in one of the first two columns and the total column on the right. Make sure that your workings make it clear where each figure has come from, for example, show a working of taxable non-savings income by deducting the personal allowance from the total non-savings income, or by deducting savings and dividend income from the total taxable income.

The following Test Your Understanding question shows both the five and the three column approach in the answer.

Test your understanding 13

Hossam

In the tax year 2021/22 Hossam has non-savings income of £53,650 together with bank interest of £2,250 and dividends of £4,000.

Calculate the income tax liability using the grid below.

Test your understanding 14

Margarita

Margarita is employed as a sales representative at an annual salary of £41,550. She is provided with a company car by her employer, which gave rise to a taxable benefit for the tax year 2021/22 of £5,700.

Margarita is a member of her employer's occupational pension scheme into which she pays 6% of her basic salary.

Margarita received bank interest of £6,500 during the tax year 2021/22.

Calculate Margarita's income tax liability for the tax year 2021/22 using this grid.

Note: You do not have enough columns here to set out a full columnar computation. You should still prepare a columnar computation in your workings. In your grid you can use the left hand columns for description and workings and simply enter your total column in the third column in the grid.

10 Tax planning

10.1 ISAs

Interest income in respect of cash deposits in an ISA is exempt from income tax.

- Individuals whose savings income is not fully covered by the savings allowance should consider investing in an ISA.

Dividend income in respect of shares held in an ISA is exempt from income tax.

- Individuals with dividend income in excess of the dividend allowance of £2,000 should consider holding shares through an ISA.

In the assessment, you may be asked to identify the effect on the income tax liability of the taxpayer taking a different course of action, such as investing in an ISA instead of an ordinary bank account. You may be asked to calculate the tax savings.

 Example

Roberta received bank interest of £1,100 from her building society account in 2021/22. Her taxable income, after personal allowance, from employment in 2021/22 was £60,000.

If Roberta had invested in an ISA instead, and had received the same amount of interest, calculate the income tax saving in 2021/22.

Solution

Roberta is a higher rate taxpayer in 2021/22 as her taxable income exceeds £37,700 so she has a savings allowance of £500. Her remaining interest of £600 (£1,100 – £500) is taxed at 40%, giving income tax of £240. If she had invested in an ISA, the interest would have been exempt, so the income tax saving would be £240.

10.2 Savings allowance and dividend allowance

Income is taxed at 0% in the following circumstances:

- Interest income which falls into the savings allowance.

- The first £2,000 of dividend income.

Individuals should consider adjusting the investments they hold in order to minimise their tax liability. For example, an individual with a considerable amount of savings income but no dividend income could invest some of the funds held on deposit in shares in order to generate tax-free dividends.

However, such decisions must be made with care as minimising the tax liability is not the only, or even the most important, consideration here. The individual must recognise that money invested in shares is not as secure as money on deposit in a bank due to the possibility that the value of the shares may fall.

10.3 Married couples and civil partnerships

Married couples and civil partners can arrange their income between them in order to minimise the total tax they pay as a couple.

If income generating assets are transferred from one spouse or civil partner to the other, the income will become taxable on the second person. This tax planning can be used to maximise the use of each individual's:

- savings allowance

- dividend allowance

- lower tax bands

- personal allowance

Test your understanding 15

Mark the following statements as true or false.

		True	False
1	Takehiro is a higher rate taxpayer. In the tax year 2021/22, he received interest income of £270 and dividend income of £1,150. The rates of income tax which Takehiro will pay on this investment income depends on how much non-savings income he has in the year.		
2	Larisa's only income is an annual salary of £57,000 and dividend income of £2,700 each year. Larisa would be better off if she were to sell shares which currently generate annual dividend income of £700 and deposit the proceeds in a bank account which would generate £600 of interest income each year.		
3	Lin earns an annual salary of £18,600 and has no other income. His husband Joe earns an annual salary of £73,000 and receives bank interest of £4,000 each year in respect of a bank deposit of £200,000. The total annual income tax liability of Lin and Joe would be reduced if Joe were to give £100,000 of his bank deposit to his husband.		

11 Summary

Calculating an income tax liability is a fiddly task with many allowances and rates to deal with.

In order to be able to prepare an accurate computation in the assessment, you should practise as many questions as you can.

Make sure you understand any differences between your answer and the model solution so that you improve as you do each question.

Test your understanding answers

Test your understanding 1

The correct answer is £1,600.

	£		£
First	1,000	taxed at 0% savings allowance	0
Next	8,000	taxed at 20% basic rate	1,600
	9,000		
Income tax liability on savings income			1,600

Test your understanding 2

Emily

Step 1 – Analyse the income.

First separate the taxable income into non-savings income, savings income and dividend income. The easiest way to do this is to identify the dividend income then the savings income. The balance (if any) of the taxable income must then be non-savings.

In this case:

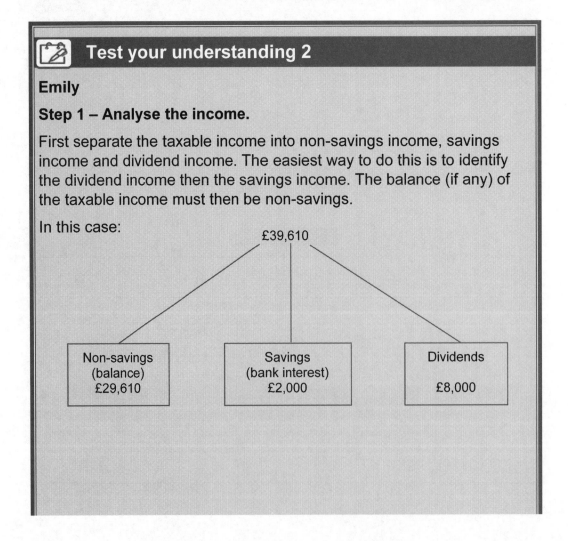

£39,610

| Non-savings (balance) £29,610 | Savings (bank interest) £2,000 | Dividends £8,000 |

Step 2 – Calculation of tax on non-savings income.

The tax liability can then be calculated, first on the non-savings income as follows:

£29,610 × 20%	£5,922

Step 3 – Calculation of tax on savings income.

The savings allowance is £500. This is because Emily's taxable income exceeds £37,700, such that she is a higher rate taxpayer.

There is £7,590 of the basic rate band left (£37,700 – £29,610 – £500).

This means that the remaining savings income of £1,500 (£2,000 – £500) all falls into the basic rate band, and will be taxed at 20%.

The tax on savings income is as follows:

	£
£500 × 0%	0
£1,500 × 20%	300
	300

Step 4 – Calculation of tax on dividend income.

The dividend allowance applies to the first £2,000 of the dividend income.

There is then £4,090 of the basic rate band remaining (£37,700 – £29,610 – £2,000 – £2,000).

This means that the next £4,090 of dividend income will be taxed at 7.5% with the balance of £1,910 (£8,000 – £2,000 – £4,090) at 32.5%.

Tax on dividend income is as follows:

	£
£2,000 × 0%	0
£4,090 × 7.5%	307
£1,910 × 32.5%	621
	928

Step 5 – In summary:

	£		£
Non-savings	29,610	× 20%	5,922
Savings			
Savings allowance	500	× 0%	0
Basic rate	1,500	× 20%	300
Dividends			
Dividend allowance	2,000	× 0%	0
Basic rate	4,090	× 7.5%	307
	37,700		
Dividends	1,910	× 32.5%	621
	39,610		
Income tax liability			7,150

 Test your understanding 3

Ralph

Step 1 – Calculation of tax on non-savings income.

The non-savings income falls into the basic rate tax band.

£10,800 × 20%   £2,160

Step 2 – Calculation of tax on savings income.

The savings allowance is £500. This is because Ralph's taxable income exceeds £37,700, such that he is a higher rate taxpayer.

There is then £26,400 of the basic rate band left (£37,700 – £10,800 – £500).

This means that the remaining savings income of £14,200 (£14,700 – £500) all falls into the basic rate band, and will be taxed at 20%.

The tax on savings income is as follows:

	£
£500 × 0%	0
£14,200 × 20%	2,840
	2,840

Step 3 – Calculation of tax on dividend income.

The dividend allowance applies to the first £2,000 of the dividend income.

There is then £10,200 of the basic rate band remaining (£37,700 – £10,800 – £14,700 – £2,000).

This means that the next £10,200 of dividend income will be taxed at 7.5% with the balance of £37,900 (£50,100 – £2,000 – £10,200) at 32.5%.

Tax on dividend income is as follows:

	£
£2,000 × 0%	0
£10,200 × 7.5%	765
£37,900 × 32.5%	12,318
	13,083

Step 4 – In summary:

	£		£
Non-savings	10,800	× 20%	2,160
Savings			
Savings allowance	500	× 0%	0
Basic rate	14,200	× 20%	2,840
Dividends			
Dividend allowance	2,000	× 0%	0
Basic rate	10,200	× 7.5%	765
	37,700		
Dividends	37,900	× 32.5%	12,318
	75,600		
Income tax liability			18,083

✿ Test your understanding 4

Lara

Step 1 – Analyse income.

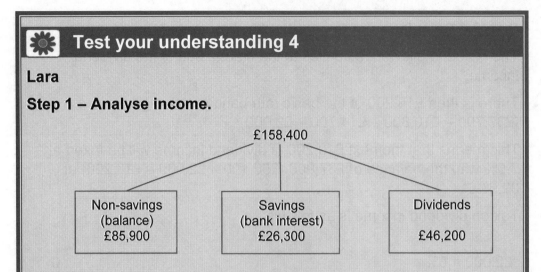

£158,400

| Non-savings (balance) £85,900 | Savings (bank interest) £26,300 | Dividends £46,200 |

Step 2 – Calculation of tax on non-savings income.

The first £37,700 of non-savings income will be taxed at the basic rate.

£37,700 × 20%   £7,540

The remainder of the income (£48,200) falls within the higher rate band.

£48,200 × 40%   £19,280

Step 3 – Calculation of tax on savings income.

The savings allowance is not available because Lara's taxable income exceeds £150,000, such that she is an additional rate taxpayer.

There is still £64,100 of the higher rate band left (£150,000 – £85,900).

This means that all £26,300 of savings income falls into the higher rate band, and will be taxed at 40%.

The tax on the savings income is as follows:

£26,300 × 40%   £10,520

Step 4 – Calculation of tax on dividend income.

The dividend allowance applies to the first £2,000 of the dividend income.

There is still £35,800 of the higher rate band left (£150,000 – £85,900 – £26,300 – £2,000).

This means that £35,800 of dividend income will be taxed at 32.5% with the balance (£8,400) at 38.1%.

Tax on dividend income is as follows:

			£
£2,000 × 0%			0
£35,800 × 32.5%			11,635
£8,400 × 38.1%			3,200
			————
			14,835
			————

Step 5 – In summary:

	£		£
Non-savings	37,700	× 20%	7,540
Non-savings	48,200	× 40%	19,280
Savings	26,300	× 40%	10,520
Dividends	2,000	× 0%	0
Dividends	35,800	× 32.5%	11,635
	————		
	150,000		
Dividends	8,400	× 38.1%	3,200
	————		
	158,400		
	————		
Income tax liability			52,175
			————

Test your understanding 5

Leon

Taxable income computation – 2021/22

	Total £
Employment income	93,000
Dividends received	15,000
Net income	108,000
Less: PA (working)	(8,570)
Taxable income	99,430

Working:

	£
Personal allowance	12,570
Less: Restriction	
(£108,000 – £100,000) × 50%	(4,000)
	8,570

Test your understanding 6

1 **True**

2 **False** – The first £1,000 of savings income is only taxed at 0% if the person is a basic rate taxpayer.

3 **False** – where PAYE has resulted in an overpayment of tax, the taxpayer will receive a repayment.

4 **False**

Test your understanding 7

Stanley

Income tax computation – 2021/22

	Non-savings £	Savings £	Dividends £	Total £
Employment income				
– Salary	102,485			
– Bonus	38,480			
– Mileage (W)	530			
	141,495			141,495
Building society interest		3,500		3,500
Dividends			29,000	29,000
Net income	141,495	3,500	29,000	173,995
Less: PA (restricted)	(0)	(0)	(0)	(0)
Taxable income	141,495	3,500	29,000	173,995
Income tax				
Non savings basic rate	37,700 × 20%			7,540
Non savings higher rate	103,795 × 40%			41,518
	141,495			
Savings higher rate	3,500 × 40%			1,400
Dividend allowance	2,000 × 0%			0
Dividend higher rate	3,005 × 32.5%			977
	150,000			
Dividend additional rate	23,995 × 38.1%			9,142
	173,995			
Income tax liability				60,577
Less: Tax deducted at source (PAYE)				(49,098)
Income tax payable				11,479

Note: there is no savings allowance because Stanley is an additional rate taxpayer.

Working: Taxable mileage allowance

	£	£
Income (11,500 × 47p)		5,405
Less: Allowable expense		
10,000 × 45p	4,500	
1,500 × 25p	375	
		(4,875)
Taxable amount		530

Test your understanding 8

Briony

Income tax computation – 2021/22

	Non-savings	Savings	Dividends	Total
	£	£	£	£
Employment income	39,295			39,295
Trading income	15,415			15,415
Property income	6,500			6,500
(£8,000 – £1,500)				
Dividends			6,710	6,710
Net income	61,210	0	6,710	67,920
Less: PA	(12,570)	(0)		(12,570)
Taxable income	48,640	0	6,710	55,350

Income tax			
Non savings basic rate	37,700	× 20%	7,540
Non savings higher rate	10,940	× 40%	4,376
	48,640		
Dividend allowance	2,000	× 0%	0
Dividend higher rate	4,710	× 32.5%	1,531
	55,350		

Income tax liability	13,447
Less: Tax deducted at source (PAYE)	(5,359)
Income tax payable	8,088

✏️ Test your understanding 9

Sally

The correct answer is £8,078.

Income tax computation – 2021/22

	£
Net income	51,615
Less: PA	(12,570)
Taxable income	39,045

Income tax

£		
37,700 × 20% (non-savings – basic rate)		7,540
1,345 × 40% (non-savings – higher rate)		538
Income tax liability		8,078

Note: The question asks for the income tax liability not the income tax payable so there is no need to deduct the PAYE.

Test your understanding 10

Jon

Income tax computation – 2021/22

	Non-savings	Savings	Dividends	Total
	£	£	£	£
Employment income – Salary	46,830			46,830
NS&I Savings Certificates				Exempt
Gambling winnings				Exempt
Building society interest		900		900
Dividends			3,100	3,100
	————	————	————	————
Net income	46,830	900	3,100	50,830
Less: PA	(12,570)			(12,570)
	————	————	————	————
Taxable income	34,260	900	3,100	38,260
	————	————	————	————

Income tax				
Non savings basic rate	34,260	× 20%		6,852
Saving allowance	500	× 0%		0
Savings basic rate	400	× 20%		80
Dividend allowance	2,000	× 0%		0
Dividend basic rate	540	× 7.5%		41
	————			
	37,700			
	————			
Dividend higher rate	560	× 32.5%		182
	38,260			
	————			————
Income tax liability				7,155
Less: Tax deducted at source (PAYE)				(6,866)
				————
Income tax payable				289
				————

Note: the savings allowance is £500 because Jon is a higher rate taxpayer.

Test your understanding 11

Marcel

Income tax computation – 2021/22

	Non-savings £	Savings £	Dividends £	Total £
Pension income	17,630			17,630
Interest on NS&I Certificates				Exempt
Government stocks		9,410		9,410
Bank interest		2,480		2,480
Dividends			6,200	6,200
Net income	17,630	11,890	6,200	35,720
Less: PA	(12,570)			(12,570)
Taxable income	5,060	11,890	6,200	23,150
Income tax				
Non savings basic rate	5,060	× 20%		1,012
Saving allowance	1,000	× 0%		0
Savings basic rate	10,890	× 20%		2,178
Dividend allowance	2,000	× 0%		0
Dividend basic rate	4,200	× 7.5%		315
	23,150			
Income tax liability				3,505
Less: Tax deducted at source (PAYE)				(1,026)
Income tax payable				2,479

Note: the savings allowance is £1,000 because Marcel is a basic rate taxpayer.

Test your understanding 12

Galina

Income tax computation – 2021/22

	Non-savings £	Savings £	Dividends £	Total £
Employment income	50,800			50,800
Bank interest		728		728
Dividends			330	330
	———	———	———	———
Net income	50,800	728	330	51,858
Less: PA	(12,570)			(12,570)
	———	———	———	———
Taxable income	38,230	728	330	39,288
	———	———	———	———
Income tax				
Non savings basic rate	37,700	× 20%		7,540
Non savings higher rate	530	× 40%		212
	———			
	38,230			
Savings allowance	500	× 0%		0
Savings higher rate	228	× 40%		91
Dividend allowance	330	× 0%		0
	———			
	39,288			
	———			
Income tax liability				7,843
Less: Tax deducted at source (PAYE)				(7,820)
				———
Income tax payable				23
				———

Note: the savings allowance is £500 because Galina is a higher rate taxpayer.

Test your understanding 13

Hossam – Five column approach

	Non-savings	Savings	Dividends	Total
	£	£	£	£
Income	53,650			53,650
Bank interest		2,250		2,250
Dividends			4,000	4,000
Net income	53,650	2,250	4,000	59,900
Less Personal allowance	(12,570)			(12,570)
Taxable income	41,080	2,250	4000	47,330
Non savings basic rate	£37,700 × 20%			7,540
Non savings higher rate	£3,380 × 40%			1,352
Savings allowance	£500 × 0%			0
Savings higher rate	£1,750 × 40%			700
Dividend allowance	£2,000 × 0%			0
Dividend higher rate	£2,000 × 32.5%			650
Income tax liability				10,242

Note: the savings allowance is £500 because Hossam is a higher rate taxpayer.

Hossam – Three column approach

		Total
	£	£
Income		53,650
Bank interest		2,250
Dividends		4,000
Net income		59,900
Less Personal allowance		(12,570)
Taxable income		47,330
Taxable non-savings income (£53,650 – £12,570)	41,080	
Non savings basic rate	£37,700 × 20%	7,540
Non savings higher rate	£3,380 × 40%	1,352
Savings allowance	£500 × 0%	0
Savings higher rate	£1,750 × 40%	700
Dividend allowance	£2,000 × 0%	0
Dividend higher rate	£2,000 × 32.5%	650
Income tax liability		10,242

Test your understanding 14

Margarita – income tax computation – 2021/22

		Total
		£
Salary and benefits (£41,550 + £5,700)		47,250
Less: 6% pension contribution (£41,550 × 6%)		(2,493)
Bank interest		6,500
Total = Net income		51,257
Less: Personal allowance		(12,570)
Taxable income		38,687
Non-savings (£47,250 – £2,493 – £12,570)	£32,187 × 20%	6,437
Savings allowance	£500 × 0%	0
Savings basic rate (£37,700 – £32,187 – £500)	£5,013 × 20%	1,003
Savings higher rate (£6,500 – £500 – £5,013)	£987 × 40%	395
Income tax liability		7,835

Note: the savings allowance is £500 because Margarita is a higher rate taxpayer.

Workings:

(W1) Income tax computation – 2021/22

	NSI	SI	Total
	£	£	£
Employment income (W2)	44,757		44,757
Bank interest		6,500	6,500
Net income	44,757	6,500	51,257
Less: PA	(12,570)		(12,570)
Taxable income	32,187	6,500	38,687

Income tax			
Non savings basic rate	32,187	× 20%	6,437
Saving allowance	500	× 0%	0
Savings basic rate	5,013	× 20%	1,003
	37,700		
Savings higher rate	987	× 40%	395
Income tax liability			7,835

(W2) Employment income

	£
Salary	41,550
Car benefit	5,700
	47,250
Less: Pension contributions (6% × £41,550)	(2,493)
Employment income	44,757

✿ Test your understanding 15

1	**False**	Takehiro's savings income is less than his savings allowance of £500 (Takehiro is a higher rate taxpayer) and his dividend income is less than the dividend allowance of £2,000. Accordingly, he will not pay any income tax in respect of his investment income regardless of how much other income he has.
2	**True**	Larisa's investment income would be £100 (£700 – £600) less if she were to adopt this strategy.
		Larisa is a higher rate taxpayer. Her income tax liability would reduce by £228 (£700 × 32.5%) if she were no longer to receive £700 of her dividend income.
		Larisa would then have £600 of savings income. She is entitled to a savings allowance of £500. Her income tax liability on the remaining £100 of savings income would be £40 (£100 × 40%).
		In total, Larisa's income tax liability would reduce by £188 (£228 – £40), which is more than the reduction in her investment income.
3	**True**	Joe's taxable savings income would be reduced by £2,000, such that his income tax liability would be reduced by £800 (£2,000 × 40%).
		Lin would have taxable savings income of £2,000. He is a basic rate taxpayer and is therefore entitled to a savings allowance of £1,000. His income tax liability on the remaining £1,000 of savings income would be £200 (£1,000 × 20%).

Gift aid and pension payments

Introduction

Tax relief is available in respect of these two types of payment. This chapter considers the amount of tax relief available and how it is given.

ASSESSMENT CRITERIA
Calculate the personal allowance for all taxpayers (3.1)
Adjust income and/or tax bands for: occupational pension schemes, private pension schemes and charitable donations (3.1)

CONTENTS
1 Donations to charity
2 Pension contributions
3 Pension payments, gift aid and personal allowances

1 Donations to charity

```
        TWO
       OPTIONS

  Payroll giving        Gift aid
```

1.1 Options available to individuals

Payroll giving – an individual can have an amount deducted from salary/wages at each pay day.

This is treated as an allowable expense when calculating employment income (see Chapter 3).

Gift aid – an individual can make regular payments or one-off payments of cash directly to charity (see 1.2 below).

1.2 Gift aid

If an individual declares a charitable payment of cash to be under 'gift aid', the amount of the donation is treated as paid net of basic rate tax which is then recoverable by the charity:

	£
Donation actually paid, say	80
Basic rate tax (20/80)	20
	———
Gross value of gift to charity	100
	———
Charity claims direct from HMRC	20
	———

If the individual is a basic rate taxpayer there is no effect on the income tax computation.

If the individual is a higher or additional rate taxpayer, higher or additional rate relief is given by extending the individual's basic rate band and increasing the higher rate limit by the gross amount of the gift aid payment.

In the above example, the taxpayer would not be subject to the higher rates (40% or 32.5%) until taxable income exceeded £37,800 (£37,700 + £100 gross gift aid).

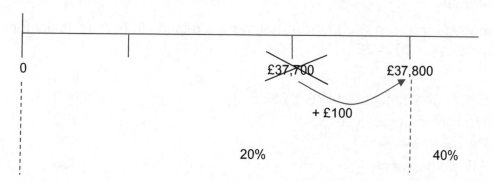

Taxpayers can elect to treat a gift aid donation as if it were paid in the previous tax year.

💡 Example

Sofia earns £70,000 p.a. and pays a total of £4,800 to a number of charities in the tax year 2021/22 under the gift aid scheme.

Calculate her income tax liability for the tax year 2021/22.

Solution

		£
Net income		70,000
Less: PA		(12,570)
Taxable income		57,430

Basic rate band: £37,700 + (£4,800 × 100/80) = £43,700

	£	
Income tax:	43,700 × 20%	8,740
	13,730 × 40%	5,492
	57,430	
Income tax liability		14,232

Test your understanding 1

Imogen

Imogen has given you the following details relating to her tax affairs for the tax year 2021/22.

	£
Salary and benefits (PAYE = £58,593)	166,040
Bank interest received	3,100
Payroll giving	2,500
Gift aid payment	6,320

Imogen is not entitled to a personal allowance (see section 3 below).

Calculate Imogen's income tax payable or repayable for the tax year 2021/22.

Approach to a question

Step 1: Consider how to treat the gift to charity

- Payroll giving deduction against employment income; or

- Gift aid: extend basic rate tax band and increase higher rate limit.

Step 2: Consider how to treat the pension payment (see below)

Step 3: Now continue with the income tax computation.

2 Pension contributions

2.1 Tax efficiency

A tax efficient way of providing for retirement is to make contributions into a registered pension scheme.

It is tax efficient for the following reasons:

- The individual gets tax relief in respect of the contributions made.

- The employer gets tax relief in respect of any contributions made, but without there being a taxable benefit for the employee.

- The income and chargeable gains generated by the funds in a pension scheme are exempt from income tax and capital gains tax.

- Part of the pension may be taken as a **tax-free** lump sum.

Registered pension schemes are available to all individuals.

Certain employed persons have a choice of provision so the full details are included in this section for all individuals.

2.2 Options available to employees

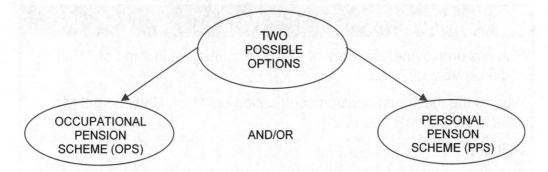

An OPS is an option only if the individual has an employer who offers such a scheme.

An OPS is also known as a company pension scheme. Such schemes were considered briefly in Chapter 3.

A PPS is an option for an employee who:

- has no OPS available from his or her employer, or

- chooses a PPS in preference to his or her employer's OPS, or

- also contributes to an OPS.

2.3 Options available to other individuals

Other individuals may save through a PPS.

2.4 Tax relief for pension contributions

All registered pension schemes are governed by the same rules, regardless of whether they are occupational or personal pensions.

An individual may make a pension contribution of any amount into a registered pension scheme or may make contributions into a number of different schemes. Tax relief will however only be available for a maximum annual amount.

The maximum total annual contribution into **all** pension schemes that an individual can obtain tax relief for is the higher of:

- £3,600, and

- 100% of the individual's relevant earnings, chargeable to income tax in the tax year.

Relevant earnings include trading profits and employment income, but not savings or dividend income.

Note that an individual with no relevant earnings can still obtain tax relief on contributions of up to £3,600.

 Example

Rob has employment income of £2,500 and interest income of £10,000 in the tax year 2021/22.

What is the maximum pension contribution on which Rob can get tax relief in the tax year 2021/22?

Solution

The maximum pension contribution on which Rob can get tax relief in the tax year 2021/22 is £3,600 – being the higher of:

		£
–	£3,600 and	3,600
–	100% of relevant earnings	
	= employment income	2,500

2.5 Method of giving tax relief for pension contributions

The **amount of tax relief** that is given for pension contributions is the same whether the contributions are to a personal pension scheme or an occupational pension scheme.

However, the **method by which the tax relief is given** is different for the two types of scheme.

2.6 Tax relief for contributions to personal pension schemes

Personal pension contributions are paid net of basic rate tax (20%).

Higher rate and additional rate income tax relief is achieved by extending the basic rate band and increasing the higher rate limit by the gross amount of the pension contribution. This is the same as the mechanism that gives tax relief for gift aid payments.

For example, if an individual pays a premium of £8,000 (net) – equivalent to a gross premium of £10,000 (£8,000 × 100/80) – the basic rate threshold is extended to £47,700 (£37,700 + £10,000).

The limit at which the taxpayer would start paying tax at the additional rates is also increased. The new limit is £160,000 (£150,000 + £10,000).

Example

Pauline's income for the tax year 2021/22 is as follows:

	£
Salary	42,650
Benefits	4,440
Bank interest received	8,000

She made a personal pension contribution of £3,200 (net) in the tax year.

Calculate Pauline's income tax liability for the tax year 2021/22.

Solution

	Non-savings	Savings	Total
	£	£	£
Employment income (£42,650 + £4,440)	47,090		47,090
Bank interest		8,000	8,000
Net income	47,090	8,000	55,090
Less: PA	(12,570)		(12,570)
Taxable income	34,520	8,000	42,520

Income tax

	£		£
Non savings basic rate	34,520	× 20%	6,904
Saving allowance	500	× 0%	0
Savings basic rate	6,680	× 20%	1,336
	41,700	(W)	
Savings higher rate	820	× 40%	328
	42,520		
Income tax liability			8,568

Working: basic rate band	
	£
Basic rate band	37,700
Add: Personal pension contribution (£3,200 × 100/80)	
(maximum contribution = 100% × £47,090)	4,000
	―――
Extended basic rate band	41,700
	―――

2.7 Method of giving tax relief for occupational pension scheme contributions

The pension contribution paid is deducted from employment income in the year of payment.

Tax relief is obtained through the PAYE system, at all rates of tax, and no further tax adjustment is required in the income tax computation other than showing the deduction against employment income (i.e. it is an allowable expense).

 Example

David received an annual salary of £43,300 and interest income of £12,000 in the tax year 2021/22.

Each year David pays 3% of his salary into his employer's registered occupational pension scheme and his employer pays a further 5%.

Explain how David will obtain tax relief for his pension contributions and calculate his income tax liability for the tax year 2021/22.

Solution

- David will pay a pension contribution of £1,299 (£43,300 × 3%) in the tax year 2021/22 on which he will obtain full tax relief, as it is less than the maximum available for tax relief of £43,300 (100% of earned income).

- David will obtain tax relief, at basic and higher rates, for the contribution through the PAYE system.

  His employer will deduct the pension contribution from David's taxable pay, in order to calculate the PAYE due.

David

Income tax computation – 2021/22

	Non-savings	Savings	Total
	£	£	£
Employment income	43,300		
Less: Pension contributions (3%)	(1,299)		
	42,001		42,001
Interest income		12,000	12,000
Net income	42,001	12,000	54,001
Less: PA	(12,570)		(12,570)
Taxable income	29,431	12,000	41,431

Income tax

	£	£	£
Non savings basic rate	29,431	× 20%	5,886
Saving allowance	500	× 0%	0
Savings basic rate	7,769	× 20%	1,554
	37,700		
Savings higher rate	3,731	× 40%	1,492
	41,431		
Income tax liability			8,932

The pension contributions made by David's employer are an exempt benefit.

Test your understanding 2

Gabrielle

Gabrielle has a salary of £54,000 per year. She pays 6% of her salary into her employer's pension scheme.

What is Gabrielle's income tax liability for the tax year 2021/22?

Approach to a question

Step 1: Consider how to treat the gift to charity (if there is one)

- Payroll giving deduction against employment income; or

- Gift aid: extend basic rate tax band and increase higher rate limit.

Step 2: Consider how to treat the pension payment:

- Allowable expense against employment income (OPS); or

- Extend basic rate band and increase higher rate limit (PPS).

Step 3: Now continue with the income tax computation.

2.8   Annual allowance

Contributions into a registered pension scheme can be made by the scheme member or any other party (e.g. an employer or spouse).

If the total contributions paid into the pension scheme exceed the annual allowance then the individual member is charged income tax on the excess.

The annual allowance is not within the scope of the assessment criteria.

2.9   Lifetime allowance

There is no restriction on the total contributions that an individual may make into a registered pension scheme. There is only a limit upon the annual contributions in respect of which tax relief will be available.

As funds in a registered pension scheme grow tax free there is also a limit, the 'lifetime allowance', which determines the maximum amount that an individual can accumulate in a pension scheme on a tax free basis.

The lifetime allowance is considered when a member becomes entitled to take benefits out of the scheme (e.g. when he becomes entitled to take a pension).

The lifetime allowance is not within the scope of the assessment criteria.

 Test your understanding 3

Paavo

Paavo has been self-employed for many years. His taxable trading profits in the tax year 2021/22 were £51,365.

He has the following investment income for the tax year 2021/22:

	£
Building society interest	1,070
Bank interest	1,750

Paavo paid a personal pension contribution of £2,800 on 13 December 2021.

Calculate Paavo's income tax liability for the tax year 2021/22.

 Test your understanding 4

Ming

Ming is employed as a teacher. For the tax year 2021/22 her employment income is £37,600. Tax deducted under PAYE was £5,020.

Her only other income in the tax year 2021/22 is £7,875 of dividend income.

She has decided to start making pension contributions.

(a) Calculate the maximum amount of tax deductible contributions that Ming could have made into a personal pension scheme for the tax year 2021/22 and the amount she would pay into the pension scheme in order to contribute the maximum.

(b) Calculate Ming's income tax payable/repayable for the tax year 2021/22 assuming she had contributed the maximum amount to her personal pension.

Test your understanding 5

Marjorie

Marjorie is employed at an annual salary of £17,000. PAYE of £1,250 was deducted in the tax year 2021/22. She was provided with a Peugeot car which gave rise to a taxable benefit of £2,330.

Other relevant information is as follows:

(1)   Marjorie has an account with the Halifax Building Society and £250 interest was credited on 31 January 2022.

(2)   Marjorie received dividends in the tax year 2021/22 of £1,500.

(3)   Marjorie paid contributions of £78 each month into her employer's occupational pension scheme throughout the tax year 2021/22.

Required:

Calculate Marjorie's tax payable/(repayable) for the tax year 2021/22.

 Test your understanding 6

Proctor

The following information is relevant to Proctor's taxation position for the year ended 5 April 2022.

(1)   His salary as managing director of Proctor (Engineers) Limited was £40,975 and his taxable benefits totalled £1,800. The company does not have an occupational pension scheme.

(2)   During the year, Proctor paid £3,200 (net) and Proctor (Engineers) Limited paid £10,000 into Proctor's personal pension scheme.

(3)   Other income:

(i)	Building society interest	£3,440
(ii)	Rental income	£9,660

Calculate Proctor's income tax liability for the tax year 2021/22.

3 Pension payments, gift aid and personal allowances

We saw in Chapter 6 that the personal allowance is reduced where a person's income exceeds £100,000.

Reference material

Some information about the limit for personal allowances can be found in the 'Allowances' section of your reference material provided in the real assessment, so you do not need to learn it.

Why not look up the correct part of the reference material in the introduction to this text book now?

When calculating the reduction, the figure of net income should be reduced by the grossed up amount of any gift aid payment or personal pension contributions.

Example

Eizo's only source of income is an annual salary of £115,000.

He makes personal pension contributions of £7,200 each year.

What is his personal allowance for the tax year 2021/22?

Solution

	£
Standard personal allowance	12,570
Less: (£106,000 (W) – £100,000) × 50%	(3,000)
Reduced personal allowance	9,570

Working: adjusted net income

	£
Salary	115,000
Less: Gross pension contributions (£7,200 × 100/80)	(9,000)
Adjusted net income	106,000

Test your understanding 7

Kurt receives a salary of £106,000 each year and pays £1,600 a year to Oxfam under gift aid.

What is Kurt's personal allowance for the tax year 2021/22?

 Test your understanding 8

Peter

Peter is employed as a sales director by Neat Limited. He earned a salary of £157,350 in the year to 5 April 2022.

He makes personal pension contributions of £22,000 (net) each year. He also makes charitable payments under the gift aid scheme totalling £15,400.

He receives bank and building society interest of £2,500.

Calculate Peter's income tax liability for the tax year 2021/22.

 Test your understanding 9

Talia

Talia has an annual salary of £53,570 per year. She wants to start contributing to a pension. Her employer operates an occupational pension scheme, whereby they will match the contribution she makes.

She decides to join and will pay £225 per month.

Calculate how much tax Talia will save in the tax year 2021/22 by contributing to this pension scheme.

Test your understanding 10

Leyla

Leyla has total income of £121,500 and contributes £7,500 per year to a private pension scheme. She would like to gift some money to charity using gift aid, but also wants to protect her full personal allowance.

What are the minimum donations Leyla can give, through gift aid, on a monthly basis to charity?

Note: round your answer to the nearest whole pound

4 Summary

- There are two tax efficient ways of giving to charity:
  - Payroll giving
  - Gift aid.

You must be able to deal with both of these.

- Pension contributions are a tax efficient way of providing for retirement.

- There are two types of pension scheme

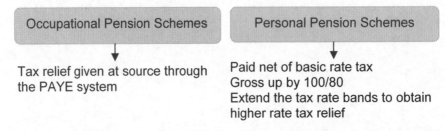

Occupational Pension Schemes	Personal Pension Schemes
Tax relief given at source through the PAYE system	Paid net of basic rate tax Gross up by 100/80 Extend the tax rate bands to obtain higher rate tax relief

- If a taxpayer with net income of £100,000 or more makes a gift aid payment or personal pension payment, the gross amount of the payment is deducted from their net income for the purposes of calculating their personal allowance.

Test your understanding answers

Test your understanding 1

Imogen

Income tax computation – 2021/22

	Non savings £	Savings £	Total £
Salary and benefits	166,040		166,040
Less: Payroll giving	(2,500)		(2,500)
	163,540		163,540
Bank interest		3,100	3,100
Net income	163,540	3,100	166,640
Less: PA (restricted)	(0)	(0)	(0)
Taxable income	163,540	3,100	166,640

Income tax

	£		£
Non savings basic rate	45,600	× 20% (W)	9,120
Non savings higher rate	112,300	× 40%	44,920
	157,900	(W)	
Non savings additional rate	5,640	× 45%	2,538
	163,540		
Savings additional rate	3,100	× 45%	1,395
	166,640		
Income tax liability			57,973
Less: Tax deducted at source (PAYE)			(58,593)
Income tax repayable			(620)

Working: Extended tax bands

Extend tax bands by £7,900 (£6,320 × $^{100}/_{80}$):

– Basic rate band £45,600 (£37,700 + £7,900)

– Higher rate limit £157,900 (£150,000 + £7,900)

Note: Imogen is not entitled to a savings allowance as she is an additional rate taxpayer.

Test your understanding 2

The correct answer is £7,736.

	£
Salary	54,000
Less: Pension contribution (£54,000 × 6%)	(3,240)
	50,760
Less: Personal allowance	(12,570)
Taxable income	38,190

Income tax

£	
37,700 × 20%	7,540
490 × 40%	196
38,190	
Income tax liability	7,736

Test your understanding 3

Paavo

Income tax computation – 2021/22

	Non-savings £	Savings £	Total £
Trading income	51,365		51,365
Building society interest		1,070	1,070
Bank interest		1,750	1,750
	———	———	———
Net income	51,365	2,820	54,185
Less: PA	(12,570)		(12,570)
	———	———	———
Taxable income	38,795	2,820	41,615
	———	———	———

Income tax

	£		£
Non savings basic rate	38,795	× 20%	7,759
Savings allowance	500	× 0%	0
Savings basic rate	1,905	× 20%	381
	———		
	41,200		
Savings higher rate	415	× 40%	166
	———		———
	41,615		
	———		
Income tax liability			8,306
			———

Notes: Basic rate band is extended by £3,500 (£2,800 × 100/80) from £37,700 to £41,200.

Paavo is entitled to a savings allowance of £500 as he is a higher rate taxpayer.

Test your understanding 4

Ming

(a)   Maximum pension contribution

The maximum personal pension contribution that Ming will obtain tax relief for is £37,600 being the higher of £3,600 and 100% of her earnings (£37,600).

Ming would pay the contribution net of basic rate tax:

i.e. (£37,600 × 80%) = £30,080.

(b)   Income tax computation – 2021/22

	Non-savings	Dividends	Total
	£	£	£
Employment income	37,600		37,600
Dividend income		7,875	7,875
	———	———	———
Net income	37,600	7,875	45,475
Less: PA	(12,570)		(12,570)
	———	———	———
Taxable income	25,030	7,875	32,905
	———	———	———

Income tax

	£		£
Non savings basic rate	25,030	× 20%	5,006
Dividend allowance	2,000	× 0%	0
Dividend basic rate	5,875	× 7.5%	441
	———		
	32,905		
	———		
Income tax liability			5,447
Less: tax deducted at source (PAYE)			(5,020)
			———
Income tax payable			427
			———

Notes: The basic rate band is extended by £37,600 to £75,300 (£37,700 + £37,600) but as Ming is already a basic rate taxpayer this does not affect the income tax calculation.

Test your understanding 5

Marjorie

Income tax computation – 2021/22

	Non-savings	Savings	Dividends	Total
	£	£	£	£
Employment income				
(£17,000 + £2,330)	19,330			
Less: Pension contributions				
(£78 × 12)	(936)			
	———			———
	18,394			18,394
Building society interest		250		250
Dividends			1,500	1,500
	———	———	———	———
Net income	18,394	250	1,500	20,144
Less: PA	(12,570)			(12,570)
	———	———	———	———
Taxable income	5,824	250	1,500	7,574
	———	———	———	———

Income tax

	£			£
Non savings basic rate	5,824	× 20%		1,165
Savings allowance	250	× 0%		0
Dividend allowance	1,500	× 0%		0
	———			
	7,574			
	———			———
Income tax liability				1,165
Less: tax deducted at source (PAYE)				(1,250)
				———
Income tax repayable				(85)
				———

Note: Contributions into an occupational pension scheme are an allowable expense against employment income.

Test your understanding 6

Proctor

Income tax computation – 2021/22

	Non-savings	Savings	Total
	£	£	£
Employment income			
(£40,975 + £1,800)	42,775		42,775
Building society interest		3,440	3,440
Property income	9,660		9,660
Net income	52,435	3,440	55,875
Less: PA	(12,570)		(12,570)
Taxable income	39,865	3,440	43,305

Income tax

	£		£
Non savings basic rate	39,865	× 20%	7,973
Savings allowance	500	× 0%	0
Savings basic rate	1,335	× 20%	267
	41,700		
Savings higher rate	1,605	× 40%	642
	43,305		
Income tax liability			8,882

Notes: The full personal pension premium gets tax relief as it is less than the maximum amount allowed of £42,775 (100% of earned income).

The basic rate band is therefore extended by £4,000 (£3,200 × 100/80) to £41,700 (£37,700 + £4,000).

Proctor is entitled to a savings allowance of £500 as he is a higher rate taxpayer.

The contributions by Proctor's employer are an exempt benefit.

Test your understanding 7

Kurt

The correct answer is **£10,570.**

	£
Standard personal allowance	12,570
Less: (£104,000 (W) − £100,000) × 50%	(2,000)
Reduced personal allowance	10,570

Working: adjusted net income

	£
Salary	106,000
Less: Gross gift aid (£1,600 × 100/80)	(2,000)
Adjusted net income	104,000

Test your understanding 8

Peter

Income tax computation – 2021/22

	Non-savings	Savings	Total
	£	£	£
Employment income	157,350		157,350
Interest		2,500	2,500
Net income	157,350	2,500	159,850
Less: PA (W)	(6,020)		(6,020)
Taxable income	151,330	2,500	153,830

Income tax

	£		£
Non savings basic rate	84,450	× 20%	16,890
Non savings higher rate	66,880	× 40%	26,752
	151,330		
Savings allowance	500	× 0%	0
Savings higher rate	2,000	× 40%	800
	153,830		
Income tax liability			44,442

Notes: The basic rate band is extended by £46,750 ((£22,000 + £15,400) × 100/80) to £84,450 (£37,700 + £46,750).

The higher rate limit will also be increased by £46,750. This increases the limit to £196,750 (£150,000 + £46,750).

The savings income nil rate band is £500 because Peter is a higher rate taxpayer.

Working: Personal allowance

The personal allowance is restricted because adjusted net income exceeds £100,000. The adjusted net income is calculated as follows:

	£
Net income	159,850
Less: Pension contributions (£22,000 × 100/80)	(27,500)
Gift aid (£15,400 × 100/80)	(19,250)
Adjusted net income	113,100
Less: Limit	(100,000)
Excess	13,100

The personal allowance is £6,020 (£12,570 − (£13,100 × 50%)).

✳ Test your understanding 9

Talia

The correct answer is **£1,080.**

Income tax liability (without pension contributions)

	£		£
Taxable income (£53,570 – £12,570)			41,000

Income tax

Non savings basic rate	37,700	x 20%	7,540
Non savings higher rate	3,300	x 40%	1,320
	41,000		8,860

Income tax liability (with pension contributions)

Taxable income (£53,570 – (£225 x 12) – £12,570)		38,300

Income tax

Non savings basic rate	37,700	x 20%	7,540
Non savings higher rate	600	x 40%	240
	38,300		7,780

Tax saving (£8,860 – £7,780) = £1,080

Note: the employer pension contribution is an exempt benefit.

Test your understanding 10

Leyla

The correct answer is £808.

	£
Total income = net income	121,500
Less: Pension contributions (£7,500 × 100/80)	(9,375)
Adjusted net income	112,125
Less: Limit	(100,000)
Excess	12,125
Gross gift aid donation	12,125
Amount paid = net amount (£12,125 × 80/100)	9,700
Monthly donation (£9,700/12)	808

National insurance contributions

Introduction

Class 1 national insurance contributions (NICs) are paid by employers and employees in respect of the earnings (excluding benefits) of the employees.

Class 1A NICs are paid by employers in respect of benefits provided to employees.

NICs are likely to be tested in every assessment.

ASSESSMENT CRITERIA	CONTENTS
Calculate Class 1/Class 1A NICs payable by: employees and employers (3.2)	1 NICs payable in respect of employees
	2 Earnings for class 1 NIC purposes
	3 Calculating class 1 contributions
	4 Class 1A contributions

1 NICs payable in respect of employees

1.1 Classes of NICs payable in respect of employees

The following national insurance contributions (NICs) are payable in respect of employees:

- Class 1 employee contributions (also known as primary contributions)

- Class 1 employer contributions (also known as secondary contributions)

- Class 1A contributions.

There are special rules relating to apprentices, younger employees, and those of state pension age, but these are not examinable.

1.2 Class 1 employee contributions

Class 1 employee contributions are a percentage based contribution levied on the gross earnings of the employee. Earnings are defined in Section 2 below.

The employer is responsible for:

- calculating the amount of class 1 employee NICs due and deducting them from the employee's wages and

- paying them to HMRC on behalf of the employees.

Note that class 1 employee contributions:

- are not an allowable deduction for the purposes of calculating the individual employee's personal income tax liability.

- do not represent a cost to the business of the employer, as they are ultimately paid by the employee. Therefore, they are not a deductible expense when calculating the employer's tax adjusted trading profits.

1.3 Class 1 employer contributions

Class 1 employer contributions are a percentage based contribution levied on the gross earnings of the employee.

Employer contributions are an additional cost of employment and are a deductible expense when calculating the employer's taxable profit.

1.4 Class 1A contributions

Class 1A contributions are also paid by employers.

They are paid in respect of the taxable benefits provided to employees.

Class 1A contributions are an additional cost of employment and are a deductible expense when calculating the employer's tax adjusted trading profits.

2 Earnings for class 1 NIC purposes

2.1 The definition of earnings

'Earnings' consist of:

- any remuneration derived from the employment
- which is paid in cash or assets which are readily convertible into cash.

The calculation of class 1 NICs is based on **gross earnings** with **no allowable deductions** (i.e. earnings before deductions that are allowable for income tax purposes, such as employee occupational pension scheme contributions and subscriptions to professional bodies).

2.2 Amounts included in gross earnings

The following are **included** in gross earnings:

- wages, salary, overtime pay, commission or bonus
- sick pay, including statutory sick pay
- tips and gratuities paid or allocated by the employer
- reimbursement of the cost of travel between home and work
- mileage allowances in excess of 45p per mile (45p threshold applies even if mileage exceeds 10,000 per year)
- vouchers (exchangeable for cash or non-cash items, such as goods).

2.3 Amounts not included in gross earnings

The following are **not included** in gross earnings:

- benefits (other than those listed above)
- tips directly received from customers
- business expenses paid for or reimbursed by the employer, including reasonable travel and subsistence expenses.

Definition

Earnings for class 1 NIC purposes are amounts paid in cash by the employer to the employee, other than tips and reimbursed expenses.

Note that dividends are not subject to NICs, even if they are drawn by a director/shareholder in place of a monthly salary.

 Example

Janet and John are employed by Garden Gnomes Ltd and both pay into the company's occupational pension scheme. Their remuneration for the tax year 2021/22 is as follows:

	Janet £	John £
Salary	30,000	55,000
Bonus	Nil	4,000
Car benefit	Nil	3,950
Employer pension contribution	2,300	4,575
Employee pension contribution	1,650	3,800

Calculate Janet and John's gross earnings for class 1 NIC purposes.

Solution

	Janet £	John £
Salary	30,000	55,000
Bonus	0	4,000
Gross earnings	30,000	59,000

Notes: The employer pension contributions are excluded as they are an exempt benefit.

The employee pension contributions are ignored as these are not deductible in calculating earnings for NIC purposes.

The car benefit is excluded as it is a non-cash benefit which will be assessed to class 1A NICs, not class 1.

Test your understanding 1

Hamza

Hamza is employed and received the following from his employer in the tax year 2021/22:

	£
Salary	35,000
Employer pension contributions	3,250
Company car – assessable benefit	3,570

In addition, Hamza incurred business travel expenses of £400.

What are Hamza's earnings for the purpose of calculating his class 1 national insurance contributions?

3 Calculating class 1 contributions

Note: When calculating NICs in the assessment, the task may ask for answers to show pounds and pence, or whole pounds only. You must follow the guidance given.

3.1 Calculating class 1 employee contributions

Employee contributions are normally calculated by reference to an employee's earnings period:

- if paid weekly, the contributions are calculated on a weekly basis.

- if paid monthly, the contributions are calculated on a monthly basis.

However, calculations can be performed on an annual basis if annual salary figures are provided.

For anti-avoidance reasons the class 1 NICs for company directors are always calculated using an annual earnings period, regardless of the frequency of payment (e.g. monthly, weekly).

In your assessment, class 1 NICs should be calculated using the annual thresholds:

- 12% on gross annual earnings between £9,568 and £50,270

- 2% on gross annual earnings in excess of £50,270.

Reference material

The national insurance rates and thresholds can be found in the 'National insurance contributions' section of your reference material provided in the real assessment, so you do not need to learn it.

Why not look up the correct part of the reference material in the introduction to this text book now?

3.2 Calculating class 1 employer contributions

Employer contributions are calculated as:

- 13.8% on all gross annual earnings above £8,840.

Note that there is:

- no upper earnings threshold
- no change in the rate of NICs payable for employer contributions.

 Example

Millie is employed by Blue Forge Ltd and is paid an annual salary of £52,000. Millie is also provided with the following taxable benefits:

	£
Company car	5,000
Vouchers for the local gym	2,000

Calculate Millie's and Blue Forge Ltd's class 1 NIC liability due for the tax year 2021/22. Show your answer in pounds and pence.

Solution

Class 1 NICs are due on annual earnings of £54,000 (salary £52,000 and vouchers £2,000). The company car is a non-cash benefit and is therefore not subject to class 1 NICs.

	£
Millie's class 1 NICs	4,884.24
(£50,270 – £9,568) × 12%	74.60
(£54,000 – £50,270) × 2%	
	———
	4,958.84
	———
Blue Forge Ltd's class 1 NICs	
(£54,000 – £8,840) × 13.8%	6,232.08
	———

Test your understanding 2

Olufemi

Olufemi is paid £10,950 each year and Amal is paid £53,440 each year.

Calculate the class 1 employee and the employer NIC liability for the tax year 2021/22. Show your answer in pounds and pence.

3.3 Employees with more than one job

Usually, if an individual has more than one employer at a time (e.g. two part time jobs), each employment is considered separately for NIC purposes i.e. the thresholds are applied separately for each job. There are exceptions for directors and if the employers are associated (e.g. if an employee works in two different branches of a fast food outlet) but these are not examinable.

 Test your understanding 3

Otto

Otto is employed part time by Seal Ltd and earns a salary of £5,300 each year. In addition, Otto is employed part time by Tortoise Ltd and earns a salary of £4,600 every year.

What are Otto's class 1 employee national insurance contributions for the tax year 2021/22? Show your answer in pounds and pence.

3.4 NIC employment allowance

Employers are able to claim up to £4,000 of relief each year from their total class 1 employer NIC payments for the business. This means

- if the total class 1 employer NICs liability does not exceed £4,000 the amount due for this will be £Nil; and

- if the total class 1 employer liability is more than £4,000 this amount can be deducted from the liability.

This allowance cannot be used against any other classes of NICs (e.g. Class 1A). It is only available to employers with total class 1 employer contributions < £100,000 in the previous tax year. However, in the assessment if there are a few employees you should assume that the prior year's employer class 1 NICs will have been below the threshold and therefore the allowance will be claimed.

Reference material

Some information about employment allowance can be found in the 'National insurance contributions' section of our reference material provided in the real assessment, so you do not need to learn it.

Why not look up the correct part of the reference material in the introduction to this text book now?

 Test your understanding 4

Clare

Clare employs three full time assistants at a salary of £20,000 p.a. each.

Calculate the total class 1 employer NICs that Clare must pay to HMRC for the tax year 2021/22 in respect of her employees. Show your answer in pounds and pence.

4 Class 1A contributions

4.1 Class 1A contributions

Class 1A contributions are paid by employers in respect of the taxable benefits provided to employees. These benefits are calculated in the same way as they are for income tax (see Chapter 4).

No class 1A contributions are payable in respect of:

- exempt benefits (i.e. those benefits which are exempt from income tax

- benefits already treated as earnings and assessed to class 1 NICs, such as remuneration received in the form of non-cash vouchers.

The contributions are calculated as:

- 13.8% on the value of the taxable benefits.

Reference material

Some information about class 1A NICs can be found in the 'National insurance contributions' section of our reference material provided in the real assessment, so you do not need to learn it.

Why not look up the correct part of the reference material in the introduction to this text book now?

Class 1A contributions are an additional cost of employment and are a deductible expense when calculating the employer's tax adjusted trading profits.

 Example

Leonel is employed by Dutton Ltd at an annual salary of £52,000.

He was provided with the following benefits in the tax year 2021/22:

	£
Company motor car	3,900
Private fuel	5,772
Subsidised meals in the company canteen	360

Calculate the class 1 employee, class 1 employer and class 1A NIC liabilities due for the tax year 2021/22 in respect of Leonel.

Ignore the employment allowance and show your answer in whole pounds only.

Solution

Class 1 NICs

	£
(£50,270 – £9,568) × 12%	4,884
(£52,000 – £50,270) × 2%	35
	___
Class 1 employee NICs	4,919
	___
Class 1 employer NICs	
(£52,000 – £8,840) × 13.8%	5,956
	___

Class 1A NICs

Leonel's taxable benefits for class 1A purposes are as follows:

	£
Company motor car	3,900
Private fuel	5,772
Taxable benefits for class 1A	9,672
Class 1A NICs (£9,672 × 13.8%)	1,335

Notes: The subsidised canteen is an exempt benefit and is therefore not subject to class 1A NICs.

 Test your understanding 5

Silke

Silke is paid £25,000 per year and had taxable benefits for the tax year 2021/22 of:

	£
Company motor car	5,250
Private fuel provided by company	4,200
Beneficial loan	2,600
Vouchers to be used at the local department store	250

The company also provided Silke with a mobile phone, which cost £135.

Contributions into her personal pension scheme were as follows:

Employer contribution	£2,540
Employee contribution	£1,380

Calculate the class 1 employee, class 1 employer and class 1A NIC liabilities due for the tax year 2021/22 in respect of Silke.

Ignore the employment allowance and show your answer in pounds and pence.

5 Summary

The main issues to beware of in relation to NICs are:

- Class 1 NICs are paid by employers and employees in respect of earnings (excluding benefits).

- The meaning of earnings for these purposes.

- How to calculate class 1 NICs.

- Class 1A NICs are paid by employers in respect of benefits provided to employees.

- Remember, when calculating NICs, you must follow the instructions in the task regarding rounding.

Test your understanding answers

Test your understanding 1

Hamza

The correct answer is £35,000.

Class 1 employee contributions are not payable on either exempt benefits (the employer pension contributions) or taxable benefits, (the company car).

No deduction is made for allowable expenses in arriving at the earnings figure.

Test your understanding 2

Olufemi

	£
Class 1 employee NICs (£10,950 – £9,568) × 12%	165.84
Class 1 employer NICs (£10,950 – £8,840) × 13.8%	291.18

Amal

	£
Class 1 employee NICs	
(£50,270 – £9,568) × 12% (maximum)	4,884.24
(£53,440 – £50,270) × 2%	63.40
	4,947.64
Class 1 employer NICs	
(£53,440 – £8,840) × 13.8%	6,154.80

Test your understanding 3

Otto

The correct answer is £0.00 as both salaries are below £9,568 per year.

 Test your understanding 4

ClareRemember that the employment allowance applies per employer not per employee.

	£
Class 1 employer NIC per employee (£20,000 − £8,840) × 13.8%	1,540.08
Total class 1 employer NIC (£1,540.08 × 3)	4,620.24
Less: Employment allowance	(4,000.00)
Total class 1 employer NIC payable to HMRC	620.24

Test your understanding 5

Silke

Class 1 NICs

	£
Salary	25,000
Vouchers	250
	_____
Cash earnings for class 1 NICs	25,250
	_____
Class 1 employee NICs (£25,250 – £9,568) × 12%	1,881.84
	_____
Class 1 employer NICs (£25,250 – £8,840) × 13.8%	2,264.58
	_____

Notes: The provision of one mobile phone per employee, and employer pension contributions, are excluded as they are exempt benefits.

The employee pension contributions are not allowable deductions in calculating earnings for NIC purposes.

The car, fuel and beneficial loan benefits are excluded as they are non-cash benefits which are assessed to class 1A NICs, not class 1.

Class 1A NICs

	£
Company motor car	5,250
Private fuel provided by company	4,200
Beneficial loan	2,600
	_____
Taxable benefits for class 1A	12,050
	_____
Employer's class 1A NICs (£12,050 × 13.8%)	1,662.90
	_____

Note: The employment allowance is deducted from the employer's total class 1 employer's NICs, not from the liability relating to one individual.

Introduction to capital gains tax

9

Introduction

In the assessment there will be a number of tasks covering various aspects of capital gains tax (CGT).

This chapter determines when we need to perform a CGT computation and how to calculate the CGT payable.

The following chapters will describe how to calculate chargeable gains.

ASSESSMENT CRITERIA
Chargeable and exempt assets (4.1)
Chargeable and exempt disposals (4.1)
Chargeable and exempt persons (4.1)
The availability of the annual exempt amount (4.3)
Offset capital losses, current year and brought forward (4.4)
Apply all rates of capital gains tax (4.4)

CONTENTS

1   Capital gains tax computation

2   Chargeable disposal

3   Chargeable person

4   Chargeable asset

5   Calculating CGT

6   Summary

1 Capital gains tax computation

1.1 The three essential elements

A capital gains tax (CGT) computation is only required if there is a:

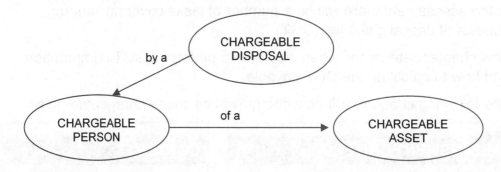

2 Chargeable disposals

2.1 Disposals

A chargeable disposal includes:

- a sale of an asset (whole or part of an asset)
- a gift of an asset
- an exchange of an asset
- the loss or destruction of an asset.

Where a gift is made the sale proceeds are deemed to be the asset's market value.

Where an asset is lost or destroyed the sale proceeds are likely to be £Nil or the insurance proceeds.

2.2 Exempt disposals

The following occasions are exempt disposals and so no CGT computation is required:

- disposals on the death of a taxpayer
- gifts of assets to charities.

3 Chargeable persons

3.1 Chargeable person

A chargeable person is:

- an individual, or
- a company (only covered in Business Tax).

Individuals who are UK resident in the tax year in which the disposal takes place are subject to capital gains tax on their worldwide gains.

Non-UK residents only pay UK CGT on land and buildings situated in the UK. Therefore, if a non-UK resident has not disposed of any qualifying UK property they will have no UK CGT liability.

In the assessment you should assume that all individuals are UK resident in questions requiring the calculation of tax.

3.2 Exempt persons

Charities do not pay capital gains tax on their disposals.

4 Chargeable assets

4.1 Exempt assets

All assets are chargeable unless they are in the list of exempt assets.

The main types of exempt asset are listed below.

Those most likely to be in an assessment are marked *.

(a) *Private residences (see Chapter 10).

(b) Gilts (e.g. treasury stock or government stock) and qualifying corporate bonds (i.e. loan notes, also known as debentures).

(c) *Wasting chattels – a wasting asset is one with an expected life of not more than 50 years, a chattel is tangible moveable property (e.g. a racehorse) (see Chapter 10). All animals in the assessment are wasting chattels.

(d) *Other chattels sold at a gain where the cost and consideration is ≤ £6,000 or less (see Chapter 10), (e.g. an antique table costing £4,000 and sold for £4,500).

(e) *Private motor cars, including vintage and veteran cars.

(f) NS&I Savings Certificates, Premium Bonds and SAYE certificates.

(g)   Shares held in an ISA (individual savings account).

(h)   Cash, legal tender in the UK.

(i)   Foreign currency bank accounts.

(j)   Medals awarded for valour, unless acquired by purchase.

(k)   Betting and lottery winnings.

(l)   Compensation or damages for any wrong or injury suffered by an individual in his or her person or in his or her profession or vocation.

Test your understanding 1

Which of the following disposals requires a CGT computation?

Select yes or no for each disposal.

1	Sale of a greyhound	Yes/No
2	Gift of shares in a limited company	Yes/No
3	Gift of a Picasso painting in a will	Yes/No
4	Sale of a vintage motor car for a substantial profit	Yes/No
5	Gift of a computer to a local charity	Yes/No
6	Sale of a holiday home in Cornwall	Yes/No

---

5 Calculating CGT

5.1   Introduction

Capital gains tax (like income tax) is calculated for the tax year.

For each individual we must undertake the following steps.

Step 1 (Chapters 10 and 11)

Calculate the gains or losses on disposals of individual assets for the tax year 2021/22 (i.e. disposals between 6 April 2021 and 5 April 2022).

For example, if four chargeable assets are disposed of, four calculations of gains or losses must be made.

Step 2

Bring together all gains and losses of the tax year and deduct the annual exempt amount then capital losses brought forward from prior years to determine the taxable gains.

Step 3

Calculate the capital gains tax payable.

5.2 The annual exempt amount

An individual has an annual exempt amount (AEA) which is applied to net chargeable gains after deduction of current year capital losses (but before the deduction of capital losses brought forward – see below).

The AEA for the tax year 2021/22 is £12,300.

> **Reference material**
>
> Some information about the annual exempt amount can be found in the 'Capital gains tax' section of your reference material provided in the real assessment, so you do not need to learn it.
>
> Why not look up the correct part of the reference material in the introduction to this text book now?

The AEA can only be relieved against chargeable gains of the current tax year. Any unused amount cannot be offset against taxable income or carried forward or back.

If a prior tax year's AEA is required in the assessment, it will be provided in the question.

5.3 Calculation of taxable gains

The pro forma shows how chargeable gains and capital losses are brought together to calculate taxable gains.

The calculation of individual gains and losses is covered in the next chapter.

	£
Chargeable gains for the year	X
Less: Current year capital losses	(X)
	———
Net chargeable gains for the year	X
Less: AEA	(12,300)
Less: Capital losses brought forward	(X)
	———
Taxable gains	X
	———

The treatment of capital losses is explained in detail below.

 Test your understanding 2

Manuel made chargeable gains and allowable losses for the tax year 2021/22:

Gain of £60,000

Gain of £12,000

Capital loss of £4,000

Calculate Manuel's taxable gains for the tax year 2021/22.

5.4 Treatment of capital losses

There is a difference in the treatment of current year capital losses and brought forward capital losses.

Current year capital losses are automatically deducted from the chargeable gains of the year. Where this results in net capital losses for the year, they will be carried forward for relief in the future.

Capital losses brought forward are automatically deducted from the first available net chargeable gains.

However, the maximum amount of brought forward losses that will be deducted is restricted to the amount required to reduce the taxable gains for the tax year to £Nil after deducting the AEA.

Any remaining brought forward loss is carried forward and automatically deducted from the next available net chargeable gains after deducting the AEA.

Finally, a capital loss arising on a disposal to a connected person (Chapter 10) can only be used against a gain on a disposal to that same connected person.

Example

Mica has the following chargeable gains and losses for the two years ended 5 April 2022.

	2020/21 £	2021/22 £
Gains	12,500	14,500
Losses	(14,000)	(2,000)

What gains (if any) are taxable after considering all reliefs and exemptions?

Solution

	2020/21 £	2021/22 £
Current gains	12,500	14,500
Less: Current losses	(12,500)	(2,000)
Net chargeable gains	0	12,500
Less: AEA	Wasted	(12,300)
Less: Capital losses b/f (Note)		(200)
Taxable gains	0	0
Loss carried forward		
(£14,000 − £12,500)	1,500	
(£1,500 − £200)		1,300

Note: the capital losses brought forward are used to reduce taxable gains to £Nil.

Test your understanding 3

Gabi has the following chargeable gains and losses for the two years ended 5 April 2022.

	2020/21	2021/22
	£	£
Gains	15,000	17,000
Losses	(17,000)	(4,000)

What are the losses carried forward (if any) at the end of each of the tax years 2020/21 and 2021/22?

 Test your understanding 4

1   Mary made a capital loss of £4,000 in the tax year 2020/21. In the following tax year she made a chargeable gain of £13,200 and a capital loss of £3,000.

How much capital loss is carried forward at the end of the tax year 2021/22?

2   What would your answer be if Mary had only made the chargeable gain of £13,200 in the tax year 2021/22 and not the capital loss?

 Test your understanding 5

Carl sold three paintings in the tax year 2021/22 making two chargeable gains of £9,900 and £12,000 and a capital loss of £2,400. Carl has capital losses brought forward as at 6 April 2021 of £3,400.

What are Carl's taxable gains for the tax year 2021/22?

5.5   Calculation of CGT payable

Taxable gains are treated as an additional amount of income in order to determine the rates of CGT. However, the gains must not be included in the income tax computation.

Where the taxable gains fall within any remaining basic rate band they are taxed at 10%; the balance of the taxable gains is taxed at 20%.

Previously you saw how the basic rate band is increased for the grossed up amount of gift aid donations and personal pension contributions. The increased basic rate band amount is also used in the CGT calculation, however this will not be examined in your assessment.

 Reference material

Some information about CGT rates can be found in the 'Capital gains tax – tax rates' section of your reference material provided in the real assessment, so you do not need to learn it.

Note that you need to use this information in conjunction with the 'Tax rates and bands' section.

Why not look up the correct parts of the reference material in the introduction to this text book now?

Example

In the tax year 2021/22 Basil has taxable gains of £14,600 in respect of quoted shares. His taxable income for the year, after deducting the personal allowance, is £35,700.

Calculate Basil's capital gains tax liability for the tax year 2021/22.

Solution

	£
£2,000 (£37,700 − £35,700) × 10%	200
£12,600 (£14,600 − £2,000) × 20%	2,520
	———
Capital gains tax liability	2,720
	———

Note that 'taxable gains' are the gains after the deduction of the AEA.

Test your understanding 6

Read the following statements and state whether they are true or false.

1   Current year capital losses are deducted before the AEA.

2   Excess capital losses can be offset against taxable income.

3   Any available capital losses must always be relieved in full.

4   Capital gains are taxed at 40% for higher rate taxpayers.

 Test your understanding 7

Misha has sold two paintings in the tax year 2021/22 making two chargeable gains of £16,900 and £12,700. Her taxable income for the year, after deducting the personal allowance, is £29,175.

What is Misha's capital gains tax liability for the tax year 2021/22?

6   Summary

6.1   Essential elements

There are three essential elements for CGT to apply:

- chargeable disposal, by a
- chargeable person, of a
- chargeable asset.

6.2   Order of calculation

To calculate CGT for the tax year:

Step 1   Calculate individual gains and losses.

Step 2   Calculate taxable gains by deducting losses (as appropriate) and the AEA.

Step 3   Calculate the CGT payable.

Test your understanding answers

🔖 Test your understanding 1

1	**No**	A greyhound is a wasting chattel (tangible moveable property with a life of < 50 years) and is therefore exempt.
2	**Yes**	Gifts are still chargeable disposals and shares are a chargeable asset.
3	**No**	Disposals on death are not chargeable disposals.
4	**No**	Cars are exempt assets regardless of whether they are sold for a profit or a loss.
5	**No**	Gifts to charity are not chargeable disposals.
6	**Yes**	A property can be exempt under PRR if it is the individual's main home, therefore a holiday home is not exempt.

📝 Test your understanding 2

Manuel

The correct answer is £55,700.

Taxable gains are defined as net chargeable gains after the deduction of the AEA, as follows:

	£
Total chargeable gains (£60,000 + £12,000)	72,000
Less: Capital loss	(4,000)
Net chargeable gains	68,000
Less: AEA	(12,300)
Taxable gain	55,700

Test your understanding 3

Gabi

The losses carried forward at the end of each of the tax year 2020/21 is £2,000; and at the end of the tax year 2021/22 is £1,300.

	2020/21 £	2021/22 £
Current year gains	15,000	17,000
Less: Current year losses	(15,000)	(4,000)
	Nil	13,000
Less: AEA	Wasted	(12,300)
Less: Capital losses b/f (Note)		(700)
		Nil
Loss carried forward		
(£17,000 – £15,000)	2,000	
(£2,000 – £700)		1,300

Note: the capital losses brought forward are used to reduce taxable gains to £Nil.

 Test your understanding 4

Mary

1   The correct answer is £4,000.

2   The correct answer is £3,100.

Explanation

1   Net chargeable gains for the tax year 2021/22 are £10,200 (£13,200 – £3,000). As this is less than the AEA, the loss brought forward of £4,000 is carried forward to the tax year 2022/23.

2   If Mary had only made the chargeable gain of £13,200 in the tax year 2021/22, losses brought forward of £900 would have been offset to reduce the taxable gain to £nil (£13,200 – £12,300 – £900). The balance of the capital losses of £3,100 (£4,000 – £900) would have been carried forward to the tax year 2022/23.

Test your understanding 5

Carl

The correct answer is £3,800.

	£
Chargeable gains for the year (£9,900 + £12,000)	21,900
Less: Current year capital losses	(2,400)
Net chargeable gains for the year	19,500
Less: AEA	(12,300)
Less: Capital losses b/f	(3,400)
Taxable gains	3,800

Test your understanding 6

1   **True**

2   **False** – Capital losses can only be set against gains.

3   **False** – Current year losses must be relieved in full. Brought forward losses are offset after the AEA and only to the extent that they bring taxable gains down to zero. Any remaining losses can continue to be carried forward.

4   **False** – Gains are taxed at 20% for higher rate taxpayers.

Test your understanding 7

Misha

The correct answer is £2,608.

	£
Chargeable gains (£16,900 + £12,700)	29,600
Less: AEA	(12,300)
Taxable gains	17,300
£8,525 (£37,700 – £29,175) × 10%	853
£8,775 (£17,300 – £8,525) × 20%	1,755
Capital gains tax liability	2,608

Calculation of individual gains and losses

Introduction

It is likely that one of the CGT tasks will require a calculation of gains on assets other than shares.

This chapter looks at the standard calculations, followed by some special rules. At least one of the special rules is likely to be included in the assessment.

ASSESSMENT CRITERIA
Chattels and wasting chattels (4.1)
Connected persons (4.1)
Calculate chargeable gains and allowable losses for: chargeable assets, part disposals and chattels (4.1)
Conditions for applying private residence relief (4.3)
Calculate net capital gains after application of relevant reliefs (4.3)

CONTENTS
1   Pro forma calculation of gains and losses
2   Special rules
3   Private residence exemption
4   Summary

1 Pro forma calculation of gains and losses

1.1 Pro forma

The following pro forma is used to calculate a chargeable gain:

	Notes	£
Gross sale proceeds	(a)	X
Less: Selling costs	(b)	(X)
Net sale proceeds		X
Less: Allowable cost	(c)	(X)
Chargeable gain	(d)	X

1.2 Notes to the pro forma

(a) Sale proceeds are usually obvious. However, where a transaction is not at arm's length (e.g. a gift) then the market value of the asset is used.

(b) Selling costs incurred on the disposal of an asset are an allowable deduction. Examples of such costs include valuation fees, advertising costs, legal fees, auctioneer's fees.

(c) The allowable cost of an asset is its purchase price plus any incidental purchase costs (e.g. legal fees) together with any capital expenditure subsequently incurred, known as enhancement expenditure, which increases the value of the asset.

If the asset was received as a gift then its cost = market value at the date of the gift.

If the asset was inherited on someone's death then the cost = probate value (market value at the date of the death, which is used for inheritance tax purposes).

(d) The gain after deducting the costs above is known as a chargeable gain.

Test your understanding 1

Paul

On 23 April 2021, Paul sold a property that was not his main residence for £145,000. He had purchased the property on 3 June 2012 for £108,000. The seller incurred fees in June 2012 of £2,000.

What is the chargeable gain arising on this disposal?

 Test your understanding 2

Alfie

Alfie bought a chargeable asset in August 2017 for £120,000. He spent £25,000 on improving the asset in February 2020. He sold the asset for £170,000 in February 2022.

The gain on this asset is:

 Test your understanding 3

Lisa bought a chargeable asset in November 2009 for £32,500, selling it in October 2021 for £56,250. She paid auctioneer's commission of 2% when she bought the asset and 6% when she sold the asset.

The gain on this asset is:

2 Special rules

2.1 Situations when special rules apply

Special rules apply in the following situations.

- Part disposals (2.2 below).

- Chattels (2.3 below).

- Connected persons (2.4 below).

- Transfers between spouses and civil partners (2.5 below).

2.2 Part disposals

When there is a disposal, it is necessary to match costs with proceeds in order to calculate the gain.

When **part of an asset is disposed of** we need a method for deciding how much of the initial purchase cost relates to the part just disposed of, so that we can calculate a gain.

 Definition

The **part disposal formula** for allocating the cost of an asset is:

$$\frac{A}{A+B}$$

where   A = the value of the part disposed of
                B = the value of the unsold remainder

Note that A is the full value of the part disposed of so if the disposal is a sale use sale proceeds **before** deducting selling expenses.

B will be provided in questions in the assessment, but the formula itself is not provided and must be learned.

Example

Kwasi disposes of part of a field which cost £6,000 as a whole. He sold one corner of the field for £8,000 incurring £200 legal costs. We need to calculate the gain.

Proceeds
£8,000

Cost of entire field
£6,000

We know the sale proceeds but not the cost of the part sold.

To calculate the gain it is necessary to **apportion part of the overall cost to the part disposed of**.

This could be done in a number of ways, e.g. based on the area of the land sold.

However, in order to make the calculation standard for all types of disposal, the part disposal formula is used.

Solution

If the remainder of the land was worth £15,000 then the chargeable gain would be calculated as follows:

	£
Proceeds	8,000
Less: Selling expenses	(200)
	———
Net sale proceeds	7,800
Less: Cost (£6,000) × $\dfrac{£8,000}{£8,000 + £15,000}$	(2,087)
	———
Chargeable gain	5,713
	———

Test your understanding 4

Whahid bought 20 hectares of land on 3 May 2008 for £28,000. On 12 December 2021 he sold 10 hectares for £45,000. The market value of the remaining land at that time was £15,000.

What is the chargeable gain arising on the disposal of the land in December 2021?

2.3 Chattels

Definition

Chattels are tangible, moveable property (e.g. a picture or a table).

A building is not a chattel as it is not moveable. Similarly, shares are not chattels – a share certificate may be tangible and moveable but the asset of value is the underlying rights conferred by the certificate. These rights are not tangible.

Definition

Wasting chattels are chattels with an expected life not exceeding 50 years. These are exempt from CGT.

Machinery is always treated as wasting. However, it will only be a wasting chattel if it is moveable.

All animals which appear in the assessment are regarded as wasting chattels.

Definition

Non-wasting chattels are chattels with an expected life of more than 50 years (e.g. antiques, works of art, jewellery).

The CGT treatment of non-wasting chattels is based on the £6,000 rules.

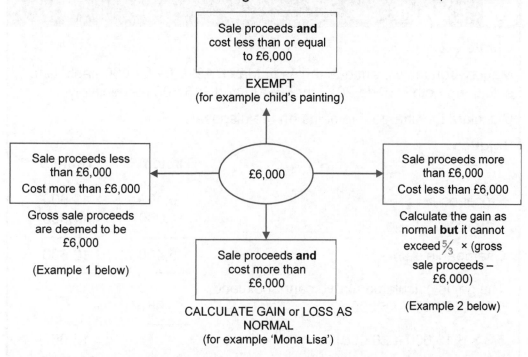

 Example

Chattels 1

Amina bought a picture in April 1994 for £10,000 plus purchase costs of £500. The market for the artist's work slumped and the picture was sold on 10 April 2021 for £500, less disposal costs of £50.

Calculate the loss on disposal.

Solution

	£
Gross sale proceeds (£500 but deemed to be £6,000)	6,000
Less: Selling costs	(50)
Net proceeds	5,950
Less: Cost (including acquisition expenses)	(10,500)
Allowable loss	(4,550)

Notice that it is the gross sale proceeds **before** deducting selling costs that are deemed to be £6,000.

Example

Chattels 2

Marjory bought two antique tables in March 1996 for £1,000 each. She sold them both in June 2021 for £6,400 and £13,600 respectively.

Calculate the chargeable gains on the disposals.

Solution

	Table A £	Table B £
Proceeds	6,400	13,600
Less: Cost	(1,000)	(1,000)
Chargeable gain	5,400	12,600
The gains calculated above cannot exceed:		
5/3 × (£6,400 − £6,000)	667	
5/3 × (£13,600 − £6,000)		12,667
Chargeable gain	667	12,600

 Test your understanding 5

Zhu

Zhu has made the following disposals in the tax year 2021/22.

(1) A painting was sold in July 2021 for £6,600. He originally bought it in February 2002 for £3,500.

(2) A house which he bought as an investment in April 1995 for £5,000 was sold in September 2021 for £75,000. In June 2000 an extension costing £10,000 was built.

(3) He sold a car for £20,000 in June 2021 that had originally cost him £43,000 in June 2011.

(4) He bought a plot of land for £8,000 in August 2004. He sold part of the land for £20,000 in January 2022. At that time the remaining land was worth £60,000.

Calculate his total chargeable gains.

Test your understanding 6

Match the following statements to the correct asset details. All of the assets are chattels and none have a life of less than 50 years.

Match the statements below with the assets disposed of.

Asset	Sale proceeds	Cost	Statement
1	£8,000	£4,000	
2	£14,000	£20,000	
3	£16,000	£7,000	
4	£4,000	£9,000	
5	£3,000	£2,000	

Statements:

Exempt asset

Calculate gain as normal

Calculate loss as normal

Sale proceeds to be £6,000

Gain restricted to 5/3 rule

2.4 Connected persons

Where a disposal is between connected persons:

(i) sale proceeds are deemed to be the market value of the asset transferred (any actual sale proceeds are ignored), and

(ii) if a loss arises on a disposal to a connected person it can only be offset against a gain made on a disposal to the **same** connected person.

Connected persons are mainly relatives and their spouses or civil partners or relatives of one's spouse or civil partner.

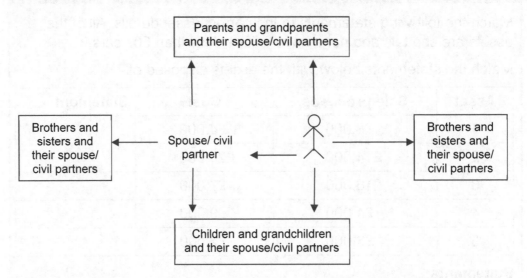

An individual is also connected with a company he or she controls and a partner is connected with his or her other business partners as well as the business partner's spouse/civil partner and relatives.

2.5 Transfers between spouses and civil partners

Whilst spouses and civil partners are clearly connected persons, the tax treatment of assets transferred from one to the other is different from the treatment of transfers between other connected persons.

On disposals between spouses or civil partners, sales proceeds are deemed to be equal to the seller's cost such that no gain or loss arises.

This figure is also used for the recipient's cost when calculating the gain on a future sale of the asset by the second spouse or civil partner.

Example

David purchased some jewellery in August 2010 for £50,000. In June 2020 he gave the jewellery to his wife Victoria when it was worth £200,000. Victoria sold the jewellery in May 2021 for £220,000.

Calculate Victoria's chargeable gain.

Solution

Disposal by David

	£
Deemed proceeds (equal to cost)	50,000
Less: Cost	(50,000)
	———
No gain or loss arises	Nil
	———

The market value at the date of the disposal to Victoria has no impact. Disposals between spouses are deemed to be at a value equivalent to the allowable cost.

Sale by Victoria

	£
Proceeds	220,000
Less: Deemed cost	(50,000)
	———
Chargeable gain	170,000
	———

 Test your understanding 7

Read the following statements and state whether they are true or false.

1   Brian sold a quarter of a plot of land. A quarter of the original cost should be deducted when calculating the chargeable gain.

2   Advertising costs are not an allowable deduction as they are revenue expenses.

3   Market value should be substituted for disposal proceeds when an asset is gifted to someone other than the spouse.

4   If Alina bought a picture for £8,000 and sold it for £3,000 her allowable loss will be £2,000.

Test your understanding 8

For each statement below, tick the appropriate treatment.

		Actual proceeds used	Market value used	No gain or loss basis
1	Erkki gives an asset to his sister in law			
2	Husband sells an asset to his wife at market value			
3	Eloise sells an asset on EBay for £8,000 when the market value is £12,000			

3 Private residence relief

3.1 General exemption

Other than business reliefs (which we do not need to consider for the Personal Tax unit) the main CGT relief available to individuals is the *private residence relief* (PRR) exemption.

If the owner occupies his or her private residence throughout the period of ownership, the gain is exempt.

If there have been periods where the owner has not lived in the property, part of the gain may be taxable

An individual who lives in more than one residence may elect for one of them to be treated as his or her main residence. This election must be made to HMRC within two years of commencing to live in the second residence.

3.2 Private residence relief

Where there has been a period of absence, the procedure is as follows.

(a) Calculate the gain on the sale of the house.

(b) Compute the total period of ownership in months.

(c) Calculate periods of occupation in months.

(d) PRR exemption = $\dfrac{(c)}{(b)} \times (a)$

The PRR exemption must be given before deducting capital losses.

 Example

Jim bought a house on 1 January 2004. Initially the house remained empty. He started to live in the house on 1 October 2011, and lived in it until he sold it on 30 September 2021.

The gain on disposal before deduction of PRR was £167,500.

Calculate the chargeable gain after PRR.

Solution

Step 1: Calculate the gain before relief.

Given = £167,500.

Step 2: Identify the total period of ownership and the period the house was occupied (lived in by Jim).

Step 3: Apply the PRR exemption.

	£
Gain before relief	167,500
Less: PRR exemption $\frac{120}{213} \times £167,500$	(94,366)
Chargeable gain	73,134

3.3 Periods of deemed occupation

Exemption is also available for the following periods of 'deemed occupation'.

(a)   The last nine months of ownership.

(b)   Up to three years of absence for any reason.

(c)   Any period spent working abroad.

(d)   Up to four years of absence while working elsewhere in the UK.

To be allowed, the absences in (b), (c) and (d) above must be preceded and followed by a period of actual occupation. No such condition applies to absence under (a) above.

For (c) and (d) the condition of actual occupation after a period of absence is relaxed where an employer requires the owner to work elsewhere immediately, thus making it impossible to resume occupation.

Example

Maksim bought a house on 1 January 2003 and sold it on 30 September 2021 making a gain before deduction of reliefs of £275,000.

During this time:

1 January 2003	– 31 December 2004	Lived in house
1 January 2005	– 30 June 2011	Employed overseas
1 July 2011	– 31 December 2015	Travelled the world
1 January 2016	– 30 September 2021	Lived in house

Solution

Step 1: Calculate the gain before relief.

Given = £275,000

Step 2: Identify:

- period of ownership
- periods of actual occupation
- periods of deemed occupation (remember preceded and followed by actual occupation).

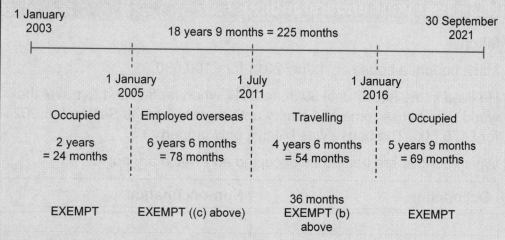

The periods of occupation before and after deemed occupation do **not** need to be **immediately** before and after (for example the employment overseas ended on 30 June 2011 and is followed by actual occupation which did not start until 1 January 2016).

Step 3: Apply PRR exemption.

			£
Gain before relief			275,000
PRR exemption			

	Months	
Occupied	24	
Employed overseas	78	
Any reason	36	
Occupied	69	
	————	
	207	out of 225
	————	

$$\frac{207}{225} \times £275,000 \qquad\qquad (253,000)$$

———————

Chargeable gain   22,000

———————

Test your understanding 9

Mitch

Mitch bought a house on 1 July 2011 for £100,000.

He lived in the house until 30 June 2017 when he decided to travel the world. The house remained empty until he sold it on 30 September 2021 for £170,000. The house was Mitch's only property.

Which periods are treated as occupied and which are not?

Occupation	Non-occupation

Test your understanding 10

Olesya

Olesya sold a house in London on 31 August 2021 and realised a gain of £144,000.

She purchased the house on 1 July 2009. She lived in the house until 31 October 2012 when she moved to Scotland for the purposes of her employment. She returned to the house on 1 January 2014.

On 1 July 2016 she left the house in order to travel around South America. She did not return to the house prior to its sale.

Calculate Olesya's chargeable gain on the sale of the house.

 Test your understanding 11

Lionel

Lionel disposes of a house which he had owned for 20 years making a gain of £200,000.

What would be the chargeable gain assuming:

1   he had always lived in the house

2   he had never lived in the house

3   he had lived in the house for three years, moved away for eight years whilst he was working elsewhere in the UK, and then lived in it for the final nine years of ownership?

4 Summary

In this chapter we have considered the pro forma calculation of the chargeable gain for an individual asset.

	£
Sale proceeds	X
Less: Allowable cost	(X)
Chargeable gain	X

In addition, special rules apply in certain situations.

For part disposals, the cost must be apportioned on the basis of the formula A/(A + B).

For disposals of chattels, the rules depend on whether the asset is wasting and whether the cost or proceeds are less than £6,000.

For connected persons, market value must be used for disposal proceeds and there are restrictions on the loss relief available.

If a taxpayer has only one house at any one time and occupies it throughout, the gain is fully exempt. Certain periods of non-occupation are deemed to be occupation.

Test your understanding answers

Test your understanding 1

Paul

The correct answer is £37,000.

	£
Sales proceeds	145,000
Less: Allowable cost	(108,000)
Chargeable gain	37,000

Note: The fees of £2,000 in June 2012 were incurred by the seller, not Paul; therefore they are not an allowable deduction.

The **chargeable** gain is **before** deducting the annual exempt amount. If asked for the **taxable** gain you should give the number after deduction of this amount.

Test your understanding 2

Alfie

The correct answer is £25,000.

	£
Disposal proceeds	170,000
Less: Cost	(120,000)
Enhancement cost	(25,000)
Chargeable gain	25,000

Test your understanding 3

Lisa

The correct answer is £19,725.

	£
Disposal proceeds	56,250
Less: Selling costs (£56,250 × 6%)	(3,375)
	52,875
Less: Cost	(32,500)
Incidental purchase costs	
(£32,500 × 2%)	(650)
Chargeable gain	19,725

Test your understanding 4

Whahid

The correct answer is £24,000.

Explanation

	£
Proceeds	45,000
Less: Cost	
£28,000 × £45,000/(£45,000 + £15,000)	(21,000)
Chargeable gain	24,000

The cost to carry forward of the remaining land is £7,000 (£28,000 − ££21,000).

Test your understanding 5

Zhu

		£	£
(1)	**Painting (non-wasting chattel)**		
	Sales proceeds	6,600	
	Less: Allowable cost	(3,500)	
		3,100	
	Chargeable gain cannot exceed:		
	$\frac{5}{3}$ × (sale proceeds – £6,000)		
	= $\frac{5}{3}$ × (£6,600 – £6,000)		1,000
	Total gains c/f		1,000

		£	£
	Total gains b/f		1,000
(2)	**House**		
	Sale proceeds	75,000	
	Less: Allowable cost		
	Original	(5,000)	
	Enhancement	(10,000)	
	Chargeable gain		60,000
(3)	**Car – exempt asset**		Nil
(4)	**Plot of land (part disposal)**		
	Sale proceeds	20,000	
	Less: Allowable cost		
	$\dfrac{A}{A+B} \times £8,000$		
	$\dfrac{20,000}{20,000+60,000} \times £8,000$	(2,000)	
	Chargeable gain		18,000
	Total chargeable gains		79,000

Test your understanding 6

Asset	Sale proceeds	Cost	Statement
1	£8,000	£4,000	Gain restricted to 5/3 rule
2	£14,000	£20,000	Calculate loss as normal
3	£16,000	£7,000	Calculate gain as normal
4	£4,000	£9,000	Sale proceeds to be £6,000
5	£3,000	£2,000	Exempt asset

Test your understanding 7

1 **False** – The A/(A + B) formula should be used to calculate the allowable cost.

2 **False** – Advertising costs are an allowable selling cost.

3 **True**

4 **True** – Proceeds will be deemed to be £6,000 as a picture is a chattel and it has been sold for less than £6,000 but bought for more. The loss will therefore be (£6,000 – £8,000) = £2,000.

 Test your understanding 8

1 Market value used as the disposal is between connected persons.

2 No gain or loss basis as a transfer between spouses. Actual proceeds are irrelevant.

3 Actual proceeds used as the sale is not between connected persons and not a deliberate sale at undervalue.

KAPLAN PUBLISHING

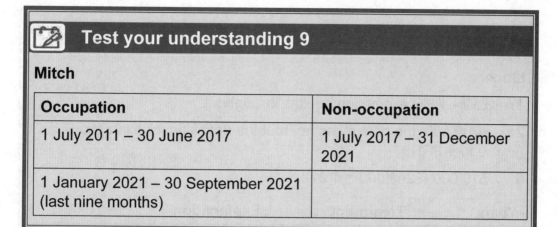

Test your understanding 9

Mitch

Occupation	Non-occupation
1 July 2011 – 30 June 2017	1 July 2017 – 31 December 2021
1 January 2021 – 30 September 2021 (last nine months)	

Test your understanding 10

Olesya

	£
Gain before relief	144,000
PRR exemption	

		Months
1 July 2009 – 31 October 2012	Occupied	40
1 November 2012 – 31 December 2013	Employed in UK	14
1 January 2014 – 30 June 2016	Occupied	30
1 July 2016 – 31 August 2021	Absent (Note 1)	9
		93

	£
93/146 (Note 2) × £144,000	(91,726)
Chargeable gain	52,274

Notes:

1 The last nine months of ownership are always treated as a period of occupation. Accordingly, the period of absence from 1 December 2020 to 31 August 2021 is deemed occupation.

   None of the beginning of the period of absence, from 1 July 2016 to 30 November 2020, can be treated as a period of occupation as Olesya did not live in the property both before and after the period of absence.

2 Olesya owned the property for a period of 146 months from 1 July 2009 to 31 August 2021.

Test your understanding 11

Lionel

1   £Nil – PRR exemption applies throughout.

2   £200,000, the house has not met the definition for exemption under PRR.

3   £10,000 (£200,000 × 1/21):

Years	Treatment	Explanation
Years 1 – 3	Fully exempt	Actual occupation
Years 4 – 11	7 years exempt, 1 year chargeable	4 years covered by working away exemption, 3 years covered by 'any reason' exemption, remaining one year chargeable
Years 12 – 20	Fully exempt	Actual occupation

Note: It is possible to claim more than one of the deemed occupation periods during the same period of absence.

Shares and securities

11

Introduction

As part of the assessment you may be required to calculate a gain on the disposal of some shares.

There are special rules applying to share disposals as it is necessary to determine which particular shares have been sold.

ASSESSMENT CRITERIA	CONTENTS
Apply matching rules for individuals (4.2)	1 The matching rules
	2 Same day and next 30 days
Account for bonus issues (4.2)	
Account for rights issues (4.2)	3 Share pool
	4 Bonus issues and rights issues
	5 Approach to assessment questions

1 The matching rules

What distinguishes a share disposal from other asset disposals is the need for matching rules.

The main reason why matching rules are needed is because the same type of shares in a company may be bought at different times and at different prices.

Hence, if only some of the shares are sold we need to know which they are in order to identify their cost.

For individuals we match shares disposed of in the following order:

- first, with shares acquired on the same day as the disposal

- second, with shares acquired within the following 30 days (using the earliest acquisition first, i.e. on a FIFO basis)

- third, with the share pool (all the shares bought by the individual before the date of disposal).

Example

Frederic had the following transactions in the shares of Earth plc, a quoted company.

1 June 1998	Bought	4,000 shares for	£8,000
30 July 2005	Bought	1,800 shares for	£9,750
20 May 2013	Bought	1,000 shares for	£8,500
15 March 2022	Sold	3,500 shares for	£36,000
20 March 2022	Bought	400 shares for	£3,900

You are required to match the shares sold with the relevant acquisitions.

Solution

	Number	Number
Shares sold		3,500
(1) Shares acquired same day		Nil
(2) Shares acquired following 30 days (20 March 2022)		(400)
		———
		3,100
(3) Share pool		
1 June 1998	4,000	
30 July 2005	1,800	
20 May 2013	1,000	
	———	
	6,800	
	———	
The disposal from the pool is therefore		
3,100 out of 6,800		(3,100)
		———
		Nil
		———

Test your understanding 1

Petra sold 200 shares in Red plc on 13 December 2021. She had acquired her shares in the company as follows:

	Number of shares
1 January 2011	650
14 February 2012	250
5 January 2022	50

In accordance with the share matching/identification rules the 200 shares sold by Petra are correctly identified as which of the following?

A   The 50 shares acquired on 5 January 2022 and then 150 of the remaining 900 shares in the pool.

B   The 50 shares acquired on 5 January 2022 and then 150 of the shares acquired on 14 February 2012.

C   200 of the shares acquired on 1 January 2011.

D   200 shares in the share pool which includes all 950 shares acquired.

Once the correct acquisition is identified, then the computation of the gains can be carried out. This is looked at in detail over the next few sections.

2 Same day and next 30 days

2.1 Calculation of the gain

The calculation of the gain on disposal is straightforward.

	£
Sale proceeds or market value	X
Less: Allowable cost	(X)
	———
Chargeable gain	X
	———

Example

Using the example details above (Frederic) calculate the gain on the sale of the shares acquired in the 30 days following the sale.

Solution

This consists of the sale of 400 shares.

Sale proceeds of £36,000 relates to 3,500 shares so must be apportioned.

The proceeds relating to 400 shares will be:

$$\frac{400}{3,500} \times £36,000 = £4,114$$

	£
Sale proceeds	4,114
Less: Cost (Given in the question)	(3,900)
	———
Chargeable gain	214
	———

The balance of the proceeds (£36,000 – £4,114 = £31,886) will be applied to shares sold from the share pool.

3 Share pool

3.1 Calculation of the pooled cost

The share pool consists of all shares in a particular company purchased before the date of disposal. It is used to calculate the cost of shares sold by reference to the average cost of all shares purchased.

The pool is set up with two columns; number (of shares) and cost. Shares purchased are added to the pool and shares sold are deducted.

- For a purchase, add the number of shares acquired to the number column and the cost to the cost column.

- For a sale, deduct the number of shares sold from the number column and an appropriate proportion of the cost from the cost column.

 Example

Using the example details above (Frederic), calculate the cost to be eliminated from the pool.

Solution

Share pool

		Number	Cost £
1 June 1998	purchase	4,000	8,000
30 July 2005	purchase	1,800	9,750
20 May 2013	purchase	1,000	8,500
		6,800	26,250
15 March 2022 disposal 3,100 out of 6,800 (Note 1)		(3,100)	(11,967)
Pool balance carried forward		3,700	14,283

Note:

(1) To calculate the amount to eliminate on disposal, multiply the total cost by $\dfrac{\text{Number of shares sold}}{\text{Total shares in pool}}$

3.2 Calculation of the gain on the share pool

The gain is calculated as proceeds less cost in the normal way:

	£
Sale proceeds	X
Less: Allowable cost	(X)
Chargeable gain	X

💡 Example

Using the details from the example Frederic, what is the gain on the share pool disposals?

Solution

Sale proceeds are £31,886 (£36,000 × 3,100/3,500).

	£
Sale proceeds	31,886
Less: Allowable cost (above)	(11,967)
Chargeable gain on share pool shares	19,919

Hence, the total chargeable gain on disposal of the 3,500 shares = (£214 + £19,919) = £20,133. An alternative way to show this would be:

	£
Total sale proceeds	36,000
Less: Allowable cost (next 30 days)	(3,900)
Less: Allowable cost (pool)	(11,967)
Chargeable gain on share pool shares	20,133

KAPLAN PUBLISHING

Test your understanding 2

Ken has carried out the following transactions in shares in Cygnet plc.

	Number	Cost £
Purchase (8 February 2004)	1,800	3,100
Purchase (12 September 2013)	1,200	4,400
Purchase (10 October 2021)	400	6,000
	Number	Proceeds
Sale (10 October 2021)	2,000	33,000

What is the chargeable gain on the sale of shares?

 Test your understanding 3

Liese bought 4,000 shares in Prokop plc for £20,000 on 5 December 2014 and a further 1,000 for £6,000 on 9 May 2020.

She then sold 2,000 shares for £16,800 on 10 July 2021 before buying 200 more on 18 July 2021 for £1,700 and a further 600 on 30 July 2021 for £4,860.

What is the amount of the chargeable gain arising on the 10 July 2021 disposal?

4 Bonus issues and rights issues

 Definition

A **bonus issue** is the distribution of free shares to existing shareholders based on existing shareholdings.

A bonus issue is included in the share pool as follows:

- The number of shares acquired is added to the number column in the share pool.

- No cost is added to the cost column.

Example

Mila bought 15,000 shares in Last Chance Ltd for £6 per share in August 2009. She received a bonus issue of 1 for 15 shares in January 2012. In November 2021 Mila sold 9,000 shares for £14 per share.

The gain on the disposal is calculated as follows.

	£
Sale proceeds (9,000 × £14)	126,000
Less: Cost (W)	(50,625)
Chargeable gain	75,375

Workings: Share pool	Number	Cost £
August 2009 purchase (15,000 × £6)	15,000	90,000
January 2012 bonus issue	1,000	
	16,000	90,000
November 2021 disposal $\frac{9,000}{16,000}$ × £90,000	(9,000)	(50,625)
Pool balance c/f	7,000	39,375

 Definition

A **rights issue** involves shareholders acquiring new shares in proportion to their existing shareholdings. The shares are not free but are usually priced at a rate below the market price.

A rights issue is included in the share pool as follows:

- The number of shares acquired is added to the number column in the share pool

- The cost is added to the cost column.

Accordingly, a rights issue is treated the same as any other purchase of shares in the share pool.

Example

In October 2021 Janusz sold 3,000 shares in Smith plc for £36,000. He had purchased 4,200 shares in June 1997 for £11,600. In August 2011 there was a 1 for 3 rights issue at £5.60 per share.

The gain on the disposal is calculated as follows.

	£
Sale proceeds	36,000
Less: Cost (W)	(10,414)
Chargeable gain	25,586

Workings: Share pool	**Number**	**Cost**
		£
June 1997 purchase	4,200	11,600
August 2011 rights issue		
(⅓ × 4,200) = 1,400 × £5.60	1,400	7,840
	5,600	19,440
October 2021 disposal $\frac{3,000}{5,600}$ × £19,440	(3,000)	(10,414)
Pool balance c/f	2,600	9,026

 Test your understanding 4

Alma

Alma acquired shares in Shark plc, a quoted company, as follows.

2,000 shares acquired on 26 June 1999 for £11,500.

On 3 October 2009 there was a 1 for 2 bonus issue.

On 23 December 2011 there was a 1 for 4 rights issue at £3 per share.

Alma sold 1,350 shares on 15 November 2021 for £30,000.

What is the chargeable gain?

5 Approach to assessment questions

In the assessment there is likely to be an eight mark task on the capital gains tax on the disposal of some shares. It is important that you enter your answer correctly into the table supplied, which could be between three and five columns, and show your workings.

In the sample assessment a four column table is supplied. The first two columns are for date and description whilst the other two columns are for numerical entry.

Example

Jason bought 3,000 shares in Viz plc for £4.20 each in December 2011.

In February 2013 he sold 2,000 of the shares for £5 each.

In July 2020 he received a 1 for 5 rights issue at £6.52 each.

In May 2021 he sold 400 shares for £45,000.

What is the chargeable gain on the shares sold in the tax year 2021/22? Your answer should clearly show the balance of shares carried forward. Show all workings.

Solution

Proceeds	45,000	
Less: Cost (pool)	(1,835)	
Gain	43,165	
Pool	**Number**	**Cost**
Dec 2011 Purchase	3,000	12,600
Feb 2013 Sale	(2,000)	(8,400)
2,000/3,000 × £12,600		
	1,000	4,200
Jul 2020 Rights issue		
1,000/5 × £6.52	200	1,304
	1,200	5,504
May 2021 Sale	(400)	(1,835)
400/1,200 × £5,504		
Balance c/f	800	3,669

Test your understanding 5

Conrad

Conrad sold all of his ordinary shares in Turnip plc on 19 November 2021 for net sale proceeds of £8,580. His previous dealings in these shares were as follows:

3 October 2015	purchased 3,500 shares for £5,250
25 July 2016	sold half of the shares for £3,000
23 May 2017	purchased 200 shares for £640
24 June 2018	took up 1 for 10 rights issue at £3.40 per share

What is the amount of the chargeable gain arising on the disposal in the tax year 2021/22?

6 Summary

Share disposals require special matching rules.

Shares sold are matched with:

- purchases on the same day
- purchases within the following 30 days
- share pool.

Bonus issues increase the number of shares held in the pool.

Rights issues affect both the number of shares held in the pool and the pool cost.

Test your understanding answers

Test your understanding 1

Petra

The correct answer is A, because the share identification rules match shares in the following priority.

1   Shares acquired on the same day as the disposal – not applicable here.

2   Shares acquired in the following 30 days – 50 shares acquired on 5 January 2022.

3   Shares in the share pool (all acquisitions prior to date of disposal).

Test your understanding 2

Ken

10 October 2021 disposal of 2,000 shares identified with:

		£
(a)	Shares acquired on the same day	400
(b)	Shares from share pool	1,600
		——
		2,000
		——

Sale proceeds are £33,000 for 2,000 shares

(a)   10 October 2021 acquisition

	£
Sale proceeds ($\frac{400}{2,000} \times £33,000$)	6,600
Less: Cost	(6,000)
	——
Chargeable gain	600

(b) Share pool

	£
Sale proceeds ($\frac{1,600}{2,000} \times £33,000$)	26,400
Less: Cost (W)	(4,000)
Chargeable gain	22,400
Total chargeable gains	23,000

Working: Share pool	Number	Cost
		£
8 February 2004 purchase	1,800	3,100
12 September 2013 purchase	1,200	4,400
	3,000	7,500
10 October 2021 disposal	(1,600)	(4,000)
Pool balance c/f	1,400	3,500

Alternative presentation

	£
Total sale proceeds	33,000
Less: Cost (same day)	(6,000)
Less: Cost (pool)	(4,000)
Total chargeable gains	23,000

☀ Test your understanding 3

Liese

10 July 2021 disposal of 2,000 shares identified with:

		£
(a)	Shares acquired in the following 30 days	
	– 18 July 2021 purchase	200
	– 30 July 2021 purchase	600
(b)	Shares from share pool	1,200
		————
		2,000
		————

Sale proceeds are £16,800 for 2,000 shares

(a) 18 July 2021 acquisition

	£
Sale proceeds (200/2100 × £16,800)	1,680
Less: Cost	(1,700)
	————
Allowable loss	(20)

(b) 30 July 2021 acquisition

	£
Sale proceeds (600/2100 × £16,800)	5,080
Less: Cost	(4,800)
	————
	180

(c) Share pool

	£
Sale proceeds (1,200/2,000 × £16,800)	10,080
Less: Cost (W)	(6,240)
	————
Chargeable gain	3,840
	————
Total chargeable gains	4,000
	————

Working: Share pool

		Number	Cost £
5 December 2014	purchase	4,000	20,000
9 May 2020	purchase	1,000	6,000
		5,000	26,000
10 July 2021	disposal	(1,200)	(6,240)
Pool balance c/f		3,800	19,760

Test your understanding 4

Alma

	£
Sale proceeds	30,000
Less: Cost (W)	(4,950)
Chargeable gain	25,050

Working: Share pool

	Number	Cost £
26 June 1999 purchase	2,000	11,500
3 October 2009 bonus issue (1 for 2) No cost so simply add in new shares	1,000	–
	3,000	11,500
23 December 2011 rights issue (1 for 4) (£3 × 750)	750	2,250
	3,750	13,750
15 November 2021 disposal $\frac{1,350}{3,750} \times £13,750$	(1,350)	(4,950)
Pool carried forward	2,400	8,800

Note: As all the shares were purchased before the date of the disposal these will all be shown in the share pool.

✿ Test your understanding 5

Conrad

The correct answer is £4,652.

	£
Proceeds	8,580
Less: Cost (W)	(3,928)
Chargeable gain	4,652

Working: Share pool

		Number	Cost
			£
3 October 2015	purchase	3,500	5,250
25 July 2016	disposal	(1,750)	(2,625)
23 May 2017	purchase	200	640
		1,950	3,265
24 June 2018	rights issue		
(1 for 10) @ £3.40		195	663
		2,145	3,928
19 November 2021 sale		(2,145)	(3,928)
		Nil	Nil

Inheritance tax

Introduction

Most inheritance tax (IHT) is collected on the death of an individual based on the value of their death estate. Some lifetime gifts may also result in an IHT liability.

This chapter covers the principles that underpin IHT, the ways in which an individual is liable to IHT and considers the IHT payable on lifetime gifts. Finally, it covers the IHT payable on the death estate.

IHT will always be tested in the assessment.

ASSESSMENT CRITERIA
Chargeable lifetime transfers (5.1)
Exempt transfers (5.1)
Potential exempt transfers (5.1)
Annual gifts, gifts to charities, marriage/civil partnership gifts, national purposes, political parties, small gifts, tapering relief (5.1)
Nil rate band and residence nil rate band (5.1)
Tax rates applicable to lifetime transfers and on the death estate (5.1)

CONTENTS

1. The charge to IHT
2. Lifetime gifts
3. Exemptions
4. IHT payable during an individual's lifetime on CLTs
5. IHT payable on lifetime gifts as a result of death
6. IHT payable on the death estate

1 The charge to IHT

1.1 Introduction

IHT is charged on:

- a **transfer of value**
- of **chargeable property**
- by a **chargeable person**.

A charge to IHT may arise:

- on the death of an individual
- on lifetime gifts where the donor dies within seven years of the date of a gift
- on certain lifetime gifts which are taxed at the date of the gift.

For the purposes of the assessment you will not be asked to perform detailed IHT calculations.

1.2 Chargeable persons

A chargeable person is an individual. All individuals are potentially liable to IHT. Companies and partnerships are not subject to IHT.

An individual who is domiciled in the UK (see Chapter 1) is liable to IHT in respect of his or her worldwide assets.

If not UK domiciled, he or she will be liable in respect of his or her UK assets only.

Note that spouses and partners in a registered civil partnership are chargeable to IHT separately.

 Definition

The **donor** is the person who makes the transfer of the asset. He or she will be the chargeable person.

 Definition

The **donee** is the person who receives the asset. This could be a trust or an individual.

1.3 Chargeable property

There are no specifically exempt assets for the purposes of IHT.

 Definition

Chargeable property includes any property to which a person is beneficially entitled

Even though an asset may be exempt for capital gains purposes (e.g. a wasting chattel), this does not mean it is also exempt for IHT purposes.

1.4 Transfer of value

 Definition

A **transfer of value** is a gift of any asset which results in a reduction in the value of the donor's estate.

To be treated as a transfer of value the transfer must be a 'gratuitous disposition'. This basically means a gift.

A bad business deal will therefore not be liable to IHT, even though there is a fall in value of the estate, as it was not the donor's intention to give anything away.

To calculate the transfer of value for IHT purposes, the **loss to donor** principle is used (also referred to as the **diminution in value** concept).

The loss to the donor, is the difference between the value of the donor's estate before and after the gift, and is the starting point for IHT calculations:

	£
Value of estate before gift	X
Less: Value of estate after gift	(X)
Diminution in value or transfer of value	X

The loss to the donor is usually the **open market value** of the asset gifted.

However, in some circumstances, the transfer of value from the donor's point of view is not necessarily the same as the value of the asset received from the donee's point of view.

This is most common with unquoted shares, where a controlling shareholding has a higher value per share than a minority shareholding.

 Example

Linda owns 6,000 shares which represents a 60% holding in Loot Ltd. On 31 December 2021 she gave a 20% holding in the company to her friend, Bob. The values of shareholdings in Loot Ltd on 31 December 2021 have been agreed for IHT purposes as follows:

Holding	Value per share
Up to 25%	£9
26% to 50%	£15
51% to 74%	£26
75% or more	£45

As a result of the gift Linda's holding of the shares in the company has fallen from 60% to 40%. We use these percentage holdings to value the shares. If 6,000 shares represented 60% of the shares in the company then after the gift she must hold 4,000 shares if her holding is 40%.

	£
Value of estate before transfer (6,000 × £26)	156,000
Less: Value of estate after transfer (4,000 × £15)	(60,000)
	———
Transfer of value	96,000
	———

Note that a lifetime gift will have both IHT and CGT consequences.

The diminution in value concept is very important but unique to IHT. The value of the asset gifted; a 20% interest in these shares (i.e. 2,000 × £9 = £18,000):

• is not relevant for IHT purposes; it is the diminution in the value of the estate from the donor's point of view which is important, but

• is important for CGT purposes; the market value of the asset gifted is always the consideration used as the starting point of the chargeable gain computation.

2 Lifetime gifts

2.1 Types of lifetime gifts

There are three categories of lifetime gifts that can be made by an individual. The three categories, and their IHT implications are:

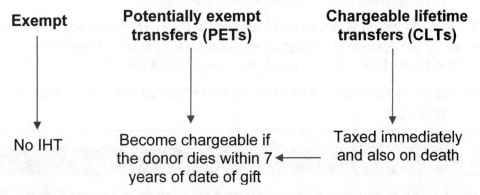

The definition of each type of gift and an overview of the way in which they are taxed is summarised in the following table.

Exempt transfers	Potentially exempt transfers (PETs)	Chargeable lifetime transfers (CLTs)
Definition		
A gift that is specifically deemed to be exempt from IHT (see below)	A gift by an individual to another individual	No definition = residual category (i.e. a gift which is not exempt nor a PET) Therefore a CLT will be a gift into most types of trust such as a discretionary trust.
During lifetime		
No IHT payable	No IHT payable	IHT to pay calculated using the lifetime rates of tax
If donor lives seven years		
No IHT payable	No IHT payable Gift becomes exempt.	No further IHT payable
If donor dies within seven years		
No IHT payable	The PET becomes chargeable on death for the first time	Possibly extra IHT, calculated using the death rates of tax

It is important to note that in practice, the majority of lifetime transfers made by individuals are either:

- exempt transfers, or

- transfers from one individual to another (i.e. a PET).

Individuals should ensure that they keep a record of the lifetime gifts they have made so that IHT can be calculated at death if necessary.

2.2 Chargeable lifetime transfers (CLTs)

A CLT is a gift which is not exempt and not a PET. They are not common in practice, but appear in assessments because they are chargeable to IHT at the time of the gift, i.e. while the donor is still alive.

In the assessment a lifetime transfer by an individual into a trust should be treated as a CLT.

 Definition

A **trust** is an arrangement where property is transferred by a person (known as the settlor) to the **trustees**, to be held for the benefit of one or more specified persons (known as the **beneficiaries**) on specified terms.

The most common example of a trust is where parents wish to give assets to their children, but not until they are adults. They therefore put the assets into a trust with the children as beneficiaries, and the assets are controlled by the trustees until the children reach a specified age.

It is not necessary to understand the workings of trusts for the assessment, only to learn that gifts into trusts are CLTs.

2.3 Potentially exempt transfers (PETs)

PETs derive their name from the fact that if the donor lives for seven years after making the gift, then the transfer is exempt (i.e. free from IHT). Therefore, at the time of such transfer, it has the potential to be exempt.

However, if the donor dies within seven years of making the gift, then IHT may become chargeable on these gifts.

Note that transfers on death can never be PETs.

Test your understanding 1

Mark the following statements as true or false.

		True	False
1	A potentially exempt transfer is chargeable to IHT unless the donor dies within seven years of the gift		
2	IHT may be charged on both potentially exempt transfers and chargeable lifetime transfers at the time of a person's death.		
3	IHT is only ever payable when a person dies.		
4	An IHT liability may arise in respect of a gift made more than seven years prior to death.		

3 Exemptions

3.1 Overview

There is no IHT payable where a gift is covered by an exemption.

The following table summarises the exemptions available for IHT that may feature in the assessment.

Exemptions available against:	
Lifetime gifts only	**Lifetime gifts and death estate**
• Small gifts exemption • Marriage exemption • Annual exemption	• Inter spouse exemption • UK charities exemption • Political parties exemption • Museums and art galleries exemption

3.2 Exemptions available for lifetime gifts only

The following exemptions are available to reduce lifetime transfers only. They do not apply to the death estate.

Reference material

Some information about lifetime exemptions can be found in the 'Inheritance tax - exemptions' section of your reference material provided in the real assessment, so you do not need to learn it.

Why not look up the correct part of the reference material in the introduction to this text book now

---

Small gifts exemption

Lifetime gifts are exempt if they are:

- an outright gift to an individual of no more than £250

- per recipient

- per tax year.

The small gifts exemption does not apply to a gift or gifts to an individual of more than £250.

Therefore, a gift of £300 will not qualify. Similarly, if an individual makes a gift of £240 to a person followed by another gift of £100 to the same person in the same tax year, neither gift will be exempt.

However, the donor can make gifts of up to £250 to any number of different recipients and they will all be exempt.

Marriage exemption

A lifetime transfer made 'in consideration of a marriage' (or registration of a civil partnership) is exempt up to the following maximum limits:

- £5,000 by a parent

- £2,500 by a grandparent or remoter ancestor

- £2,500 by a party to the marriage or civil partnership to the other party

- £1,000 by anyone else.

The exemption is conditional on the marriage or registration of the civil partnership taking place.

KAPLAN PUBLISHING

The annual exemption

The annual exemption (AE) is an exemption available against lifetime transfers and operates as follows:

- The AE:
    - exempts the **first £3,000** of lifetime transfers in any one tax year
    - is applied chronologically to the first gift in the tax year, then (if there is any left) the second gift and so on
    - must be applied to the first gift each year, even if the first gift is a PET and never becomes chargeable.
- Any unused AE:
    - may be carried forward to the next year
    - however, it can be carried forward for one year only, and
    - can only be used after the current year's AE.
- The maximum AE in any one year is therefore £6,000 (£3,000 × 2).
- If other exemptions are available they are given before the AE.

Example

Julie made the following lifetime gifts:

(a)   31 August 2019, £600, to her son

(b)   31 October 2019, £800, to a trust

(c)   31 May 2020, £2,100, to a trust

(d)   30 November 2020, £1,100, to a trust

(e)   30 April 2021, £5,000, to her daughter.

Calculate the transfer of value after AEs for each of the gifts.

Solution

	PET 31.8.19 2019/20 £	CLT 31.10.19 2019/20 £	CLT 31.5.20 2020/21 £	CLT 30.11.20 2020/21 £	PET 30.4.21 2021/22 £
Tax year of gift					
Transfer of value	600	800	2,100	1,100	5,000
Less: AE					
2019/20	(600)	(800)			
2018/19 b/f	(–)	(–)			
2020/21			(2,100)	(900)	
2019/20 b/f				(200)	
2021/22					(3,000)
2020/21 b/f					(Nil)
Transfer of value	Nil	Nil	Nil	Nil	2,000

The unused AE from the tax year 2018/19 is available in full (£3,000) however in can only be carried forward for one year and is not utilised in the tax year 2019/20, therefore it is lost.

The unused AE from the tax year 2019/20 is £1,600 (£3,000 – £600 – £800). £200 of that is utilised in the tax year 2020/21, and the remaining £1,400 is lost.

The AE for the tax year 2020/21 is utilised in full in that tax year therefore there is no brought forward AE available in the tax year 2021/22 to offset against the gift in that year.

Test your understanding 2

Calculate the chargeable amount (i.e. after the deduction of all available exemptions) in respect of each of the following cash gifts which were made on 1 June 2021.

		Gift £	Chargeable amount
1	Lance Lance's gift was to his brother. Lance had not made any gifts prior to 1 June 2021.	7,400	
2	Carrie Carrie's gift was to her daughter at the time of her wedding. Carrie's only previous gift was £2,300 to her son on 1 October 2020.	12,200	
3	Pinto Pinto's gift was to a friend. On 1 May 2021 Pinto gave £14,000 to his brother.	£170	

3.3 Exemptions available for lifetime transfers and the death estate

Inter-spouse exemption

Transfers between spouses or between partners in a registered civil partnership are exempt:

- regardless of the value of the transfer, and

- whether they are made during the individual's lifetime or on death.

Other exemptions

All gifts to the following, regardless of their value, are exempt from IHT:

- UK charities

- Qualifying political parties

- Museums and art galleries.

This means that where an individual leaves a gift to one or more of these organisations in his or her will, the amount of the gift(s) must be deducted from the value of the assets in the death estate.

Test your understanding 3

In the situations set out below it should be assumed that no annual exemptions are available to the donor.

Tick the appropriate column for each of the gifts

	Gift	Not exempt	Partly exempt	Fully exempt
1	£520 from Tim to his friend Martha.			
2	£218,000 from Serena to her husband.			
3	£1,600 from Marie to her friend Eric on his wedding day.			
4	A painting worth £1,700,000 from Nadiya to The National Gallery.			

Test your understanding 4

Mark the following statements as true or false.

		True	False
1	Ashraqat makes a gift to a trust. The gift will only become chargeable to inheritance tax if she dies within seven years of making a gift.		
2	Precious made a gift of £20,000 to her grandson on occasion of his wedding in July 2021. Prior to this she had made one lifetime gift of £240 to her nephew in May 2020. The chargeable amount on the gift to her grandson is £11,500.		
3	David makes a gift of £280,000 to his husband. He has made no previous lifetime gifts. The chargeable amount will be £274,000.		

4 IHT payable during an individual's lifetime on CLTs

4.1 The procedure to calculate the lifetime IHT on a CLT

Lifetime IHT may be payable when an individual makes a gift into a trust.

The lifetime tax should be calculated on each gift separately, in chronological order, as follows:

(1) Calculate the chargeable amount of the gift:

	£
Value of estate before gift	X
Less: Value of estate after gift	(X)
	―――
Transfer of value	X
Less: Specific exemptions	
(e.g. spouse/charity)	(X)
Marriage exemption	(X)
Annual exemptions	(X)
	―――
Chargeable amount	X
	―――

The transfer of value in the above calculation will often be simply the value of the gift.

(2) Calculate the amount of nil rate band available after deducting gross chargeable transfers in the previous seven years (see below).

(3) Calculate the excess of the chargeable amount over the available nil rate band.

(4) Calculate tax on this excess at either 20% or 25% depending on whether the donor or the donee will pay the tax (see below).

(5) Calculate the gross amount of the gift to carry forward for future computations.

4.2 The nil rate band

All individuals are entitled to a nil rate band (NRB) and are taxed on the value of gifts in excess of the NRB, so the NRB is the maximum value of lifetime and death gifts, which can be gifted without incurring any IHT liability.

For lifetime calculations, the NRB applicable at the time of the gift should be used, which for the tax year 2021/22 is £325,000.

Reference material

Some information about nil rate band can be found in the 'Inheritance tax – tax rates' section of your reference material provided in the real assessment, so you do not need to learn it.

Why not look up the correct part of the reference material in the introduction to this text book now

4.3 The appropriate rate of tax

The appropriate rate of tax to apply to lifetime gifts depends on who has agreed to pay the tax due.

Donee pays the tax

If the trustees of the trust (i.e. the donee) agree to pay the tax:

- the gift is referred to as a **gross gift**, and

- the appropriate rate of tax is 20%.

Reference material

Some information about the lifetime rate can be found in the 'Inheritance tax – tax rates' section of your reference material provided in the real assessment, so you do not need to learn it.

Why not look up the correct part of the reference material in the introduction to this text book now

Donor pays the tax

If the donor agrees to pay the tax:

- The gift is referred to as a **net gift**.

- As a result of the gift, the estate of the donee is being reduced by:

  - the value of the gift, and

  - the associated tax payable on the gift.

- Accordingly the amount of the gift needs to be 'grossed up' to include the tax that the donor has to pay.

- The appropriate rate of tax is therefore 25% (i.e. 20/80ths of the net gift). This figure is not included in the tax tables provided in the real assessment, so you need to learn it.

- The gross transfer to carry forward is the net chargeable amount plus any IHT paid by the donor.

In summary, the rate of tax on the value of CLTs in excess of the NRB is:

Payer		Appropriate rate
Trustees of the trust	Gross gift	20%
Donor	Net gift	25% (or 20/80)

Note that the tax due on a CLT is primarily the responsibility of the donor.

 Example

Li

Li made a gift into a trust on 13 June 2021 of £366,000.

She has made no previous gifts.

Calculate the amount of lifetime IHT due on the gift, assuming:

(a) the trustees of the trust have agreed to pay the tax.

(b) Li has agreed to pay the tax.

Solution

(a) Trustees have agreed to pay the tax

	£
Gift	366,000
Less: AE 2021/22	(3,000)
Less: AE 2020/21 b/f	(3,000)
	———
Chargeable amount	360,000
Less: NRB	(325,000)
	———
Excess of chargeable amount over NRB	35,000
	———
IHT (£35,000 × 20%)	7,000
	———

Note: Gross amount to carry forward for future computations 360,000

(b)	**Li has agreed to pay the tax**	
	Excess of chargeable amount over NRB as in (a)	35,000
	IHT (£35,000 × 25%)	8,750
Note:	Gross amount to carry forward for future computations (£360,000 + £8,750)	368,750

4.4 The seven year accumulation period

The NRB is available for a 'seven year accumulation period'.

In order to calculate the IHT liability in respect of a CLT it is necessary to look back seven years and calculate how much NRB is available to set against that particular gift.

For lifetime calculations, to calculate the NRB available at any point in time, it is necessary to deduct the total of the gross amounts of all other CLTs made within the previous seven years from the NRB.

However, you will only be tested on basic calculations in the assessment.

 Test your understanding 5

Dana

Dana made a gift into a trust on 1 September 2021 of £380,000. This was Dana's only gift in the tax year 2021/22.

She has made gross chargeable transfers of £86,000 in the seven years prior to the tax year 2021/22 including gifts of more than £3,000 in the tax year 2020/21.

Calculate the amount of lifetime IHT due on the gift, assuming:

(a) the trustees of the trust have agreed to pay the tax.

(b) Dana has agreed to pay the tax.

4.5 Summary of lifetime calculations

Remember, whilst the donor is alive:

- only calculate IHT on CLTs.

- tax is due at 20% if the trustees pay, and 25% if the donor pays.

- PETs are not chargeable at this stage, but they do use the annual exemptions.

5   IHT payable on lifetime gifts as a result of death

5.1   IHT on gifts within seven years of death

On the death of an individual, an IHT charge may arise in relation to lifetime gifts made **within seven years of death** as follows:

- PETs become chargeable for the first time.

- Additional tax may be due on CLTs.

The IHT payable on lifetime gifts as a result of death is always paid by the recipient of the gift:

Type of gift:	Paid by:
CLT	Trustees of the trust
PET	Donee

5.2   The available NRB

The NRB available on the death of an individual is:

- the NRB for the tax year of death (rather than the tax year of the gift)

- plus any unused proportion of the NRB of their spouse or civil partner who has already died

- less any gross chargeable transfers in the previous seven years (you will not be required to calculate this figure).

Note that the unused proportion of a spouse's NRB can only be utilised when calculating tax at death, **not** during the donor's lifetime.

 Example

Erica was widowed on the death of her husband Arnie on 21 June 2010.

35% of Arnie's NRB was used when calculating the IHT due at the time of his death.

Erica died on 23 May 2021.

Erica had made gross chargeable transfers of £40,000 in the seven years prior to her death.

Calculate Erica's available NRB at the time of her death.

Solution

	£
NRB at the date of death	325,000
NRB transferred from Arnie (£325,000 × 65%)	211,250
Erica's gross chargeable transfers in the seven years prior to death	(40,000)
NRB available to Erica	496,250

5.3 Calculating the death IHT on lifetime gifts

The death tax should be calculated on a gift within seven years of death as follows:

(1) Calculate the **gross chargeable amount** of the gift.

(2) Calculate the **available NRB** (as set out above).

(3) Deduct the available NRB from the gross chargeable amount of the gift.

(4) Calculate the **death tax** on the excess at 40%.

(5) Calculate and deduct any **taper relief** available (see below).

(6) For CLTs, deduct any **lifetime IHT paid**.

(7) If required by the question, state who will pay the tax (see below).

5.4 Taper relief

Note that taper relief applies to both CLTs and PETs.

Where IHT is chargeable on any lifetime transfer due to death, the amount of IHT payable on death will be reduced by taper relief:

- where more than three years have elapsed since the date of the gift

- by a percentage reduction according to the length of time between

   - the date of the gift, and
   - the date of the donor's death.

Reference material

Some information about taper relief can be found in the 'Inheritance tax – tapering relief' section of your reference material provided in the real assessment, so you do not need to learn it.

Why not look up the correct part of the reference material in the introduction to this text book now

	% reduction
3 years or less	0
Over 3 years but less than 4 years	20
Over 4 years but less than 5 years	40
Over 5 years but less than 6 years	60
Over 6 years but less than 7 years	80

For gifts made seven or more years before death there is no IHT payable on death, so taper relief is not relevant.

5.5 Deduction of lifetime IHT paid

For CLTs, any lifetime IHT already paid can be deducted from the liability calculated on death.

However, no refund is made if the tax already paid is higher than the amount now due on death.

At best, the deduction of lifetime tax paid will bring the liability on death down to £Nil.

 Example

On 15 July 2014 Mirela made a transfer of £365,000 into a trust. Mirela agreed to pay the IHT due in respect of this gift. She has made no other lifetime transfers. The NRB in 2014/15 was £325,000.

Mirela died on 30 May 2021.

Calculate the IHT due on the lifetime gift as a result of Mirela's death.

Solution

Lifetime IHT payable

The gift was made to a trust meaning it is a CLT. Lifetime tax would have been payable when the gift was made.

	£
Transfer of value	365,000
Less: AE 2014/15	(3,000)
AE 2013/14	(3,000)
	————
Net chargeable amount	359,000
NRB at date of gift (no gifts in the previous seven years)	(325,000)
	————
Taxable amount	34,000
	————
Lifetime IHT due (£34,000 × 25%)	8,500
	————
Gross amount to carry forward for future computations (£359,000 + £8,500)	367,500
	————

IHT payable on death

	£
Gross chargeable amount (above)	367,500
Less: NRB at death (no gifts in the previous seven years)	(325,000)
	————
Taxable amount	42,500
	————
IHT due on death (£42,500 × 40%)	17,000
Less: Taper relief (£17,000 × 80%)	(13,600)
(15 July 2014 to 30 May 2021 is 6 – 7 years)	
	————
	3,400
Less: IHT paid in lifetime on CLT – restricted	(3,400)
	————
IHT payable on death	0
	————

Note: Deducting lifetime IHT cannot result in a repayment, and so the deduction is restricted to the amount required to reduce the liability to £Nil.

Test your understanding 6

Ximena

Ximena made a gift into a trust on 13 September 2017 of £420,000. This was Ximena's only lifetime gift. She agreed to pay any lifetime tax arising. The NRB in 2017/18 was £325,000.

Ximena died in July 2021.

Calculate the amount of IHT due on the gift:

(a) during Ximena's lifetime.

(b) as a consequence of Ximena's death.

6 IHT payable on the death estate

6.1 The death estate computation

On the death of an individual, an IHT charge arises on the value of his or her estate at the date of death.

 Definition

The **death estate** includes all assets held at the date of death. There are no exempt assets so anything owned by the deceased should be shown.

The value of assets brought into an individual's estate computation is normally the open market value (OMV) of the asset at the date of death (known as the probate value).

The gross chargeable value of an individual's estate is calculated using the following pro forma:

Pro forma death estate computation

	£	£
Freehold property		X
Less: Mortgage		(X)
		─────
		X
Business owned by sole trader/partnership		X
Stocks and shares (including ISAs)		X
Government securities		X
Insurance policy proceeds		X
Leasehold property		X
Motor cars		X
Personal chattels		X
Debts due to the deceased		X
Cash at bank and on deposit (including ISAs)		X
		─────
		X
Less: Debts due by the deceased	X	
Outstanding taxes (e.g. IT, CGT due)	X	
Funeral expenses	X	
	─────	(X)
		─────
Less: Exempt legacies		(X)
		─────
Gross chargeable estate		X
		─────

Exempt legacies

The only exempt legacies are to:

- spouse or civil partner
- UK charities
- qualifying political parties
- museums and art galleries.

6.2 The procedure to calculate the IHT on the death estate

The procedure to calculate the IHT on the death estate is as follows.

(1) Deal with the IHT on lifetime gifts within seven years of the date of death first before looking at the estate computation.

(2) Calculate the gross chargeable estate value.

(3) Calculate the amount of the residence nil rate band (RNRB) available (see section 6.3 below).

(4) Calculate the amount of NRB available after deducting the figure for GCTs in the previous seven years (you will not be required to calculate this figure).

(5) Calculate the tax on the excess at 40%.

(6) If required by the question, state who will pay the tax.

6.3 Further points regarding IHT payable on the death estate

The RNRB

The RNRB is available if the deceased leaves a home in his or her death estate that he or she lived in at some point to a direct descendant, e.g. son or granddaughter. It applies from 6 April 2017 and is deducted in the death estate computation before applying the NRB.

The RNRB is not available against lifetime gifts and is restricted to the lower of:

- £175,000

- the value of the property (net of any repayment mortgage).

📑 Reference material

Some information about the residence nil rate band can be found in the 'Inheritance tax – tax rates' section of your reference material provided in the real assessment, so you do not need to learn it.

Why not look up the correct part of the reference material in the introduction to this text book now

---

The NRB

The NRB available to an individual on death of £325,000 is first used to calculate the death tax on lifetime gifts, and then any remainder is set against the death estate.

The seven year accumulation period

The seven year accumulation period applies in a similar way to the death calculations on lifetime gifts. The NRB must be reduced by the total of the gross amounts of all chargeable gifts made within the previous seven years.

The death rate of tax

The death rate of IHT is 40%. This is charged on the excess of the estate over the NRB available.

 Example

Sara died on 15 June 2021 leaving a gross chargeable estate valued at £427,000 (including her home, valued at £100,000).

(a) Calculate the IHT liability arising on Sara's estate assuming she made no lifetime transfers and left her entire estate to her brother.

(b) What if Sara had gross chargeable transfers of £147,000 in the seven years prior to her death?

(c) How would your answer to part (b) have changed if Sara had left her estate to her daughter rather than her brother?

Solution

(a) No lifetime transfers

	£	£
Gross chargeable estate value		427,000
NRB at death	325,000	
Less: GCTs in 7 years pre-death	(Nil)	
Less: NRB available		(325,000)
Taxable amount		102,000
IHT due on death (£102,000 × 40%)		40,800

Note: the RNRB is not available as a brother is not a direct descendent.

(b)   Lifetime transfers = £147,000

	£	£
Gross chargeable estate value		427,000
NRB at death	325,000	
Less: GCTs in 7 years pre-death	(147,000)	
Less: NRB available		(178,000)
Taxable amount		249,000
IHT due on death (£249,000 × 40%)		99,600

(c)   Lifetime transfers = £147,000 plus availability of the RNRB

	£	£
Gross chargeable estate value		427,000
Less: RNRB (lower of £175,000 and £100,000)		(100,000)
NRB at death	325,000	
Less: GCTs in 7 years pre-death	(147,000)	
Less; NRB available		(178,000)
Taxable amount		149,000
IHT due on death (£149,000 × 40%)		59,600

Note: the RNRB is available as a daughter is a direct descendent.

 Test your understanding 7

Dmitriy

Dmitriy died on 23 April 2021 leaving a gross chargeable estate valued at £627,560 (which included a home valued at £150,000) which he bequeathed to his girlfriend.

Dmitriy had made gross chargeable transfers of £222,000 in the seven years prior to his death.

Calculate the IHT liability arising on Dimitriy's estate.

6.4　Transfer of RNRB

Any unused RNRB can be transferred to the surviving spouse or civil partner on the death of the first spouse or civil partner.

It is always an unused percentage that is transferred and you will be told what proportion of the RNRB was utilised on the first spouse's death in the assessment.

Where the spouse/civil partner died before 6 April 2017 100% of the RNRB will be available to transfer to the second spouse, since the RNRB was not yet available on the first spouse's death.

 Reference material

Some information about the residence nil rate band can be found in the 'Inheritance tax – tax rates' section of your reference material provided in the real assessment, so you do not need to learn it.

Why not look up the correct part of the reference material in the introduction to this text book now

 Test your understanding 8

Malik

Malik died on 1 July 2021 and left an estate of £950,000, including a home valued at £360,000 to his son. Malik's civil partner James died in 2015 and 58% of his NRB was used when calculating the IHT at the time of his death.

Malik had made gross chargeable transfers of £92,000 in the seven years prior to his death.

Calculate the IHT liability arising on Malik's estate.

6.5　Payment of IHT on the death estate

IHT on the death estate is initially paid by the executors.

The tax is paid from the estate, and so it is effectively borne by the person who inherits the residue of the assets (known as the residuary legatee) after the specific legacies have been paid.

A summary of the payment of tax is shown below:

Recipient/asset	Paid by	Suffered by
Spouse	N/A – exempt	N/A – exempt
Specific UK assets	Executors	Residuary legatee
Residue of estate	Executors	Residuary legatee

 Test your understanding 9

Adele

Adele died on 31 December 2021 leaving an estate worth £820,000 including a home worth £240,000. From her estate she left £20,000 to a charity and the rest to her children.

Adele's only lifetime gift had been a gift of a holiday home worth £100,000 (after deduction of available exemptions) to a trust in October 2020.

Calculate the IHT liability arising on Adele's death and state who is responsible for paying this.

7 Summary

IHT may be charged on:

- chargeable lifetime transfers whilst the donor is alive
- all gifts within seven years of death
- the death estate.

The taxable amount is:

- the transfer of value
- less exemptions
- less the available NRB.

It is important to learn:

- the meaning of chargeable lifetime transfer and potentially exempt transfer
- when the exemptions are available
- the calculation of the available NRB
- the rate at which IHT is paid in the different situations.

You should then practise calculating:

- lifetime IHT due in respect of a chargeable lifetime transfer
- IHT due on death in respect of a lifetime gift
- IHT due in respect of the death estate.

Test your understanding answers

 ### Test your understanding 1

1   **False** – A potentially exempt transfer is chargeable to IHT unless the donor **survives the gift by at least seven years**.

2   **True** – Both potentially exempt transfers (PETs) and chargeable lifetime transfers (CLTs) made within the seven years prior to death may give rise to an IHT death tax charge. CLTs may also give rise to a lifetime tax charge

3   **False** – IHT may be payable whilst a person is alive in respect of a chargeable lifetime transfer.

4   **True** – A chargeable lifetime transfer may result in an IHT liability at any time in a person's life and not just in the seven years prior to death.

Test your understanding 2

Chargeable amounts

		£
1	**Lance**	
	Gift	7,400
	Annual exemption 2021/22	(3,000)
	Annual exemption 2020/21 b/f	(3,000)
	Chargeable amount	1,400
2	**Carrie**	
	Gift	12,200
	Marriage exemption	(5,000)
	Annual exemption 2021/22	(3,000)
	Annual exemption 2020/21 b/f (£3,000 – £2,300)	(700)
	Chargeable amount	3,500

3	Pinto	
	Gift	170
	Small gifts exemption	(170)
	Chargeable amount	Nil

Test your understanding 3

	Gift	Not exempt	Partly exempt	Fully exempt
1	£520 from Tim to his friend Martha.	✓		
2	£218,000 from Serena to her husband.			✓
3	£1,600 from Marie to Eric on his wedding day.		✓	
4	A painting worth £1,700,000 from Nadiya to The National Gallery.			✓

1   This gift exceeds £250, such that the small gifts exemption is not available.

2   The whole of this gift is covered by the spouse exemption.

3   A marriage exemption of £1,000 is available in respect of this gift.

4   The whole of this gift is covered by the exemption available in respect of gifts to museums and art galleries.

Test your understanding 4

1   **False** – In your assessment you should assume all gifts to trusts are chargeable lifetime transfers. An immediate charge to IHT arises on these.

2   **True** – The gift in May 2020 would have been covered by the small gifts exemption. This means for the gift in June 2021 the marriage exemption plus the 2021/22 and 2020/21 annual exemptions can be offset. The chargeable amount is £11,500 (£20,000 – £2,500 – £3,000 – £3,000).

3   **False** – Gifts to an individual's spouse or civil partner are exempt in full.

Test your understanding 5

Dana

(a)   Trustees have agreed to pay the tax

	£
Gift	380,000
Less: AE 2021/22	(3,000)
Chargeable amount	377,000
Less: NRB (£325,000 – £86,000) (See note)	(239,000)
Excess of chargeable amount over NRB	138,000
IHT (£138,000 × 20%)	27,600

The annual exemption for the tax year 2020/21 will have been used against the gifts in that tax year.

Note: When a question provides the value of the GCT this means any available exemptions have already been deducted.

(b)   Dana has agreed to pay the tax

	£
Excess of chargeable amount over NRB as in (a)	138,000
IHT (£138,000 × 25%)	34,500
Note: Gross amount to carry forward for future computations (£377,000 + £34,500)	411,500

Test your understanding 6

Ximena

(a) Lifetime tax due

	£
Gift	420,000
Less: AE 2017/18	(3,000)
Less: AE 2016/17	(3,000)
Chargeable amount	414,000
Less: NRB	(325,000)
Excess of chargeable amount over NRB	89,000
IHT (£89,000 × 25%)	22,250

Note: Gross amount to carry forward for future computations (£414,000 + £22,250) — 436,250

(b) Death tax

	£
Gross amount from lifetime tax working as in (a)	436,250
Less: NRB (2021/22)	(325,000)
Excess of chargeable amount over NRB	111,250
IHT (£111,250 × 40%)	44,500
Less: Taper relief (£44,500 × 20%)	(8,900)
	35,600
Less: Lifetime tax paid	(22,250)
Tax payable on death	13,350

Note: Ximena survived for 3 to 4 years after the gift into the trust. Therefore the tapering relief reduction is 20%. The tapering relief percentage reductions can be found in your tax tables.

Test your understanding 7

Dimitriy – IHT on death estate

	£
Gross chargeable estate	627,560
Less: NRB (£325,000 – £222,000)	(103,000)
Taxable amount	524,560
IHT due on death (£524,560 × 40%)	209,824

Note: the RNRB did not apply as although Dimitriy left a home in his death estate he did not leave it to a direct descendent.

Test your understanding 8

Malik – IHT on death estate

	£
Gross chargeable estate	950,000
Less: RNRB (£175,000 × 200%)	(350,000)
Less: NRB ((£325,000 × 142%) – £92,000)	(369,500)
Taxable amount	230,500
IHT due on death (£230,500 × 40%)	92,200

Note: Malik was able to make use of James's RNRB and the unused 42% of James's NRB to reduce his death estate. He could make full use of the total RNRB of £350,000 as the home he bequeathed was worth more than £350,000 and was left to his son.

Test your understanding 9

Adele

	£
Lifetime gift	100,000
Less: NRB	(100,000)
	———
Excess over NRB	–
Gross chargeable estate	820,000
Less: Bequest to charity	(20,000)
	———
	800,000
Less: RNRB (Lower of £175,000 and £240,000))	(175,000)
Less: NRB (£325,000 – £100,000)	(225,000)
	———
Taxable amount	400,000
	———
IHT due on death (£400,000 × 40%)	160,000
	———

The tax due on the estate is payable by Adele's personal representatives.

Note: The RNRB is available as the estate included a home that was left to a direct descendant.

MOCK ASSESSMENT
Q2022

1 Mock Assessment Questions

You have 2 hours to complete this mock assessment.

This assessment contains 10 tasks and you should attempt to complete every task.

Each task is independent. You will not need to refer to your answers to previous tasks.

The total number of marks for this assessment is 100.

Read every task carefully to make sure you understand what is required.

Where the date is relevant, it is given in the task data.

You may use minus signs or brackets to indicate negative numbers UNLESS task instructions say otherwise.

You must use a full stop to indicate a decimal point.
For example, write 100.57 NOT 100,57 or 100 57

You may use a comma to indicate a number in the thousands, but you don't have to. For example, 10000 and 10,000 are both acceptable.

If rounding is required, normal mathematical rounding rules should be applied UNLESS task instructions say otherwise.

Task 1 (10 marks)

This task is about principles and rules underpinning tax.

You work for a firm of accountants. Your employer has become aware that one of your clients, Alexander, has deliberately reduced his property income figure in his 2021/22 tax return by not including income from one of his rental properties.

(a) Define what is meant by tax evasion, tax avoidance and tax planning. Identify which of these Alexander has been involved in and explain what the potential penalties are.

(5 marks)

(b) Suggest the actions your firm should take if Alexander refuses to declare this income.

(5 marks)

Task 2 (14 marks)

This task is about income from employment.

Laurel and Gabrielle both had the use of company cars during 2021/22. All necessary information in respect of each car is detailed below.

	Laurel	Gabrielle
Number of months available	6 months	12 months
Car registration date	10/12/19	20/06/20
Fuel details	Hybrid petrol with electric range of 75 miles	Diesel
CO2 emissions	45g/km	109g/km
Cost price	£36,000	£25,500
List price	£37,100	£26,400
Employee contribution to cost of the car	£5,500	No
Employee contribution to use of the car	£50 per month	No
Private fuel provided by the employer	No	Yes
Employee contribution to private fuel	N/A	No

(a) **Complete the table below to show Laurel and Gabrielle's taxable benefits in kind for the cars for 2021/22. Show monetary answers in whole pounds only.**

(6 marks)

	Laurel		Gabrielle	
	Scale charge %	Amount £	Scale charge %	Amount £
Scale charge percentage				
Taxable benefit on the provision of the car				
Taxable benefit on the provision of the fuel				

Below is a list of benefits that Daley Ltd has provided to its employees during 2021/22.

(b) **Enter the taxable benefit in kind for 2021/22 for each benefit in the box provided. Enter your answer in whole pounds only. If your answer is zero, enter '0'.**

(5 marks)

	Taxable benefit in kind £
On 6 June 2021 Sue was provided with a flat to live in, which had been purchased by her employer in 2020 for £126,000. The flat has an annual value of £2,500 and is not job-related accommodation.	
Engelbert is loaned the use of a television by his employer, Daley Ltd. The television cost £650 when first provided on 1 May 2021. Engelbert does not have any business use of the television but he does pay £5 per month to Daley Ltd for the use of the television from 1 May 2021.	
A car parking space in a multi-storey car park near Daley Ltd's business premises was provided to Jason throughout 2021/22. The provision of this costs Daley Ltd £820.	
Laura receives an interest free loan of £14,000 on 6 January 2022.	

(c) **Identify whether the following statements are true or false.**

(3 marks)

	True	False
Alix paid 5% of her salary into an occupational pension scheme. This is an allowable deduction from her employment income.		
Teddy uses his own car for business purposes. During 2021/22 Teddy travelled 9,000 business miles and his employer paid him a mileage allowance of 40p per mile. Teddy has taxable income of £450 for the purposes of tax.		
Hannah received a bonus of £1,250 on 1 June 2021 for her employer's financial year ended 31 December 2020. This bonus will be taxed on Hannah in the 2021/22 tax year.		

Task 3 (10 marks)

This task is about income from investments and property.

The information below relates to the investment income received during 2021/22 by two taxpayers.

(a) Complete the following sentences. Enter your answer in whole pounds only. If your answer is zero, enter '0'. (4 marks)

(i) Lorena received a dividend of £18,000 from her shares in Ash Plc, and a further dividend of £2,000 from an investment in a stocks and shares ISA. Her other taxable income, after the personal allowance, totalled £78,000.

Lorena's income from dividends, on which tax will be paid, is:

£ [   ]

The total tax payable on her dividends will be:

£ [   ]

(ii) Magnus received £2,200 of interest on his building society account. His other taxable income, after the personal allowance, is £36,000. The total tax payable by Magnus on his interest will be:

£ [   ]

Pablo owns and rents out two properties during 2021/22. Relevant information on the properties is shown below. Pablo has elected to be assessed on his property income using the accruals basis.

(b) Complete the table below to show taxable rent and allowable expenses for these properties in 2021/22. Enter your answer in whole pounds only. If your answer is zero, enter '0'.

(4 marks)

Property		Taxable rent £	Allowable expenses £
Duncombe Way	Duncombe Way was let from 1 January 2022 for rent of £1,400 per month. The rent was paid in advance on the 1st of each month. On 1 January 2022 Pablo paid insurance of £1,100 for the year ended 31 December 2022.		
Chandlers Close	Chandlers Close was let until 30 November 2021 for rent of £11,400 per year. On 1 December 2021 Pablo moved into the property. The annual cleaning costs for the property were £960. Pablo also paid £2,400 for repairs in June 2021.		

(c) Identify whether the following statements are true or false.

(2 marks)

	True	False
An additional rate taxpayer pays tax on interest at 40%.		
A landlord has tax allowable expenses of £1,800 relating to their rental property. They should claim the property allowance instead of claiming relief for these if they would like their property income to be assessed in the most tax efficient way.		

Task 4 (14 marks)

This task is about income tax payable.

During the tax year 2021/22 Yasmeen has the following income:

	£
Income from employment	101,600
Property income	18,000
Dividends received	10,600

Yasmeen has losses from property brought forward from 2020/21 of £17,800.

During 2021/22 Yasmeen paid 6% of her income from employment into her employer's occupational pension scheme. Her employer paid 8% of her salary into the same scheme. Yasmeen pays £1,640 to Oxfam each year through the gift aid scheme.

During 2021/22 Yasmeen paid £29,880 in PAYE.

Calculate her total income tax payable or repayable for the tax year 2021/22 using the table set out below. Show your answers in whole pounds only. **(14 marks)**

KAPLAN PUBLISHING

Task 5 (6 marks)

This task is about national insurance contributions.

Anita and Abraham are employed by Fir Ltd. Anita's gross salary for 2021/22 was £28,400 and Abraham's was £84,200.

(a) **Complete the following sentences. Ignore the employment allowance. Enter your answer in whole pounds only. If your answer is zero, enter '0'.** **(4 marks)**

The total class 1 National Insurance contributions payable by Anita in 2021/22 are:

£

The total class 1 National insurance contributions payable by Abraham in 2021/22 are:

£

The total class 1 National insurance contributions payable by Fir Ltd in respect of Anita and Abraham's earnings are:

£

(b) **Identify whether the following statements are true or false.**
(2 marks)

	True	False
Class 1A national insurance contributions are payable by employees in respect of the benefits they receive.		
Earnings for the purposes of calculating class 1 national insurance contributions are before the deduction of pension contributions.		

Task 6   **(8 marks)**

This task is about tax planning.

You work for a firm of accountants and are advising some of your clients about the impact of certain proposals on their income tax liability for 2021/22.

Complete the following sentences. Enter your answer in whole pounds only. If your answer is zero, enter '0'.   **(8 marks)**

(i)   Nadia is a higher rate taxpayer. She is provided with a company car which has a scale charge percentage of 23%.

Nadia is also provided with free petrol for both business and private mileage. The cost of the petrol used on private journeys by Nadia is £1,800 per year.

If Nadia's employer stopped providing her with petrol for private journeys she would be better off by:

£

(ii)   Caleb, an additional rate taxpayer, has inherited £70,000. He currently has no investments and has decided he wants to invest in shares.

Caleb wants to know how much tax he will pay if he invests all his money in shares. He has determined that they will pay on average a return of 3.5% per year. You tell Caleb that his tax liability on his investments will be:

£

(iii) Giselle has net income of £60,000. She is considering contributing to a personal pension scheme. If Giselle pays a total of £3,360 into her personal pension scheme in 2021/22 she will save tax of:

£

(iv)   Masumi is a higher rate taxpayer. Her employer has offered her two benefits to choose between as part of her employment package for 2021/22:

1.   A mobile phone worth £700 or

2.   Use of a plasma television for the tax year. The TV will cost her employer £3,200;

She has asked your advice regarding these two options.

The mobile phone will increase her income tax liability by:

£ ☐

The television will increase her income tax liability by:

£ ☐

Task 7 (10 marks)

This task is about capital gains tax principles.

(a) Identify whether the following disposals are chargeable or exempt from capital gains tax. (3 marks)

	Chargeable	Exempt
Olivia makes a gift of a painting worth £30,000 to her daughter		
Daniel leaves a house worth £5 million in his death estate to his niece		
Adelaide sells a share in a racehorse for £30,000		

Edgar sold four assets to unconnected persons during 2021/22. The proceeds and cost of each asset are shown in the table below.

(b) Show whether the sale of each asset below results in a taxable gain, an allowable loss or is exempt for capital gains tax. The amount of the gain or loss should be entered in the final column, with a zero '0' being entered if you think the asset is exempt.

Do not leave any cells blank. Do not use brackets or minus signs. Enter your answer in whole pounds only.

(4 marks)

Asset	Proceeds £	Cost £	Gain/loss/exempt	Amount of gain or loss £
Car	8,000	14,200		
Vase	2,200	6,000		
Painting	8,040	3,650		
Sculpture	6,400	8,200		

Aditi bought 20 acres of land for £130,000 in June 2015. In February 2021 she sold four acres for £60,000. The remainder of the land had a market value of £180,000 in February 2021.

(c) Calculate the gain on the sale of the land. Enter your answer in whole pounds only.

(3 marks)

	£
Proceeds	
Cost	
Gain	

Task 8 (8 marks)

This task is about capital gains tax: disposals of shares.

Mai holds shares in Galaxy Ltd and has made a number of transactions over the years. Details of the transactions are:

Event date	Details
1 April 2016	Purchased 3,500 shares for £16,800
10 November 2018	1 for 4 rights issue at £3.60 per share
13 September 2019	Sold 475 shares for £6 per share
20 January 2021	1 for 3 bonus issue
18 May 2021	Sold 4,200 shares for £8.50 per share

Calculate the gain Mai made on the sale of shares in 2021/22, clearly showing the balance of shares and their value to carry forward.

All workings must be shown in your calculations. Enter your answer in whole pounds only. You have been give more space than you need.

Task 9 (10 marks)

This task is about capital gains tax: reliefs and exemptions.

(a) **Identify whether the following statements about capital gains tax are true or false.** (4 marks)

	True	False
Capital losses can be offset against taxable income if the taxpayer has no capital gains in the year.		
The last nine months of ownership of an individual's private residence are always exempt from capital gains tax.		
Capital losses cannot be carried back.		
Each partner in a married couple is entitled to his, her or their own annual exempt amount.		

Jenna's only income in 2021/22 is property income of £49,500, after the deduction of the personal allowance. She made the following gains and losses during 2021/22, none of which relate to residential property.

	Chargeable gain £	Allowable loss £
Asset 1	24,100	
Asset 2 – sold to Jenna's brother		4,000
Asset 3		8,000
Asset 4	12,200	

(b) Complete the following sentences in respect of Jenna's capital gains tax liability in 2021/22. Enter your answer in whole pounds. If your answer is zero, enter '0'.　　　(3 marks)

The total amount that Jenna will pay capital gains tax on, after all allowances in 2021/22 is:

£ [   ]

The amount of capital gains tax payable by Jenna in 2021/22 is:

£ [   ]

Neil had the following capital gains and losses in the last few years.

Year	Annual exempt amount £	Capital gains £	Capital losses £
2019/20	12,000	37,400	51,200
2020/21	12,300	16,300	13,500
2021/22	12,300	25,500	11,400

(c) Complete the following sentences. Enter your answer in whole pounds only. If your answer is zero, enter '0'.　　(3 marks)

The amount chargeable, if any, to capital gains tax for 2021/22 is:

£ [   ]

The amount of losses, if any, to carry forward to 2022/23 is:

£ [   ]

Task 10 (10 marks)

This task is about inheritance tax

(a) **Identify whether the following statements about inheritance tax (IHT) are true or false.** (5 marks)

	True	False
No IHT liability can arise in respect of a gift made more than seven years prior to death.		
In the tax year 2021/22 Ryan made a single gift to Danielle of £420. The small gifts exemption will not be available in respect of this gift.		
A chattel with a value of no more than £6,000 is exempt from IHT.		
The residence nil rate band is not available in respect of lifetime gifts.		
April died in June 2020 leaving all her estate to her wife, Alix. Alix died in March 2021. The nil rate band available on Alix's death is £650,000.		

(b) **Complete the following statements that relate to inheritance tax (IHT). If appropriate, enter your answer in whole pounds only. If your answer is zero, enter '0'.** (3 marks)

On 1 May 2021 Guiseppe gave his niece £8,000 on her wedding day. Guiseppe has made no previous lifetime gifts.

The chargeable amount (after the deduction of all available exemptions) of the gift made on 1 May 2021 is:

£

Andre made two lifetime gifts. In June 2020 he made a gift of £2,500. In October 2021 he made a further gift of £4,200. The chargeable amount of the gift in October 2021 is:

£

Monica left an estate of £820,000 (including her home which had a value of £200,000) to her daughter. She had made no previous gifts. The taxable amount of her estate for the purposes of inheritance tax will be:

£

Craig lives in the UK and has made two gifts in 2021/22. The first gift was to his nephew and the second to his cousin. These are the only lifetime gifts he has made.

(c) **Complete the table below showing whether these gifts would be a chargeable lifetime transfer (CLT), an exempt transfer (ET) or a potentially exempt transfer (PET).** **(2 marks)**

Date	Details of the gift	Value £	CLT/ET/PET
08 June 2021	Car	22,000	
24 December 2021	Cash	200	

KAPLAN PUBLISHING

2 Mock Assessment Answers

Task 1

(a) Alexander

Tax planning involves legal methods to minimise a tax liability. It is acting within the intention of Parliament when the legislation was passed.

Tax avoidance also involves using legal methods to minimise a tax liability, but it is not acting within the spirit of tax law.

Tax evasion is committed when a taxpayer uses illegal methods to minimise his, her or their tax liability.

Alexander has committed tax evasion. The likely penalties are prison and/or a fine.

(b)

If Alexander refuses to disclose this income my firm should cease acting for him.

Due to the duty of confidentiality we cannot disclose this income to HMRC ourselves unless our engagement letter gives us permission to do so.

We will need to tell HMRC that we have ceased to act for him but not the reason why.

We should ensure all communications with Alexander are in writing.

Task 2

(a)

	Laurel		Gabrielle	
	Scale charge %	Amount £	Scale charge %	Amount £
Scale charge percentage	5%		29%	
Taxable benefit on the provision of the car		503		7,656
Taxable benefit on the provision of the fuel				7,134

Workings

(W1)   Scale charge for Laurel

As Laurel has a hybrid car with emissions under 51g/km the relevant percentage can be picked up from the tax tables. An additional 1% is added to this as the car was registered before 6 April 2020.

4% + 1% = 5%

(W2)   Car benefit for Laurel

In calculating the car benefit we use the list price (not cost). A deduction can be made for Laurel's capital contribution but this deduction is capped at £5,000.

(£37,100 - £5,000) × 5% = £1,605.

As the car was not available for the full tax year the benefit is time apportioned. Laurel's contributions towards the use of the car are deducted from the benefit.

£1,605 × 6/12 – (£50 × 6) = £503

(W3)   Scale charge for Gabrielle

As the emissions of the car exceed 55g the relevant percentage must be calculated. A 4% supplement is added on as the car has a diesel engine:

15 + 4 + (105-55)/5 = 29%

(W4)   Car benefit for Gabrielle

The car benefit is calculated as list price multiplied by scale charge percentage:

29% × £26,400 = £7,656

(W5)   Fuel benefit for Gabrielle

When fuel is provided for private journeys when using a company car an additional benefit is calculated. The same scale percentage as for the car benefit is multiplied by the fuel base figure (found in the tax tables).

29% × £24,600 = £7,134.

(b) Daley Ltd

	Taxable benefit in kind £
On 6 June 2021 Sue was provided with a flat to live in, which had been purchased by her employer in 2020 for £126,000. The flat has an annual value of £2,500 and is not job-related accommodation.	2,933
Engelbert is loaned the use of a television by his Daley Ltd. The television cost £650 when first provided on 1 May 2021. Engelbert does not have any business use of the television but he does pay £5 per month to Daley Ltd for the use of the television from 1 May 2021.	64
A car parking space in a multi-storey car park near Daley Ltd's business premises was provided to Jason throughout 2021/22. The provision of this costs Daley Ltd £820.	0
Laura receives an interest free loan of £14,000 on 6 January 2022.	70

Workings

(W1) Sue

£2,500 + ((£126,000 – £75,000) × 2%) × 10/12 = £2,933

(W2) Engelbert

(£650 × 20%) × 11/12 – (£5 × 11) = £64

(W3) Jason

A car parking space provided at or near the place of work is an exempt benefit.

(W4) Laura

As Laura is paying less than the official rate of interest (2% - this can be found in your tax tables) a taxable benefit arises.

£14,000 × 2% × 3/12 = £70.

(c)   Alix

	True	False
Alix paid 5% of her salary into an occupational pension scheme. This is an allowable deduction from her employment income.	✓	
Teddy uses his own car for business purposes. During 2021/22 Teddy travelled 9,000 business miles and his employer paid him a mileage allowance of 40p per mile. Teddy has taxable income of £450 for the purposes of tax.		✓
Hannah received a bonus of £1,250 on 1 June 2021 for her employer's financial year ended 31 December 2020. This bonus will be taxed on Hannah in the 2021/22 tax year.	✓	

Notes:

A payment into an occupational pension scheme made by an employee is an allowable deduction from employment income.

Teddy is paid less than the approved mileage allowance (this can be found in your reference material). The difference of £450 (9,000 × 5p) is an allowable deduction from employment income, not taxable income.

Employment income is taxable on the receipts basis. As the bonus was received between 6 April 2021 and 5 April 2022 this will be assessed in the 2021/22 tax year.

Task 3

(a)   Tax on interest and dividends

(i)   Lorena's taxable income from her dividends is £18,000.

The dividends from an ISA are exempt from tax.

Her tax on dividends is £5,200.

Lorena will be entitled to a dividend allowance of £2,000. Due to her level of other income she is a higher rate taxpayer. Her tax is calculated as:

(£2,000 × 0%) + (£16,000 × 32.5%) = £5,200

(ii)   Magnus' tax on his interest is £440.

Magnus has £1,700 left of his basic rate band. As some of his income will be taxed at the higher rate he is entitled to a personal savings allowance of £500. This uses his remaining basic rate band first. His income tax is:

(£500 × 0%) + (£1,200 × 20%) + (£500 × 40%) = £440.

(b)   Pablo

Property		Taxable rent £	Allowable expenses £
Duncombe Way	Duncombe Way was let from 1 January 2022 for rent of £1,400 per month. The rent was paid in advance on the 1st of each month. On 1 January 2022 Pablo paid insurance of £1,100 for the year ended 31 December 2022.	4,200	275
Chandlers Close	Chandlers Close was let until 30 November 2021 for rent of £11,400 per year. On 1 December 2021 Pablo moved into the property. The annual cleaning costs for the property were £960. Pablo also paid £2,400 for repairs in June 2021.	7,600	3,040

Note:

For an individual taxpayer rental income is automatically assessed on the cash basis. As Pablo has elected to be assessed under the accruals basis rent is taxed as earned, and expenses are deductible as accrued.

The cleaning costs will not be allowable for the period Pablo himself lived in the property.

Workings

(W1) Duncombe Way – taxable rent

£1,400 × 3 = £4,200

(W2) Duncombe Way – allowable expenses

£1,100 × 3/12 = £275

(W3) Chandlers Close – taxable rent

£11,400 × 8/12 = £7,600

(W4) Chandlers Close – allowable expenses

(£960 × 8/12) + £2,400 = £3,040.

(c)   True or false

	True	False
An additional rate taxpayer pays tax on interest at 40%.		✓
A landlord has tax allowable expenses of £1,800 relating to their rental property. They should claim the property allowance instead of claiming relief for these if they would like their property income to be assessed in the most tax efficient way.		✓

Note:

An additional rate taxpayer will pay tax at 45% on interest.

The property allowance is £1,000. A taxpayer can elect to claim this instead of allowable expenses. Here as the actual expenses are more than the allowance this election should not be made.

Task 4

Yasmeen – Income tax payable

	Non-savings income	Dividends	Total
	£	£	£
Employment income	101,600		101,600
OPS (101,600 × 6%)	(6,096)		(6,096)
Property income (18,000 – 17,800)	200		200
Dividends		10,600	10,600
Net income	95,704	10,600	106,304
Less: PA £12,570			
Less: ½ (£106,304 – £2,050 – £100,000)	(10,443)		(10,443)
Taxable income	85,261	10,600	95,861
Basic rate band:			
(£37,700 + £2,050)			
Non-savings – basic rate	39,750	× 20%	7,950
Non-savings – higher rate	45,511	× 40%	18,204
	85,261		
Dividends – allowance	2,000	× 0%	0
Dividends – higher rate	8,600	× 32.5%	2,795
Income tax liability			28,949
PAYE			(29,880)
Income tax repayable			(931)

The property loss is offset against property income.

The gift aid payment is grossed up to £2,050 (£1,640 × 100/80). This reduces the net income for the purpose of calculating the personal allowance and extends the basic rate band.

Task 5

(a) Anita and Abraham

The total class 1 National Insurance contributions payable by Anita in 2021/22 are £2,260

(£28,400 - £9,568) × 12% = £2,260.

The total class 1 National insurance contributions payable by Abraham in 2021/22 are £5,563.

	£
(£50,270 - £9,568) × 12%	4,884
(£84,200 - £50,270) × 2%	679
Total	5,563

The total class 1 National insurance contributions payable by Fir Ltd in respect of Anita and Abraham's earnings are £13,099.

	£
Anita	
(£28,400 – £8,840) × 13.8%	2,699
Abraham	
(£84,200 - £8,840) × 13.8%	10,400
Total	13,099

(b) True or false

	True	False
Class 1A national insurance contributions are payable by employees in respect of the benefits they receive.		✓
Earnings for the purposes of calculating class 1 national insurance contributions are before the deduction of pension contributions.	✓	

Task 6

(a)

(i) Nadia

The correct answer is **£463**.

Nadia's income tax liability in respect of the free petrol is:

£24,600 × 23% × 40% = £2,263.

If she stopped receiving the free petrol she would be £463 (£2,263 – £1,800) better off.

(ii) Caleb

The correct answer is **£171.**

Caleb's investments will generate income of:

£70,000 × 3.5% = £2,450.

Caleb is entitled to a dividend allowance of £2,000. As he is an additional rate taxpayer the rest of the tax on his investment will be charged at 38.1%.

(£2,000 × 0%) + (£450 × 38.1%) = £171.

(iii) Giselle

The correct answer is **£840.**

Giselle has taxable income of:

£60,000 - £12,570 = £47,430.

This means currently £9,730 (£47,430 - £37,700) of her income is taxed at the higher rate.

By making a personal pension contribution her basic rate band is extended by the gross contribution:

£3,360 × 100/80 = £4,200.

This means £4,200 of her income will be taxed at 20% rather than 40%. The tax saving is:

£4,200 × (40% - 20%) = £840.

(iv) Masumi

The mobile phone will increase her income tax liability by **£0.**

A mobile phone is an exempt benefit so has no tax implications.

The television will increase her income tax liability by **£256**.

Use of an asset creates a benefit at 20% of market value for each year it is used. The tax is calculated as:

£3,200 × 20% × 40% = £256.

Task 7

(a) Chargeable or exempt

	Chargeable	Exempt
Olivia makes a gift of a painting worth £30,000 to her daughter	✓	
Daniel leaves a house worth £5 million in his death estate to his niece		✓
Adelaide sells a share in a racehorse for £30,000		✓

Notes:

A gift of an asset is a chargeable disposal. The asset is deemed to be sold at market value.

Assets left on death are not subject to capital gains tax. A charge to inheritance tax may arise.

A racehorse is an exempt asset for capital gains tax.

(b) Gain or loss

Asset	Proceeds £	Cost £	Gain/loss/exempt	Amount of gain or loss £
Car	8,000	14,200	Exempt	0
Vase	2,200	6,000	Exempt	0
Painting	8,040	3,650	Gain	3,400
Sculpture	6,400	8,200	Loss	1,800

Notes:

A car is always exempt for capital gains tax purposes.

A vase is a non-wasting chattel. As it has both sales proceeds and cost not exceeding £6,000 this is also exempt.

Workings:

(W1) Painting

	£
Proceeds	8,040
Less: Cost	(3,650)
Gain	4,390

$(£8,040 – £6,000) × 5/3 = £3,400$

Chargeable gain	£3,400

(W2) Sculpture

The loss is calculated as:

£6,400 - £8,200 = (£1,800)

(c)   Aditi

	£
Proceeds	60,000
Cost	(32,500)
Gain	27,500

The cost is calculated as:

£130,000 × £60,000/(£60,000 + £180,000) = £32,500.

Task 8

Shares

		£	
Sales proceeds	(£8.50 × 4,200)	35,700	
Less: Cost (pool)		(14,364)	
Chargeable gain		21,336	
Pool		Number	Cost (£)
Apr 2016 Purchase		3,500	16,800
Nov 2018 Rights	1 for 4 at £3.60	875	3,150
		4,375	19,950
Sept 2019 Sale	475/4,375 × £19,950	(475)	(2,166)
Balance c/f		3,900	17,784
Jan 2021 Bonus	1 for 3	1,300	Nil
		5,200	17,784
May 2021 Sale	4,200/5,200 × £17,784	(4,200)	(14,364)
Balance c/f		1,000	3,420

Task 9

(a) True or false

	True	False
Capital losses can be offset against taxable income if the taxpayer has no capital gains in the year.		✓
The last nine months of ownership of an individual's private residence are always exempt from capital gains tax.	✓	
Capital losses cannot be carried back.	✓	
Each partner in a married couple is entitled to his, her or their own annual exempt amount.	✓	

(b) Jenna

The total amount that Jenna will pay capital gains tax on, after all allowances in 2021/22 is **£16,000.**

The amount of capital gains tax payable by Jenna in 2021/22 is **£3,200.**

	£
Gains (24,100 + 12,200)	36,300
Less: Capital losses	(8,000)
	———
Net gains	28,300
Less: AEA	(12,300)
	———
Taxable gains	16,000
	———
CGT at 20%	3,200
	———

Jenna cannot use the loss in respect of the disposal to her brother against gains generally, but only against future gains on assets sold to her brother.

The rate of CGT is 20% because Jenna is a higher rate taxpayer.

(c) Neil

The amount chargeable, if any, to capital gains tax for 2021/22 is **£0.**

The amount of losses, if any, to carry forward to 2022/23 is **£12,000.**

Current year capital losses cannot be restricted.

In 2019/20 £37,400 of the capital losses will be used against gains. This will leave:

£51,200 – £37,400 = £13,800 to carry forward.

Current year losses are used before brought forward capital losses.

In 2020/21 offsetting the current year capital losses leaves a net amount of: £16,300 – £13,500 = £2,800.

This will be covered by the annual exempt amount so none of the brought forward capital losses will be used in this year.

In 2021/22 net gains before offset of the annual exempt amount are:

£25,500 – £11,400 = £14,100.

Brought forward losses are used after offset of the annual exempt amount. This means we can use:

£14,100 – £12,300 = £1,800.

This will leave no gains in charge to tax and mean that Neil continues to carry forward losses of:

£13,800 – £1,800 = £12,000.

Task 10

(a) True or false

	True	False
No IHT liability can arise in respect of a gift made more than seven years prior to death.		✓
In the tax year 2021/22 Ryan made a single gift to Danielle of £420. The small gifts exemption will not be available in respect of this gift.	✓	
A chattel with a value of no more than £6,000 is exempt from IHT.		✓
The residence nil rate band is not available in respect of lifetime gifts.	✓	
April died in June 2020 leaving all her estate to her wife, Alix. Alix died in March 2021. The nil rate band available on Alix's death is £650,000.	✓	

Notes:

1 An IHT liability can arise in respect of a chargeable lifetime transfer at any time in the donor's lifetime.

2 The small gifts exemption is only available in respect of gifts of no more than £250 per donee per tax year.

3 Such an asset would be exempt for the purposes of CGT but not for IHT.

4 The residence nil rate band is only available when an individual leaves a residence on death to a direct descendent.

5 On death any unused nil rate band from the deceased's spouse can be claimed. As April used none of her nil rate band, the amount available on Alix's death is:

200% × £325,000 = £650,000.

(b) Guiseppe

The answer is £1,000.

	£
Gift	8,000
Less: Marriage exemption	(1,000)
Annual exemption – 2021/22	(3,000)
Annual exemption – 2020/21	(3,000)
Chargeable amount	1,000

Andre

The answer is £700.

The 2020/21 annual exemption will be offset against the June 2020 gift leaving £500 to carry forward.

The chargeable amount for the October 2021 gift is calculated as:

	£
Gift	4,200
Less: Annual exemption – 2021/22	(3,000)
Annual exemption – 2020/21	(500)
Chargeable amount	700

Monica

The answer is £320,000.

As Monica has left a residence to her direct descendant on death she can claim the residence nil rate band and the general nil rate band. The taxable amount of her estate will be:

	£
Gross estate	820,000
Less: Residence nil rate band	(175,000)
Nil rate band	(325,000)
Taxable amount	320,000

(c) Craig

Date	Details of the gift	Value £	CLT/ET/PET
08 June 2021	Car	22,000	PET
24 December 2021	Cash	200	ET

Although a car is exempt for the purposes of CGT, there are no exempt assets for IHT.

If total gifts to an individual in a tax year do not exceed £250 the small gifts exemption applies.

INDEX